Of Bowmen and Battles

Of Bowmen and Battles

By Hugh D. H. Soar

Edited by 'Ted' Bradford

Edited by Ted Bradford
First Published in Great Britain in 2003 by
The Glade Ltd.,
62 Hook Rise North, Tolworth, Surrey KT6 7JY, England

Copyright © THE GLADE LTD 2003

All rights reserved. No part of this publication may be reproduced, stored in any retrieval system, or transmitted by any means, without the prior permission (in writing) of the Publisher, nor otherwise be circulated in any form of binding or cover other than which it is published.

ISBN 0 9517645 1 9

Printed and Bound in Gt. Britain by Simpson Drewett and Company Ltd.
70 Sheen Road, Richmond, Surrey TW9 1UF

FOR ALL THOSE LONGBOWMEN WHO HAVE GONE BEFORE!

ACKNOWLEDGEMENTS

The Author, Editor and Publishers would like to thank the following for their permission to reproduce their illustrations:

Paul Hitchens, Wolfgang Bartle, The Temple Press

and
The Towton Longbowmen
Mark Stretton, Gwynn Zucca, Jez Hartley and Alan Edwards
for their co-operation and help in the Photographic sessions and
Ray Ore for his Graphics input

Front Cover:
Mark Stretton, attired as an archer of the 1415 Battle of Agincourt period, holding his warbow which, at full draw, puts 150lbs on his back

CONTENTS

Acknowledgements .... *v*

List of Illustrations and Plates .... *viii*

Foreword .... *x*

Introduction .... *xii*

PART 1	BOWS AND BOWMEN 1
	The Macclesfield 100 7
PART 2	ENTER THE WAR-BOW 9
	The Year of Destiny, 1066 — Battles of: Gate Fulford 12
	Stamford Bridge 15
	Hastings, 1066 19
PART 3	THE DRAGON IN THE WEST 25
	Rise of Gruffydd ap Cynan — Battles of: Mynydd Cam & Anglesey 26
	Battle of Orewin Bridge 31
	Rise and Campaign of Owain Glyndwr — Battle of Bryn Glas (Pilleth) ... 35
PART 4	THE HAMMER OF THE NORTH 41
	Flower of Scotland 43
	Battle of Boroughbridge 47
	Battle of Dupplin Moor 53
	Battle of Halidon Hill 57
PART 5	SEA AND SHORE 63
	The Sea-Battle of Sluys 65
	Stalemate at Morlaix., 1342 71
	The Affair at Auberoche 75
	The Affair at Blanchetache 79
PART 6	THE SUN SETS ON FRANCE 83
	Siege of Harfleur; 86
	Siege of Caen and Rouen 89
	Battle of Verneuil 95
	The Orleans Experience 98
	The Battle of Patay 102
PART 7	SKIRMISH AND AMBUSCADE 107
	The Ambush of Nibley Green, 1469 109
	The Western Rebellion 115
	The Battle of Blatchington Hill 119
	Thomas Wyatt's Rebellion 123
PART 8	DAWN AND DUSK 127
	Battle of Lewes 129
	The Battle of Najera. 133
	The Battle of the Spurs, 1513 137
	The Battle of Tippermuir 141

PART 9	SCOTLAND THE BRAVE	145
	The Battle of Falkirk	148
	The Battle of Bannockburn	150
	The Battle of Nevilles Cross	156
	The Battles of Otterburn and Homildon Hill	158
	The Battle of Shrewsbury	161
	The Battle of Flodden	166
PART 10	AGAINST ALL ODDS	173
	The Battle of Crecy	177
	The Battle of Poitiers	182
	French Accounts of the Battle of Agincourt	188
PART 11	A CROWN OF ROSES	196
	The First Battle of St. Albans	199
	The Second Battle of St. Albans	202
	The Battle of Towton	208
PART 12	RESURGAM IN PACE	213
	The Double Armed Man	216
GLOSSARY OF TERMS		xxxix
INDEX		xli
REIGNING MONARCHS		xlvi

LIST OF ILLUSTRATIONS AND PLATES

	Stringing the Bow — Ready for Action	xiv
	Saxon Archer taken from the Bayeux Tapestry	10
	A Saxon Archer c. 1066, as imagined by the author	13
Map —	The Battle of Stamford Bridge, September 25, 1066	14
Map —	The Battle of Hastings, October 14, 1066	18
	Nocking the Arrow Preparatory to Drawing the bow	24
Map —	The Battle of Orewin Bridge, December 3, 1282	32
Plate 1 —	*Norman Archer, Hastings 1066*	xv
Plate 2 —	*Geoffrey de Chargny, Poitiers 1356*	xvi
Plate 3 —	*An English Archer of the Poitiers Campaign, 1356*	xvii
Plate 4 —	*Uniform and Equipment of an English Archer, 1375-1435*	xviii
Plate 5 —	*An English mounted Archer of the Agincourt Campaign, 1415*	xix
Plate 6 —	*King Henry V, Agincourt, 1415*	xx
Plate 7 —	*Guillame de Bartel, Bearer of the Oriflamme, Agincourt, 1415*	xxi
Plate 8 —	*Sir Thomas Erpingham, Captain of Archers, Agincourt, 1415*	xxii
Map —	The Battle of Bryn Glas (Pilleth); June 22, 1402	36
	His arrows placed within easy reach the archer draws back to loose	39
	Drawing the bow string back to his ear the archer is ready	40
Map —	Possible site of the Battle of Stirling Bridge, 1297	43
Map —	The Battle of Boroughbridge, 1322	48
Map —	The two stages of the Battle of Dupplin Moor, 1322	52
	On board ship, an archer prepares for battle at sea	62
Map —	The Sea-Battle of Sluys, 1340	66
Map —	The Battle of Morlaix, 1342	70
Map —	The Battle of Auberoche, 1344	76
	Defending Auberoche Castle	78
Plate 9 —	*A French Knight, circa 1370-1400*	xxiii
Plate 10 —	*English Archer, circa 1400-1435*	xxiv
Plate 11 —	*Tudor Archer of the Reign of Henry VIII: The 'Mary Rose', 1545*	xxv
Plate 12 —	*A bowman of the Duke of Somerset's Retinue, circa 1470*	xxvi
Plate 13 —	*'Companions.' English Archers on the march, circa 1400-1425*	xxvii
Plate 14—	*Lord John of Aumont ('The Brawler'), 1415*	xxviii
Plate 15 —	*English Archers in Defensive Position, circa 1400-1430*	xxix
Plate 16 —	*'Skeleton 16.'*	xxx
	Defending the Ramparts	84
	The Siege of Caen	88
Map —	The Battle of Verneuil	94

	A startled stag suddenly burst from cover	103
	Attacked by French cavalry, the English Archers fight for their lives	104
	An Arrow is drawn from the back quiver . . . !	106
Map —	The Battle of Nibley Green, 1469	109
	Ambush and Assassination of Lord Lisle by Black Will at Nibley Green	112
	Black Will Long, Leader of the Dean Foresters and reputed Assassin	113
Plate 17—	Gwynn Zucca in the livery of Lord Ferrers	xxxi
Plate 18 —	Paul Hitchen in the costume of an Agincourt Archer	xxxii
Plate 19 —	Alan Edwards and Jez Hartley in the livery of Lord Fauconberg	xxxiii
Plate 20—	'Together!' the forces of two Lords join up and wait for orders	xxxiv
Plate 21 —	Mark Stretton, having put the stakes in the ground, adds a pointed end	xxxv
Plate 22 —	'Loose!' The English Archers prepare to loose	xxxvi
Plate 23 —	'Draw!' Gwynn demonstrates the two-finger draw with a heavy bow	xxxvii
Plate 24 —	Moving in for hand-to-hand fighting!	xxxviii
Map —	The Battle of Fenny Bridges	118
Map —	The Battle of Blatchington Hill, 1545	119
Map —	The Battle of Lewes, 1264	130
Map —	The Battle of Najera	135
Map —	The Battle of the Spurs, 1513	138
Map —	Scotland, showing the locations of the major Battle	146
Map —	The two-day Battle of Bannockburn, 1314	151
	Mounted Archers from Wales and the English Shires	154
	Cavalry approaching to attack a group of English Archers	159
Map —	The Battle of Shrewsbury, 1403	161
Map —	The Battle of Flodden, 1513	169
	Armed with his close-quarter weapons	174
Map —	The Battle of Crecy, 1346	178
	On the March! The English army gets ready for a chevauchée	183
Map —	The Battle of Poitiers, 1356	186
Map —	The Battle of Agincourt, 1415	189
	Preparing to shoot the Arrow Storm, Agincourt, 1415	192
	Damage to the French Cavalry after the Arrow Storm, Agincourt, 1415	194
Map —	The Second Battle of St. Albans, 1461	203
	As the enemy approaches the Archer takes point-blank aim	207
	The wars are over. Time to unstring the bow	212
	At rest! The fighting has finished. The Archer rests!.	214

FOREWORD

SOME two to three years after starting the Archery magazine 'The Glade' I, being very interested in the longbow and its history in war, decided to write a few articles about its use in battle, based on my memories of lessons learned in school. I wrote some 20 articles covering battles in which the English and Welsh bowmen took part and, getting more into the subject, I started to do a little research. Consequently, especially in the realm of battles in these islands, I started contacting the Town Halls, Libraries and Archives asking for information about the battle(s) that took place in the area.

It was not long before I found myself giving more time to the subject and getting less for the editing of the magazine so, along with the wish to get these series written more professionally and, in part, to give myself more time to devote to the editing of 'The Glade,' I decided to approach my friend Hugh Soar and ask him if he would like to take over the series and undertake to cover the war-bow battles of the past.

I have known and been associated with Hugh David Hewitt Soar (known to archers around the world as "Hugh") for a good number of years, several of which he had been writing a series of articles for 'The Glade' archery magazine. His chosen subject was 'All About Longbows' in which he gave us an insight into the Victorian era's association with the 'English Longbow' and accounts of tournaments and events of that bygone age.

Hugh's contribution to 'The Glade' has been a huge success and he has followers in over 100 countries world-wide. Many letters acknowledging readers' appreciation of Hugh's series have and, still are, being received in 'The Glade' office. Another reason for asking him to continue the series!

As stated above, I (along with many another Englishman) am deeply interested in our history and heritage, especially with our association with the 'war bow' and its use in the battles of the medieval period. Having known Hugh for several years and being aware of his rather substantial knowledge of the subject, his large library of books and artefacts concerned with both archaeological, medieval and modern bows, I apprised him of my thoughts and 'suggested' that he might like to have a go!

This he has done and in his own inimitable style!! He has tackled the subject in a way that no other writer has (as far as I am aware) in that the 'Battles' are not in Chronological order, rather they are brought to you in a series of 'themes.' In these, the principal conflicts — their beginnings, their middles and the final results — are laid out in detail in an authoritative and interesting format and, to add a little spice to this story of the war bow, certain items have been taken from actual happenings, at different time periods and added to the end of some of the battle accounts.

In this book, Hugh has brought contemporary accounts of the events into the text which, in some cases, give quite humourous accounts of life as it was in those days! He also draws on his own imagination and questions events if, in his opinion, they might not be as quite popularly supposed. This questioning leaves those so inclined, to start asking questioning for themselves and then, possibly, seeking for answers.

For myself, I am pleased that I asked Hugh to start this venture and, I trust, you the reader, will be also.

I commend 'Of Bowmen and Battles' to you.

Ted Bradford
January, 2003
Surrey, England

From the 'Boke for a Justice of the Peace' 1559. 'And that al bowstaves of ewe be open. and not solde in bundles nor close. . . ."

IBID. . . "That no man kepe anie crosbowe or handgunne In his house, or elsewhere, upon payne of enprisonmente and to forfaite xii (s?) to the kinge, excepte he have landes and except makers of crosse bowes, whiche may kepe them to sell, and shoot in them for assaye. and exept them that dwell within vi. miles of th sea costes or in the English marches nere Scotlande which male kepe them for defence of their house and goodes and also their ships . . . And except merchauntes that have them to sell."

INTRODUCTION

TO PREPARE and subsequently to publish a popular account of the many battles in which the English war-bow and its accompanying battle-shaft (the 'Crooked Stick' and 'Grey Goose Wing' of poetry and story) featured has not been an easy task. My thanks go to Ted Bradford, Editor of the International archery magazine 'The Glade,' whose faith in my ability has not always been matched by my own. To Veronica-Mae whose support has been invaluable; to my good friends Wolfgang Bartl for the drawings, Mark Stretton and his fellow members of The Towton Longbowmen, Paul Hitchens for the colour paintings and finally, to J.G., H.G. and A.G. and sundry others, whose varied degrees of help and enthusiasm have been the catalyst for its eventual completion.

If in consequence there are errors of fact — or indeed of fiction — within the pages, then the fault is plainly mine.

What I have endeavoured to do, however, is to set down for the general reader of archery related history, a lightly written synopsis of over 30 engagements — from skirmish to set-piece battle — in which English, Welsh and Scottish bowmen have featured. Rather than presenting these to strict chronology, as might be expected in a book about battles, I have departed from convention to group Parts, not by date but, by theme. The success or otherwise of this departure you, the reader, will decide.

The time span thus covered ranges between 1066 and 1644; six-hundred years that saw the emergence of the great war-bow; the zenith and the nadir of its fame. That it slipped but slowly from the military scene is a tribute as much to those who kept faith in its continued ability to master opposition, as to those who made it and those who shot in it. For it was European thought that changed the established order of things and brought about its eventual demise. An archery related circumstance with a peculiarly contemporary ring.

The war-bow has known many vernacular names during its long and lively life. To today's readily recognised 'long-bow' may be added "bend-bow," "noble-bow," "English bow," "hand-bow," "round-bow," and "lugg," its various names in earlier times. But for all our intimate knowledge of its devastating effect, we know little of its early life.

True, we have a fruitful harvest from the Tudor war-ship 'Mary Rose,' and expert interpretation from — amongst others — the late Professor Pratt and Dr. Hardy; but the weapons whose secrets are thus revealed are latecomers to the scene. What would Archer Antiquarian and bowyer alike not give for knowledge of those weapons with which the great defensive battles of Crecy, Agincourt and Poitiers were fought?

It is to the credit of our innate national attitude to change that the long-bow is still with us. In recreational form it's true but, through the dedication and faith of an ever-increasing fraternity of archers we still can know the pleasure and the frustration attendant upon it.

In the words of Roger Askham: *"I praye Godde that all archers usinge shootinge honestlye, and all manner of men that favour artillerie, maye live continually in healthe and merrinesse."*

What better dedication can there be for a book about the long-bow, than to those merry archers who shoot in it today.

HUGH DAVID HEWITT SOAR: AD 2002
Research Consultant: Traditional Archery.

STRINGING THE BOW — READY FOR ACTION

Part 1

Bows and Bowmen

Early Bows
Evidence from Robin Hood
Arrow Profiles
Arrowheads

Part 1

BOWS AND BOWMEN

OF ALL weapons throughout the ages, it is fair to say, I think, that the bow and arrow carries the most charisma and, of the genre, none more so than the English long-bow. Still capable of misting many an eye when martial matters are foremost, it was, and is, the simple weapon of the people. Lacking perhaps the reverence accorded a Samurai's sword, or the awesome destruction of an Anglo-Saxon battle-axe in the brawny hands of those who tamed its strength, it humbled all, without distinction of birth, breeding or estate. Warrior king and peasant alike, each fell to the longbow and its murderous bodkin-pointed battle-shaft.

Known variously throughout its chequered history as the 'hand-bow,' the 'bend-bow,' the 'English bow,' 'the Crooked Stick'[1] and the 'lugg'[2] — most often to distinguish it from the Continental arbalest, or crossbow — our erstwhile national weapon still stirs deep feelings of martial pride at victories gained against huge odds.

This book is a compendium of combats in which the long-bow and those who used it feature. In some the bow was dominant, in others auxiliary to the outcome. Ambush, skirmish or set-piece battle however, each is here.

But firstly, when did it all start, this love affair with our English bow? Some might see priapic posturing and infer a Freudian significance, others the simple triumph of nature over science. Let us look for its beginnings.

The origins of the bow are lost in time. Imagination rules, untrammelled by fact or for that matter, artifact. Someone, somewhere, experimented with what may once have been a plaything and, with vision beyond his years, created the forerunner of the simple bow which we now know.

When was this? If we only knew. With the possible exception of the 'Clacton point,'[3] a broken, middle Palaeolithic ambiguity over which academics and others argue fruitlessly and, which may or may not have been a partial bow-limb, the earliest substantive evidence is from the Neolithic period of some 12,000 to 14,000 years ago.

This comes not from artifacts but from cave drawings which show in graphic detail

---

[1] A poetic allusion: 'England were but a fling, but for the crooked stick and the grey goose wing.' (The war-arrow was fletched with feathers from a goose.)

[2] This word refers correctly to a bell-rope, but a vernacular meaning relates to the drawing, or 'lugging' of the bow string.

[3] For a mention in context, see 'The Archaeology of Archery,' ISBN 0 9517 645 00: Dr. Alf Webb.

the use of bows in warfare and for hunting; this latter illustrating a system defunct only in historic times, since the 'bow and stable' culling of medieval deer[4] owes its origins to practices developed millennia before.

A study of those few early bows, or parts of bows, recovered and conserved in Northern Europe, shows there to have been two quite dissimilar and distinct profiles, each with their particular cross-section. On the one hand shaped with recognisably deep cambered sides ('high stacked' as we would say today), on the other, a much flatter, wider section, not unlike the bows of certain North American Plains Indians.

Contrasting types, each with its detractors and its devotees; distinguished in modern terms as English long-bow and American flat-bow.

Curiously, a limb of each type has been excavated from peat bogs within the Somerset levels here in England. That of a flat sectioned weapon of heroic proportion recovered from Meare Heath, of which sufficient survives to allow its recent reconstruction and tillering by a professional bowmaker and, that of a 'D'-sectioned longbow, from nearby Ashcott Heath.

Each is of broadly similar age (carbon dating technique has indicated 2665BC +/- 150 years) suggesting two quite disparate bow-making traditions within a short distance of each other. One might speculate on reasons for such fundamental differences. The flat-bow is an efficient weapon compared to a 'D'-sectioned bow, technically superior in cast. A replica Meare Heath bow has shot a reconstructed Neolithic arrow over 160 yards, a distance perhaps achievable by a replica Ashcott longbow. We do not know, for to the author's knowledge no such example has yet been made. Our interest whetted, we wait to see.

There is, of course, the Alpine 'Ice-man's' bow — by carbon dating 5,300 years of age. Again, a true long-bow, it too begs our replication. What would have been it's draw-weight? What cast would it have had? What distance would it have made?

Perhaps in early times one weapon served for hunting, warfare and for personal protection; we cannot know for certain since too few examples have survived but, if one arrow served a common purpose then reason suggests one bow might have done the same.

As man emerged from Dark Age mists and records started to be kept, we trace four deviations from the simple bow. Archaeologists may seek for proof and seek in vain, for there is little there to see; however, antiquarians recognise the Hunting bow and its variant, the lighter Birding bow; the War-bow; the Peasant's or Drover's Bough bow for personal defence and the Recreational bow, with its variants for Butt and Distance shooting.

So, how do we know of these variants? Be prepared to look askance, for amongst the antiquarian's source material and about as far from science as it is possible to get, are the Ballads of 'Robin Hood.' Within these old tales can be found much ancient archery lore. Here are mentioned the 'birding bow,' the 'bough bow,' the 'butt bow' and the 'distance bow.'

In one variation of the Ballad 'Robin Hood and the Forresters,' dating it is believed

---

[4] An efficient method of culling a herd for food or sport, or both, whereby archers were placed at 'stable stands,' i.e., by trees or other cover. Deer funnelled towards them by beaters were shot as they passed.

from the 17th Century or earlier, Robin, as a young man, is visiting Nottingham Town. Whilst there he meets some Foresters who make fun of him when he says that he is to take part in an archery tournament. They are scornful of his light bow, to which he replies:

> "This is my birding bow,
> Which I carry by the way.
> But I have two stronger bows at home,
> At home in Merry Loxley."

It is Little John who owns the 'bough bow' though. In the early tale of 'Guy of Gisborne,' he is trying to stop the Sheriff and his men from taking Will Scarlett who is escaping from the law. At the crucial point however, John's bow breaks! Its failings are neatly summarised by the Ballad's author who, like his audience, was no doubt familiar with its characteristics.

> "Then John bent up his long bende-bowe,
> And fetteled hym to shote,
> The bow was made of tender boughe,
> And fell downe at hys foote."

Although well suited to personal defence and as 'maids of all work,' bows made from the boughs of trees have long been considered inferior to those made from the bole, or trunk. Roger Askham dismisses the bough as a source of good bow-wood, preferring wood from either a sapling or the trunk. Draw-weight for weight, factual experiment shows a bough bow to be appreciably slower in cast than one from the trunk, comparison through a chronograph suggesting 160 feet per second as against 170 feet.

The brief description of a bow suited to distance shooting comes from the tale of 'Robin Hood and Queen Catherine' (the longer, and arguably [more] complete rendering of the Forresters Manuscript; the reference is omitted from the Broadside version). For various reasons the ballad has been dated to the 17th Century and the archery contest, as described, seems to be consistent with that time.

The match is made at '15 score' (yards is presumed, although paces is a possibility). Distance shooting required then, as it does now, a strong bow and a matched shaft, and Robin has suitably equipped himself and his three companions: Little John, who for reasons of anonymity is called 'Clifton,' Much ('Midge' in the ballad) and Will Scathlock.

> "They had bowes of ewe and strings of silk
> Arrows of silver chest,
> Black hats, white feathers, all alike
> Full deftly were they drest."

The reference to yew is understandable, because then — as now — *taxus baccata* (or *taxus brevifolia*) was recognised as the best wood for long-bows. However, the allusion to silk is interesting in the context of today's insistence upon the inert bowstring. A certain degree of elasticity was deemed a virtue in earlier times; silk was also considered quieter than hemp in operation and thus was favoured for hunting bows. Modern experiment with a silk string has shown it to deliver an arrow faster through a chronograph than does a string of the man-made material Dacron, conventional for today's long-bows.

Arrows of 'silver chest' is an unusual reference to a certain wood from which, we can assume, shafts of quality were made in the 17th Century. Rather surprisingly, in fact, if it is the 'Sugarcheste' mentioned by Roger Askham in his 'Toxophilus' as an arrow wood, since he dismisses it, along with *". . . Brasell, Turkiewood, and Fusticke . . ."* as making *". . . Dead, heavye, lumpish, hobbling shafts. . ."*

The anonymous author of 'L'art d'archerie,' written 50 years earlier than 'Toxophilus,' offers birch or cherry wood but not 'sugar,' or indeed, 'silver' chest. Interestingly however, he does refer to 'baking' arrow steles, presumably to both harden and lighten and, whilst that remained practice until at least the 18th Century (vide Roberts 'The English Bowman,' 1801) it awaits trial by those fletchers who serve our present distance shooters.

We recognise four arrow profiles: 'Bobtailed' (or to give them an alternative name, 'rush-grown,' since 'bob-tailed' was a pejorative expression in earlier times). Tapering from the point to the string nock, these were used with special heads for war. Many arrows recovered from the Tudor warship 'Mary-Rose' were bobtailed.

The others were: 'Breasted,' tapering from string nock to point, for distance shooting; 'Parallel,' for forest hunting and 'Barrelled' (or tapered) from mid-point to either end, to fly true — for a barrelled shaft is less prone to vibration en route to the target.

With these profiles came many arrowheads, each shaped and with their purpose clear. 'Bodkin' points, slim tapered cylinders, hardened and often needle sharp to pierce mail and 'jack' alike. 'Broadheads,' large and small, with or without barbs, for embarrassing cavalry or killing unharnessed (unarmoured) men and deadly against those who manned ships. Some with crescent heads, called 'Forkers,' used for game and hunting, a favourite with poachers since they could be recovered if the beast was not brought down. Others, the great 'Swallow-tails' or 'Horse-heads.' Each capable of inflicting dreadful wounds.

'Blunts' of horn or wood: used against birds for sport or small game for the pot and designed to kill by impact. The only heads allowed in forest places.

At recreation, for Butt, Rood, Hoyles or Prick shooting, conically shaped 'Crow bills' of horn, 'Silver spoon' or 'Ridged' points — 'piles' as we know them today. Designed to enable a consistent draw-length, these latter helped with accuracy

This was the formidable armoury of the common man; the weapons which brought about a fundamental change in body armour and raised the English fighting man to a position he has seldom lost. Used with determination, by soldiers whose valour was unsurpassed, the influence of the English war-bow and its battle-shafts on the outcome of medieval campaigns was in disproportion to its simplicity. Not until the advent of the breech loading rifle would such carnage, as was seen on those early fields of war, be again created.

It is appropriate here, as at any point in this story, to dwell for a while on the English war bow and its origins. However, the subject is fraught with xenophobic pitfalls and one treads carefully. No-one can say for sure who, when or where was the bowmaker who created the weapon the name of which, more than almost anything, is synonymous with England. That it first emerged in the Welsh Marches is a possibility — even a probability; the military need was recognised. Anglo-Norman warfare made more and more use of the bow and, material was present in abundance.

The Anglo-Saxon had used the bow regularly in hunting and, to a lesser extent, in warfare. Early woodcuts show a shorter weapon than the later war-bow and this is consistent with its primary hunting purpose. It is unnecessary to discard the myth that this bow was short, it is necessary only to understand it. Surviving examples of the war long-bow measure around 6´ 5˝ (or some 2 metres) in length. No Saxon bows survive — although occasional traces have been found during excavations of burial sites, indicating a length of about 5´ 6˝ (165cms) — quite co-incidentally the minimum length required of the present long-bow by the British Long-Bow Society. Viking bows recovered from the Nydam site are of this length or a little longer.

There is a correlation between bow length and draw-weight. Assessment of the Nydam bows has suggested a draw-weight of some 50lbs — adequate enough for hunting, and well capable of penetrating mail, or even light armour in close confrontations, as experiments witnessed by the writer have demonstrated. However, a perceived need to disrupt advancing cavalry at longer distance revealed the inadequacy of the lighter bow; it was this need to consolidate and develop tactics to thwart the attacks of mounted men-at-arms that led to the development of the heavier and more substantial weapon, with its weightier arrow. Creating mayhem amongst the horses at a reasonable distance from the waiting infantry was the prime purpose of the war-bow and remained so for generations.

With reason and need defined, the military men looked for means and they had not far to search. The Welsh bow was a powerful weapon, suitable for sudden ambush, if, less capable of distance. Whether it was of yew we do not know — Geraldus Cambrensis (Gerald of Wales) mentions Wych Elm, an adequate enough wood, but lacking the effectiveness of a combination of tension and compression capability present in Yew. But the bow was there and, of more importance perhaps, so were the men who could both draw and use it.

Archery was, of course, not new to warfare in Continental Europe. Although by themselves they could not have won Hastings, the massed archers deployed so effectively by Duke William, helped significantly in the attrition of the shield wall. As later experience was to show, with one or two exceptions, archers alone did not win battles; their role was to disrupt and disorientate, to disorganise and break the cohesion of cavalry or infantry attack. Arrows did not necessarily kill outright; it was the sepsis they brought in their wake that maimed and killed.

THE MACCLESFIELD 100

THERE ARE two components to an archer — the weapon and the man. Men there were in numbers, capable of drawing the heavy bow; Welsh at first — steeped in the culture of warfare, their weapons crude and unsophisticated — joined as time passed by Saxon forest bowmen from Derbyshire and Nottinghamshire, whose forté lay in the accuracy of their shooting and who matched the Welsh in ambush skills. Whilst from Cheshire, came the 'Macclesfield 100,' that elite body of archers who drew a special wage of 3d a day in 1277 and served Edward I longer than any other levy.

For Edward — he it was whose commitment to the bow began its steady rise to fame — needed strong shots to man his armies. The task before him was to teach his archers to make and keep a length. To do this required bows of quality. A man's hunting bow, strong but slow of cast, might be made from a bough but, the great war-bow was to be made from the bole of the tree — or from a sapling. From this source alone would come distance shooting; the men who would fashion the weapons would soon learn their skill.

By law of Henry I: an archer whilst legitimately practising his skill but who accidentally killed a man, would not be held culpable of his murder if he had first warned by calling 'faste' (stand fast). A belated recognition of the potential of massed archery was followed by Henry III's Assize of Arms in 1252. This signalled the beginning of the bow and arrow as the weapon of the common soldier; all males between 15 and 60 were to keep weapons, including bows. The Statute of Winchester in 1285 confirmed the provisions of the Assize of Arms and, nine years later, came the first reference to a maker of bows in London when, in 1293, Ivo le Bowyere was called to account for a crime at Westminster. He was a Freeman of the City of London and as such, a man of good standing; a position, incidentally, which stood in his favour at his indictment.

That all the better bows were not made of yew is illustrated by a 13th Century record from Cornwall. For, in 1284, Robert Fitzwalter sold 1/3rd of his moiety of the manor of Treverue (Truro) to Sir Richard de Hywish (Huish?) and Matilda his wife, to be held of the King *'in capite'* and by the service of rendering a bow of Laburnum or 8d yearly. The appearance of this weapon would certainly have been rather special and, although lacking the elastic modulus of yew, would have cast well. Laburnum is still a favoured wood today. One may imagine the royal personage disporting his bow at game, or perhaps the butts, attracting glances of admiration even if his performance was less than exciting

Hand bows, progenitors of the great war-bow, were in regular use in Norman armies and were used to effect at the siege of Alençon in 1118 and at Brémule in 1119 (although here the evidence is perhaps circumstantial) but, more particularly, at Bougthérolde in 1124, where a central line of dismounted men-at-arms supported by flank archers, preluded the Crecy formation of two centuries later.

The cross-bow, with the mercenaries who used it, still figured prominently in Norman military thinking, until ultimately superseded by the heavy war-bow, as confidence in the tactical use and manufacture of that weapon increased. Aspirant English bowmen there were in number by then but, quantity does not necessarily equate with quality and it was to be some time before numerically the balance of mustered archers favoured England rather than Wales.

Principal References and Further Reading:

'THE MAN IN THE ICE,' Konrad Spindler, 1994 Weidenfeld & Nicolson: ISBN 0 297 81410 9

'THE BOW, SOME NOTES ON ITS DEVELOPMENT, SECOND EDITION,' Dr. Gad Rausing, 1997 Simon Archery Foundation: ISBN 0 9503199 5 3

'ROBIN HOOD, POEMS SONGS AND BALLADS,' Joseph Ritson. 1885 The Ballantyne Press:

'ROBIN HOOD, THE FORRESTER MANUSCRIPT,' Ed.: Prof: Stephen Knight: 1998 D.S.Brewer Camb. ISBN 0 85991 436 4

'TOXOPHILUS, OR THE SCHOLE OF SHOTINGE,' Roger Askham, Simon Archery Foundation. Reprint: 1985 ISBN 0 9503199 0 9

'L'ART D'ARCHERIE.' Transl.: Henri Gallice. See Henri Stein: 'Archers d'Autrefois: Archers d'Aujourd'hui.' Paris 1925. See also, Eng. transl.: Col. Walrond: 'Archer's Register' 1902/3.

From Walter Michael Mosely's 'An Essay on Archery': ". . . our old archers held their bows well **beeswaxed** in order to fix them in their hands . . ."

IBID . . . "Bows used for 'fire arrows' were lower braced than others to give a slower cast."

Part 2

Enter the War-Bow

The Year of Destiny, 1066
The Battle of Gate Fulford
The Battle of Stamford Bridge
The Battle of Hastings

SAXON ARCHER TAKEN FROM THE BAYEUX TAPESTRY

Part 2

ENTER THE WAR-BOW

FOR MANY thousands of years the bow served both the hunter and the warrior. Indeed in early pre-history the distinction between human and animal prey, between hunting and warfare, would have been fundamentally blurred. The rock paintings in Eastern Spain portraying groups of archers in combat against each other, depict haphazard affairs that seemingly differ little from similar scenes of archers slaughtering Ibex. The bow, whether simple or complex, was essentially a dual-purpose weapon; it could strike and strike hard in aggressive combat and provide in the hunt but, equally, it could defend against attack.

And so matters might well have remained; for when warfare was synonymous with ambush, or at best close contact, what use was there for a specialised weapon? Hunting with bows was conducted at short range as true hunting should be. The lone hunter, perhaps with his dog, would stalk his prey with the utmost dexterity and despatch it at a modest distance. Ishi, the last of the Yana Indians of California, and a living representative of the Stone Age, took pride in stalking and calling his prey. His shooting skills were confined to short distances and there is no reason to believe that his remote ancestors were any different.

However, as technology advanced, so edged weapons with their capacity for maiming developed. The bow — stand-off weapon of Neolithic European man — gave way in later times to hand-to-hand engagements with swords, daggers and axes; an accepted style of warfare which persisted in Scandinavia and Saxon England. Projectiles — javelins and thrown spears, accompanied by other less sophisticated missiles, opened the proceedings with archery — where present — a peripheral activity intended to embarrass rather than disrupt the opposing side. Only in early sea war-fare perhaps, was the bow elevated to more than an auxiliary weapon, a disordering softener indulged in before the boarding party got down to serious business. An arrangement which was to mature in later times, after the worth of archery had been recognised by military tacticians.

The descriptions of campaigns and their battles which follow, trace the usage of the long-bow across the years and its increasing and then declining significance in warfare, as man found and developed newer, if not always more effective, means of finishing his fellows.

THE YEAR OF DESTINY, 1066 AD

IT IS A curious fact that, etched into the subconscious of most English folk — deeper even than the number of their car, telephone, or the date of their wedding anniversary, are four figures that to other Nations would be a meaningless jumble. They are of course, 1, 0, 6 & 6. Individually of no significance, quite useless as aids in the National Lottery; together they mark a definitive turning point in English history.

If ever a year might justifiably be called momentous it was A.D. 1066. Within the space of 10 months it saw the death of three kings and the triumph of a duke; three major battles — two of homeric proportion and intensity — and the termination of Anglo-Saxon succession in England.

The 'dramatis personæ' who strode the stage in this power struggle were dominant men by any standard: Edward the Confessor by the strength and piety of his will; Godwin, Earl of Wessex, tempestuous leader of the West Saxon host and his son, Harold, warrior and aspirant king; Tostig Godwinson, Earl of Northumbria, Harold's disaffected brother, despoiler of churches and distinctly no better than he should be; King Harald Sigurdson of Norway, a giant Viking with attitude; Earls Morcar and Edwin, loyal Saxons who, with the Mercian fyrd thwarted Tostig's plans for invasion and, waiting in the wings, a finger in every pie, the wild-card: Duke William of Normandy, bastard son of Robert the Devil and Herleve, the tanner's daughter.

Edward, 'The Confessor', whose death in January 1066 set the show rolling, was son to Ethelred the Redeless (the ill counselled) dubbed by history the 'Unready,' a sustainable if not an etymologically accurate play on words. Married to Earl Godwin's daughter, he remained celibate, thereby denying Godwin his chance to be grandfather to an English king and directly precipitating the events that followed.

There was thus no direct heir to the English throne. The closest legitimate successor was a child: Edward's nephew, Edgar the Atheling.

It having been decided in Council that with storm clouds brewing in Scandinavia and Normandy, England needed the guidance of a man at the helm rather than a child and with a distinct lack of acceptable candidates, Harold, son of Godwin, Earl of Wessex, was offered and readily accepted the post. Although his curriculum vitæ was perhaps no worse than those of others and better than some, the choice was by no means universally approved. Brother Tostig, exiled by Harold for making a thorough nuisance of himself, was less than happy with it, as was the formidable Harald Sigurdson, King of Norway, whose claim (though tenuous in the extreme) was nevertheless backed by considerable Viking muscle.

Whilst, biding his time off-stage, the morality of his title equal in his own mind to that of Harold, stood William the Bastard, Duke of Normandy.

The scene set and Harold enthroned, events unfurled. Tostig Godwinson, ever a thorn in his brother's side and exiled to Flanders, appeared off the South Coast with a fleet of 60 ships and raided Sandwich. Raising the Southern fyrd and anxious to scotch this early threat to his throne, Harold prepared to meet him. Having arrived by sea however, Tostig as quickly departed and a frustrated Harold had perforce to chase him to Norfolk. Although his slippery brother once more eluded royal capture, he and his substantial army of Flemings were finally pinned down in the vicinity of the Humber and thoroughly trounced by Earls Edwin and Morcar and the Mercian levy.

Tostig escaped to Scotland; his shipmen and what was left of his army deserted and things quietened down for a month or two. In the meantime, however, Duke William had not been idle. In meticulous preparation for his challenge to the throne he had built ships and interested a number of fellow Normans in an entrepreneurial expedition to Harold's England. In anticipation of this unwelcome interest, Harold had mustered his butse-carles (or boat-men) to counter it and a formidable English fleet waited to greet William and his get-rich-quick comrades in arms.

A SAXON ARCHER C. 1066, AS IMAGINED BY THE AUTHOR

ENTER THE WAR-BOW — GATE FULFORD & STAMFORD BRIDGE

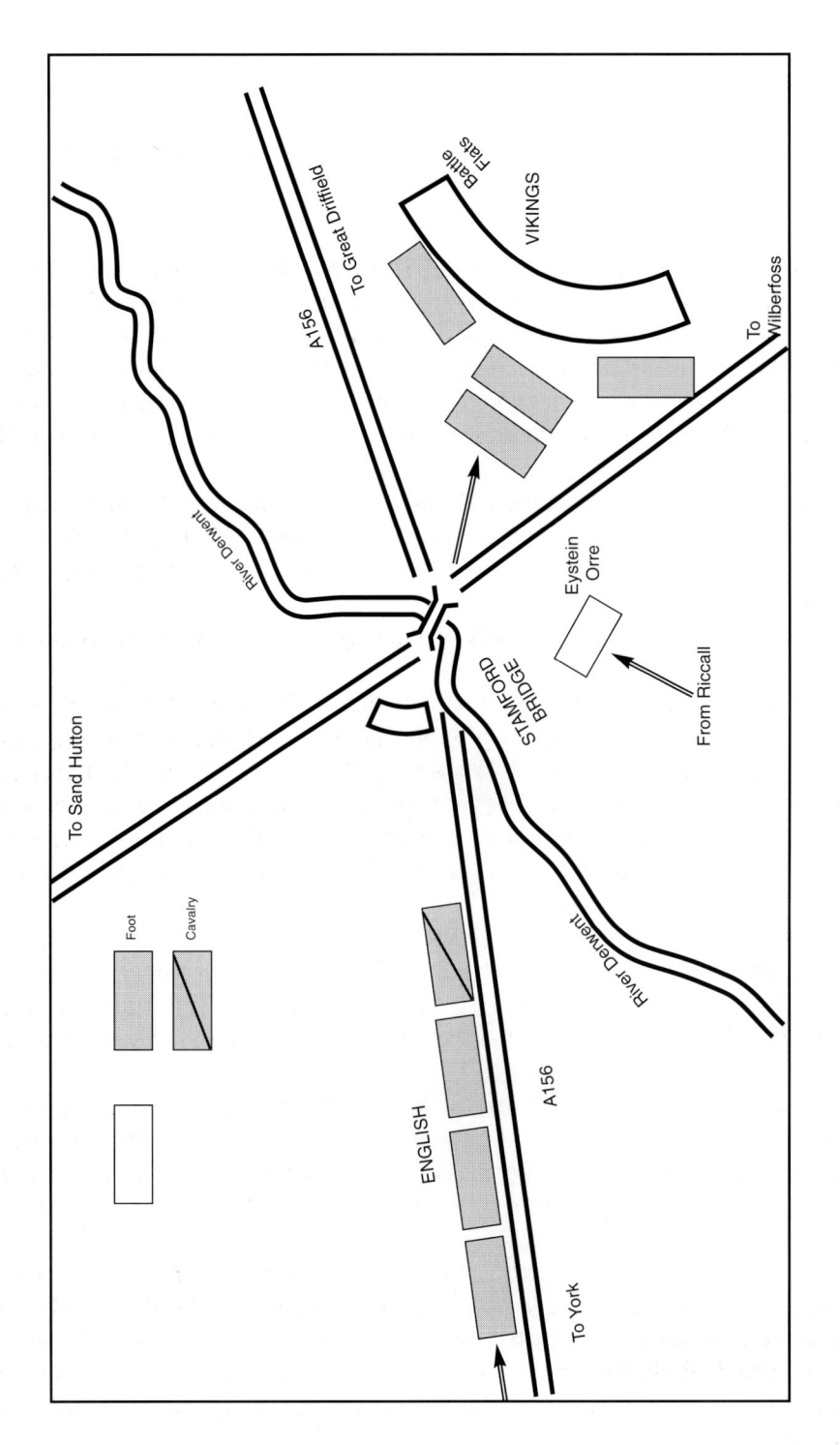

THE BATTLE OF STAMFORD BRIDGE
September 25, 1066

BATTLES OF GATE FULFORD & STAMFORD BRIDGE

ENTER ONCE more the ubiquitous Tostig. Smarting from his defeat earlier, he had thrown in his lot with Norway and re-appeared in the Humber estuary, accompanied this time by a huge Norwegian battle-fleet, loaded to the gunwhales with Viking warriors and commanded in person by King Harald Sigurdson, nicknamed 'Hardrada' (hard counsel). A competent general and a giant of a man — he is said to have been seven feet tall — his very presence inspired awe in his foes and reassurance in his friends.

This shipborne army of Norwegian fighting men was met, close to the village of (Gate) Fulford (near York) by the Northern and Midland fyrd, led by Earls Edwin and Morcar, supported by the Yorkshire fyrd. To Tostig's evident satisfaction, matters this time went his way.

The ANGLO-SAXON CHRONICLE records laconically: "... the Norwegians had the victory..."

Understandably perhaps, the Norse Saga-men made rather more of the event. From them we learn that Harald and Tostig deployed their men along the River Ouse, close to the village, placing the strongest of their army by the river and the weakest adjacent to a muddy ditch. The reason for this apparently strange tactic seems to have been to induce the Saxons to cross the ditch, for it was at this point that the Norwegian army gave way, feigning flight and thus encouraging the home team to cross in pursuit. (Note: We shall meet this ploy again.)

It was now that Harald Sigurdson raised his war-banner, the fearsome 'Land-Ravager' and sounded the charge. With the ditch now behind them, after fighting valiantly hand to hand, the Saxons were forced back and defeated in a hotly-contested engagement. The first major confrontation of the year had occurred. There would be two more!

Told of the outcome, and conscious of what might become a ground-swell of popular support for the Norwegians — since amongst the Northern population were many with Scandinavian roots, whose loyalties were not necessarily to a Southern Saxon King — Harold had perforce to tackle the situation and, moreover, do so promptly.

This he did with characteristic despatch. Leading his house-carles (professional fighting men sworn to his support) and gathering up and dusting off the defeated locals, he arrived at York in time to catch his errant brother and the victorious Hardrada virtually unprepared. Both the Anglo-Saxon Chronicle and the Northern scalds, or saga-men, recount the ensuing conflict. The former pragmatically, as was its way, the latter poetically.

Having defeated Earls Morcar and Edwin on the previous Wednesday, on Sunday,

September 24th, the Norwegian King had marched to York Castle to make the necessary arrangements for the formal declaration of his personal agenda and inter alia, that of Tostig, at Stamford on the following day. Preliminaries arranged to his satisfaction, he had returned to base.

Monday duly dawned, warm and sunny and the army moved off with Harald and Tostig at its head. There was no thought of danger; men wore little or no armour and carried only personal arms: helms, shields, swords, spears and bows and arrows. Conversation was light, a pleasant sense of 'joie de vivre' filled the air and all was jolly.

Matters were soon to take a downward turn however. On their way to the rendezvous Harald Sigurdson and Tostig were conscious of a mildly worrying cloud of dust on the horizon. A cloud moreover lit by the occasional flash of sun on armour. With what in hindsight seems an ingenuous faith in his immediate family, Tostig reassured the King that these were just a few relations arriving early to greet him. An explanation accepted by Harald with perhaps just a tinge of doubt. Family? Certainly! Greeting? Yes! But this was no friendly get-together; brother Harold had arrived post-haste, had spent the night at York and, in full battle order, was en route to deal terminally with sibling Tostig and his Norwegian friend.

The battle of Stamford Bridge was short, sharp and, although by no means an easy Saxon victory, was nevertheless decisive. According to legend, King Harald was struck in the throat by a Saxon arrow and expired on the spot. Tostig fared no better and, by the end of the day, Harold Godwinson had disposed of two contenders for his throne.

The conflict is enigmatic in that the Norse account speaks of Saxon cavalry and sharpened spears placed in the ground against them. It also emphasises the use of archery by both sides. Although each reported tactic has been disputed — for the Saxon host did not use cavalry tactically — it is evident that the house-carles were mounted, if only for speed of movement. Equally, the use of archery by the Northern fyrd is perhaps more likely than in the South, where the bow was less prominent and there seems little reason to doubt its employment by Harold's men here. Evidence certainly exists for the bow's use militarily in early Scandinavian history.

There seems no doubt that the Norwegians were taken by surprise and, it is to their credit, that they put up such a valiant struggle. Harald and Tostig were hastily grouping their army to the East of the Derwent River, thereby obliging Harold first to take the bridge. If legend is right, this was valiantly held for some time by just one Viking who single-handedly slew a number of Harold's house-carles, thus giving valuable time for his comrades to form into battle-order.

This brave man, whose name was seemingly unknown and is not recorded by the Saga-men, was at last killed by a spear thrust from below the bridge, delivered by an enterprising Saxon in a borrowed boat.

The sagas tell of a Norwegian line of battle arranged in two ranks with two wings that, bending back, met together to form a wide ring of equal all-round thickness, locked shields making an impenetrable wall. To their front spears were set at angles in the ground, the first rank aimed at a rider, the second at his horse. Their King, his housemen, and the 'Land Ravager' banner were in the centre. Tostig, with his own troops, was a short distance away. The Norwegian archers, without spears and with little or no reserve of arrows, were directed to stand close to the King.

The conflict seems to have progressed in three phases. Firstly, the Normans broke from the shield wall to engage the Saxons more directly. It is said of Hardrada that he himself led this charge *"...hewing down with both hands so that neither helmet nor armour could withstand him . . ."*

With defeat staring Harold Godwinson in the face, the day was saved by Saxon archers, one of whom — or so says the Saga — hit and killed King Harald with an arrow through the windpipe.

As the scald wrote later:

> *". . . The King whose name ill-doers scare*
> *The gold-tipped arrow would not spare . . ."*

Overall control, with custody of the 'Land Ravager' then passed to Tostig and, after a pause for breath on both sides, during which the remaining Northmen were offered peace and Tostig a sizeable chunk of Northern England (a proposition scornfully rejected by the Norsemen, if not perhaps by their surrogate leader, who may have seen Nemesis approaching) it all began again. Once more the fighting was exceptionally fierce and during this the unfortunate Tostig was slain.

In the meantime however, hurried word had been got back to those Norwegians still at their Riccall base and, headed by trusted leader Eystein Orre, who now took responsibility for 'Land Ravager,' a relieving force arrived post haste in full panoply of battle, exhausted but ready for the fray. This very nearly proved a turning point in Norse fortunes for, despite tiredness after a long forced march, Eystein and the reinforcements rallied the flagging Vikings and renewed their confidence.

A combination of Saxon tenacity and Norwegian weariness eventually settled the outcome however. The few remaining Norsemen straggled back to their ships in disarray to make tracks for home. It is said that of the 300 (some accounts say 500) ships that brought the army, just 24 sailed away.

With brother Tostig and Harald Sigurdson safely out of the frame, King Harold Godwinson had now just one contender for his throne with whom to deal. Duke William of Normandy — and he was on his way!

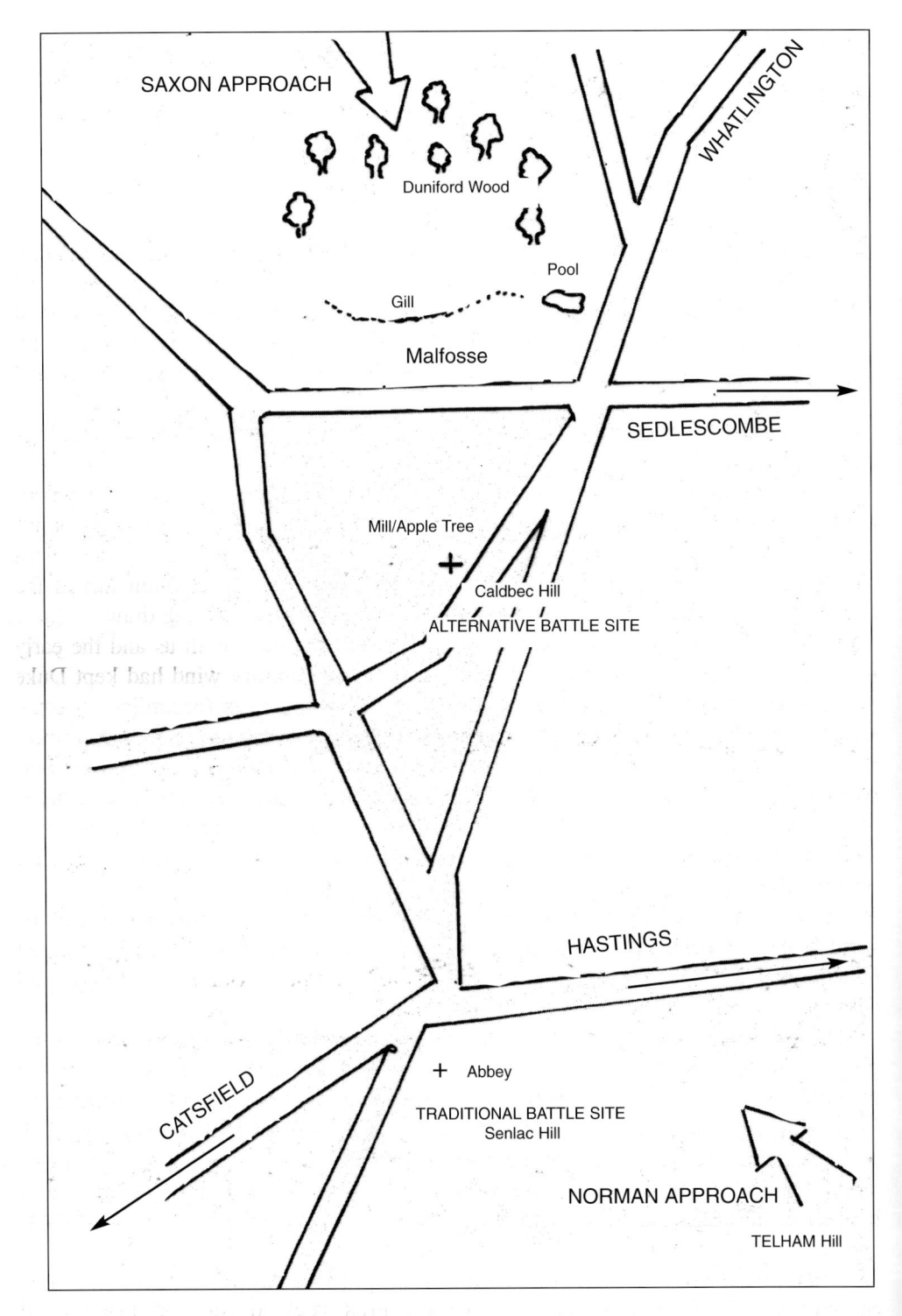

BATTLE OF HASTINGS, October 14th, 1066

HASTINGS, 1066

IF ANY English King could be said to have gained his throne by sheer hard graft, then Harold, elder son of Earl Godwin of Wessex must be among the principal contenders. One of four competing candidates, each with a pedigree bearing at least superficial scrutiny, each with a track record of determined skulduggery, Harold — by astute leadership and inspired force of arms — had, at Stamford Bridge, eliminated two.

But Stamford Bridge was now history; the stage was set for the final act. Hastings was yet to come.

Now it is commonplace for us English to regard our fickle climate with phlegmatic ambivalence. Accustomed as they were to mud and steady rain on important occasions, our stolid warrior bowmen were well prepared for Agincourt. Whilst both in happier days and modern times, the vagaries of weather have often turned the certainty of National defeat at cricket and other games into ego-salving draw.

There have been occasions though when luck has not been with us and the early Autumn of 1066 A.D. was one such time. Although a contrary wind had kept Duke William of Normandy and his army away from Saxon shores (according to some accounts for around a month), during that time those butse-carles or sea-borne soldiers who manned Harold's anti-invasion fleet were getting distinctly twitchy about their harvest. Thus, with desertion looming and some degree of self-interest — since much of the harvest was on Godwin land — coupled with no immediate signs of activity from William, Harold had little choice but to disband his off-shore soldiers to care for their on-shore livelihoods.

So it was that, with what amounted to open sea in front of him and a favourable wind at last, Duke William of Normandy, holy relics around his neck and, no doubt butterflies in his stomach, prepared to sail for Saxon England, Harold Godwinson and destiny.

From its assembly at Dives-sur-Mer, the voyage of William's fleet to its departure point at St. Valery-sur-Somme had not been without incident. Vessels were lost and men drowned. William chose not to publicise the fact however, perhaps to avoid denting morale in an army by now stagnating from enforced inaction. On September 27th he departed, accompanied by the precious war-horses of his cavalry, encouraged no doubt by the prognosis of his soothsayer who forecast victory — correctly as it happened, although one feels there to have been a certain restriction of available choice.

Thus it was, with the wind now to his advantage and no naval force with which to contend, by the following day the entrepreneurial William and his fleet lay off Pevensey Bay, ready to land.

The journey had been comparatively trouble-free; few men had been lost overboard, although it is noteworthy that these included the soothsayer who, to be charitable to him, seems to have overlooked his own fate whilst concentrating upon the broader picture.

Disembarkation on the 28th was not entirely uneventful since William stumbled on the uneven beach and fell to his knees; an episode not unconnected perhaps with his breakfast of mulled wine. He made little of the event however and archers, men-at-arms, palfreys and war-horses were soon assembled in good order on the shore.

Whilst Harold may have been unprepared for the invasion — suggested by the lack of a welcoming fyrd — he was quickly apprised of William's appearance and, with characteristic speed and firmness of purpose, he and his housemen departed there and then from York for London and Southern parts.

The Duke meanwhile had moved along the coast, burning and pillaging as he went. There was method in this action; Pevensey and Hastings were Godwin territory and it was Harold's family land that was being despoiled. There are few things better calculated to bring a hot-tempered Saxon to the boil than to have someone making free with his possessions and King Harold Godwinson was no exception. Without real foothold, William was vulnerable and he knew it. He needed action, the earlier the better. Moreover, he knew how to get it.

Although Harold had stopped off at London before continuing his march South, he and his elite force of victorious house-carles were inevitably tired. They had fought and won a major battle against formidable opposition by the slenderest of margins and, although morale was no doubt buoyant in consequence, it is fair to presume that ranks were significantly depleted and required restoring to full strength; whilst the southern fyrd needed to be raised and told where to muster to provide essential auxiliary back-up force.

This may be relevant to the apparent lack of Saxon bowmen amongst the troops. Historically the strength of English archery has come substantially from the North. No particular reason is offered for this, although it may be that the bow was less a feature of everyday life in the South than in the colder, harder North, with predatory Scots permanently in the offing. But the surmise is dangerous. (The writer is a Southern archer by accident of birth, but with entrenched Northern roots and dare go no further along that road!)

Whilst Harold was re-grouping his military strength in London, William had been busily examining potential battle sites. Although he could influence the matter by the positioning of his army, the final choice would fall to Harold who, with his mounted troops, was even then making his way by night through the Wealden Forest towards Hastings, seemingly with the (unfulfilled) object of surprise.

Arriving at the forest edge by dawn, Harold surveyed the scene. The assembly point is believed to have been an old apple tree; a convenient place at the conjunction of three of the Hundreds of the Rape of Hastings, and a meeting place which would have been familiar at least to local military leaders. Once there, Harold had to decide upon the site which he would defend and, in this he may have had limited choice, since far from being surprised, wily William was by all accounts ready and waiting.

It is here that we move into the heady world of legend and fiction, interspersed with little hard fact; for despite tradition so deep-set as to be virtually immutable, there is limited concrete evidence for the battle-site at Senlac Hill. No 11th Century source for the battle was by an eye-witness and there is another local possibility in Caldbec Hill — equally as defensible against cavalry attack and unfavourable to archery, besides being somewhat closer to the forest edge and thus affording shelter in the event of the unthinkable.

However, the 12th Century Chronicle of Battle Abbey is naturally precise about the site, the Memorial to Harold stands where legend had it that he fell. A spot, chosen originally by a group of monks sent by William for the purpose, was subsequently changed, allegedly by personal command of the Conqueror; although it is said by the Chronicler that he did not actually revisit the scene of his triumph.

Let us leave the discussion there, before it becomes heated. As Professor Jim Bradbury, who covers the matter fully in his recent book[1] mentions, there are vested interests whose ire would be roused above and beyond boiling point if long-held belief were ever to be faulted.

By circumstance, or by choice, wherever it was that he set his personal banner (the 'Fighting Man') and with it the Wyvern Dragon of Wessex (rallying Standard of the West Saxons), Harold marshalled his men in traditional Saxon fashion. Facing the Norman army were his house-carles, picked men who formed the shield wall. Armed with two-handed, broad-bladed battleaxes, wielded left-handed, backed up by keen-edged swords, this elite force of dismounted professional infantry were formidable foes whose worth was respected by all who had met them. William would have had no doubt of their abilities.

Behind the well-trained body of house-carles ranked the less disciplined fyrd, armed with a variety of weapons and missiles which, until stocks ran out, were hurled over the heads of the front rank into the opposition. One presumes — indeed one hopes — that aims were accurate and that in the heat of the moment, javelins, throwing hammers and other assorted items actually reached the other side. There must have been occasion when a short, overly-enthusiastic Saxon pitched his rock into the unsuspecting back of a large house-carle, followed one supposes by a sharp intake of breath and an immediate apology.

The battle is traditionally said to have begun at 9 a.m. with a volley of arrows from William's archers, directed by pre-arranged signals and verbal command. Although there is a belief (supported by the text of one account) that crossbows as well as hand-bows were in use, their bolts aimed directly at faces and penetrating Saxon shields — none is depicted on the Bayeux Tapestry and the matter remains unproven.

However, unlike the heavier arrow, which retains a capacity to wound or even kill over its full trajectory, the comparatively light bolt relies upon initial velocity for effect. With no evidence of lath (prod) weight to guide, if they were indeed used, the

---

[1] Professor Bradbury devotes several pages of his book to the consideration of an alternative site adjacent to or on Caldbec Hill for the battle. Those open-minded enough to entertain the thought are recommended at least to contemplate his thesis.

assumption is that these were stirrup crossbows and spanned by hand, or perhaps by gaffle.

Thus, with the need for a flat trajectory, discharge of the first volley of arrows/bolts may have taken place at short range. It would be convenient to the crossbowmen if they were out of range of the thrown missiles — bearing in mind an upward slope to the ground and the stated penetration of shields, it may be that contention began at no further than 50 or 60 yards or even closer. If the purpose of a crossbow attack — assuming that it happened at all — was to cause a disruption of the shield wall, as some accounts of the battle's early stage suggest, then the object may have been to buy more space for the cavalry to assemble and charge.

Dwelling for a further moment on the crossbow: if such an attack did precede the first cavalry charge then it is reasonable to believe that an arrow-storm from hand-bow-men accompanied it. However, whilst the crossbow with its flat trajectory would need to have been discarded to avoid damaging the knights, arrow volleys aimed above their heads could readily continue during the cavalry action and, perhaps, intermittently throughout the engagement, to the embarrassment of both house-carle and fyrd alike.

Interestingly, it has been suggested by one eminent authority that arrows shot into the air would be largely ineffective since they would *". . . have lost their force. . . ."* Those familiar with the matter would disagree. A two-ounce arrow descending at above 32 feet per second is effective over its full range; it does not float gently to earth. To prove the point, if one may be forgiven the pun, a replica (Viking) shaft, shot at 45°, has been observed by the writer to penetrate seven inches into the earth on its landing some 160 yards away. Enough one feels to make the case.

As an aside and relevant to Saxon archery (or the apparent lack of it), attention is sometimes drawn to a feature of the Bayeux Tapestry where a soldier is shown lying down with an arrow in his face. Accepting that a Norman is shown — by no means a certainty — this is an indication perhaps that the few Saxon archers present at least contributed something.

With battle joined, the axes wielded by Harold's housemen brought carnage to Norman horse and rider alike and Round One of the fighting went distinctly Harold's way. The slope of the hill, whether Senlac or Caldbec, was against William, deadening the effect of his cavalry charge. His initial assault ended in ignominious failure and, with rumours of his death spreading rapidly through the ranks, very nearly total defeat.

The effective rallying of his troops was a measure of William's charismatic personality. Lifting his visor at this point, he revealed his face for all to see and, at the head of a force revitalised and with confidence restored, he led a further series of cavalry charges against the by now disintegrating shield wall. There seems little doubt that Round Two was won by William.

The battle now entered its final phase. Leofwin and Gyrth, Harold's loyal brothers, with other senior leaders, had been killed earlier and Harold alone stood firm until, if we are to believe the Tapestry and legend, he was struck in the face by an arrow. Although the outcome was still finely balanced, with principal Commanders and many other lesser leaders now out of the frame, the shield wall — depleted by constant cavalry charge and the attention of the Norman archers — faltered and finally broke.

Harold was brought down and killed, the fyrd disintegrated and fled whilst, as required by their oath, the remaining house-carles fell around their dead leader, fighting bravely until the last.

The Tapestry, which depicts Norman cavalry in pursuit of the fyrd, shows inter alia, a mounted archer shooting whilst he rides, whilst two of the fleeing Saxons are drawn with arrows in their faces; an indication of William's military tactics and the importance which he attached to the bow. Were the curiously named 'Archer Wood,' 'Battle Wood' and 'Deadmen's Wood' adjacent to the site perhaps evocative of the rout?

Enigma abounds in descriptions of the battle, not least in the final phase, where there is reference to the 'malfosse' (literally evil ditch) and the death there of an unspecified number of Norman horsemen. The location of this feature has been identified (or so reports an authority upon the battle) as lying 600 yards to the North of Caldbec Hill (favoured by him as an alternative site for the battle itself) behind Virgin's Lane and close to a pool. It is a natural gully, and is named Oakwood Gill. For fear though that we dent legend, we must leave matters there.

DESTINY. It is a measure of this Year of Destiny 1066 A.D. that although near a thousand years have passed, we English still recall its aftermath. For William the Bastard, Duke of Normandy, victor at Hastings, bears a unique title in our long history. We know him simply as . . . the "Conqueror."

POSTSCRIPT. There was a curious ambivalence about William's victory. Hastings gave him the English throne, but it by no means gave him England's heart. The wisest of men, he recognised the quality of the fighting men he challenged, whilst they recognised the quality of his leadership. It was not long before they formed a significant part of his armies; it was after all a Saxon soldier who later saved his life in the heat of battle. As is our nature, we English absorbed 11th Century Norman aristocracy as we had absorbed Norse barbarism a century before.

Principal References and further reading:

Gad Rausing THE BOW, SOME NOTES ON ITS ORIGIN AND DEVELOPMENT. Reprinted by the Simon Archery Foundation, Manchester Museum. ISBN 0 9503199 5 3. 1999

Saxton Pope. HUNTING WITH THE BOW AND ARROW. Reprinted by Wolfe Publishing Co., Prescott, Arizona. ISBN 1-879356 05 8. 1991

Jim Bradbury. THE BATTLE OF HASTINGS. Sutton Publishing. ISBN 0 7509 1291 X. 1998

Folio Society. THE BAYEUX TAPESTRY AND THE NORMAN INVASION. 1973.

NOCKING THE ARROW PREPARATORY TO DRAWING THE BOW

Part 3

The Dragon in the West

The Battle of Anglesey
The Battle of Orewin Bridge
The Battle of Bryn Glas

Part 3

THE DRAGON IN THE WEST

IT IS SAID of us English that we accept change with equanimity. That may be so and despite the valiant efforts of Hereward the Wake and others further North to dispute a fundamental change to the status quo, the stoic English peasant may have cared very little whether his master swore a Saxon or a Norman oath before he cracked his whip.

Matters were more than a little different in the Welsh fastnesses, for 11th Century Wales was a violent place. The Cymry of those times, rather like today's Irish, thrived on internecine conflict and, with the ultimate prize a Princedom, much effort was expended in its achievement by those sufficiently high in the running to care.

This is the story of one such contender, Gruffydd ap Cynan and his attempts to seize and hold his birthright, the Princedom of Gwynydd. But before we begin the tale, we should examine the political and military temperature of the time.

MEDIEVAL Wales, like its neighbour England, was no cohesive whole. Nationalism, as we know it today, was rudimentary. Unification was a thing imposed by Authority upon a peasantry whose concept of National identity extended little further than the next village or, in the case of the Cymry, an adjacent mountain.

Philanthropists were as rare as hen's teeth. With a few notable exceptions, those in the driving seat of power were more used to catering for 'Number One' than their dependants.

Welsh society and economy revolved around the local leader, or petty Prince, the 'tywysog.' He claimed and, dependant upon his personality, largely received, loyalty from those under his protection; whilst he coveted and usually acquired (invariably by military means) the goods and chattels of his neighbour — possessions themselves often bearing more than a hint of blood.

The 'War Song of Dinas Vawr,' a poem by Thomas Love Peacock exemplifies the simplicity of this thought process:

"The mountain sheep are sweeter,
But the valley sheep are fatter,
We therefore deemed it meeter
To carry off the latter.

We made an Expedition
We met a host and quelled it,
We forced a strong position
And killed the men who held it."

Welsh economy was essentially fluid. Summers were spent on the mountain, winters below, in the valley; all and sundry upped stakes and moved with their possessions when the time came. A built-in mobility which served the Welsh well on many occasions when a truculent Marcher Lord had expansionist plans, or an exasperated Monarch was driven to retaliate against raids on his property.

It was very largely a military bond that tied able-bodied men to their leader. War was an expected way of life and something at which the warrior Celt had always excelled. Battle tactics almost invariably involved the ambush — virtually an art-form to the medieval Welsh and a facet of warfare that later English monarchs were not slow to copy.

An onrush of spearmen backed by accurate archery in a mountain forest fastness; this was the last thing that the members of many an English raiding party bent on retribution saw, before a premature meeting with their Maker.

The scenario now set, our story opens in Dublin with the birth of Gruffydd (Griffith to us English). Whilst his mother was of Scandinavian royalty — a fact not always as helpful as it might have been in future confrontations with his rivals — his father Cynan traced a Welsh descent through more than 100 generations back to Adam and thus, to God. A mite more than adequate, even in those litigious days, for the princely prerogative.

Armed with this pedigree and having achieved manhood, Gruffydd left Dublin en route for Wales and his birth-right. Through many vicissitudes, including the battle of Gwaed Erw (in English, the Bloody Field) he established his right as Prince of Gwynedd — the starter as it were for 10, and (so his History tells us) he ruled his people "... *with an iron rod, gloriously in the Lord.* ..."

All was fine for a time. However, Norman influence was now well beyond Offa's Dyke; military architecture, manned by Norman soldiery, was fast becoming a permanent and unwelcome part of the national landscape. Determining to do something destructive about matters, Gruffydd, with a large host (a loose term, conveniently used) arrived at the gates of Castel Rhuddlan and in a fiercely fought engagement, during which many of the mailed and mounted Norman men-at-arms "... *fell from their horses in fighting and many foot-soldiers also.* ..." he, with his spearmen and archers, plundered the castle's Bailey and burnt it.

The status quo thus restored, at least for the time being — for permanence was no part of the shifting political and military scene in those far-off days — Gruffyd returned to governance and the iron rod of office.

Feelings however were running high amongst those opposed to his style of management and whilst he was on a visit to the family home in Ireland, 52 of his personal followers and guard (the history is quite precise) were massacred by dissidents.

The effect of this was electric. From out of the woodwork came one Trahearn,

Gruffyd's arch-enemy and rival contender for the Princedom. He, with the men of Powys "... *a multitude of forces* ..." and aided by traitors, attacked Gwynedd in strength. A great battle took place at which Gruffydd was reluctantly persuaded to return to Ireland; in other circumstances perhaps, that would have been that!

However, Gruffydd was not as other men. Conscious no doubt of his impeccable pedigree and refusing to bow to what might be thought by lesser mortals to be the inevitable, he called upon the family firm for support and, with his confidence bolstered by 30 ship-loads of Danes and Irish (a heady combination calculated to deal comprehensively with the opposition), he returned with enthusiastic determination to the fray.

Sadly however, matters again did not go his way. Although Trahearn wisely moved away to Merioneth, Gruffydd's ertswhile colleagues, unhappy about the share-out of spoils, rose against him, sacking Anglesey; the great adventure ended ignominiously back in Ireland.

Norman Lords, charged by the King with the maintenance of law and order in the Marches, were becoming less than happy with the marauding Welsh and, Gruffydd, being temporarily out of circulation, Hugo (the Stout), Earl of Chester, with others (including, let it be said the men of Powys) invaded the Llyn peninsular, ravaging the land and killing the people.

After some time (history says eight years) the redoubtable Gruffydd, undeterred by the whims of fortune, tried once more to get back on terms with his birthright. Accompanied again by Irish, Danes and Britons but this time under the protection of King Diarmuid (a Royal Irish gentleman more than accustomed to dealing with wayward kinsmen), Gruffydd set foot anew upon Welsh soil.

Once there, he was met by Rhys ap Tewdyer, King of the Deheubarth (and remote ancestor of Henry VII, Henry VIII, et al) who sought his help to rid his kingdom of the men of Gwent. These, accompanied by Norman crossbowmen and others, were making free with his possessions.

Ever one with an eye to expansion, Gruffydd demanded (and was reluctantly given) half of Rhys' territory in exchange for martial aid. Preliminaries thus successfully concluded, the battle of Mynydd Cam was short but monumental in its intensity. Gwent warbows and Norman crossbows were together matched against Danish battle-axes and the spears and lances of North Walians. Trahearn, usurper of Gwynedd and bane of Gruffydd, was paunched by an Irishman named Gwcharki and died on the field, together with 25 of his mounted guard.

Now left in comparative peace, Gruffydd reigned successfully for a short while (the history says a few days). All was not as it might be however. A hitherto trusted follower, one Meirion Goch (the Red) betrayed him to the Normans and Hugo, Earl of Chester, locked him up and metaphorically threw away the key.

With Gruffydd out of action, the Earls of Chester and Shrewsbury (Hugo the Stout and Hugo the Brave) set about establishing law and order, Norman fashion, in Gwynedd — and Anglesey in particular; building castles and manning them with horsed men-at-arms and archers on foot.

For Gruffydd, however, things were about to take a turn for the better. Sprung from captivity by a faithful retainer who found him wandering around the market place in Chester (no place for a Welshman, irrespective of his rank) and who personally guided him to Anglesey, he was once more quickly back in business as a thorn in Norman flesh.

But the horizon was darkening perceptibly. William Rufus, successor to the Conqueror, was less than happy with the re-vitalised Prince. Leading a host of Norman, Anglo-Saxon and Welsh soldiery, with attendant baggage, he made his way laboriously over Offa's Dyke. Once on Welsh soil however, Gruffydd, well versed in Welsh warfare, laid ambush after ambush — the form of fighting in which his countrymen excelled — and a discomfited Norman army was eventually obliged to retreat with much loss and little gain for its trouble for, if the history is to be believed, just one Welsh cow made the journey across Offa's Dyke to England from its home pasture.

The art of good management however is delegation and, to assuage dented pride and salvage something from the exercise, King William deputed his two Earls to continue where he had failed. Accordingly another army was prepared and the two Hugos set out once more to pin the elusive Gruffydd down for good.

This latter, well aware of the situation, retired with two trusted Lords to Anglesey to await developments, having prudently ordered 16 boat-loads of Irish Danes to take the brunt. However, here things went seriously adrift. The Irish, having sized up the potential opposition, re-wrote their terms of reference and appeared aggressively in front of, rather than behind Gruffydd.

Faced with the desertion of a substantial part of his army, the Prince did the only thing possible in the circumstances. He returned to Ireland — history says just for one day. A certain pinch of salt may be necessary here however, for he was certainly back in good time and, before long, face-to-face with both vengeful Hugo's, fully conscious of their Royal mandate.

Let us consider the scenario. It is early morning. A low mist is rising. His back to the sea and with a substantial force about him (including inter alia, the erstwhile otherwise contracted Danes) is a bellicose Hugo the Stout puffing slightly from his exertions. With him, fully equipped for battle is Hugo the Brave.

Before them both are three unhappy Welsh Lords. Nemesis is in the air. However, by one of those chance twists of fate which from time to time change history, help was unexpectedly at hand.

As the Welsh bard had it ". . . *by the Providence of God . . .,*" moving slowly through the grey swirling mists of Menai en route to the mainland and territorial expansion, loomed the fearsome dragon-prows of huge Viking longships. It was King Magnus Barefoot's Royal Norwegian battle-fleet, crammed to the gun-whales with sealers and whalers and grab-what-you-can opportunists drawn from the coasts and fjords of Norway — King Magnus in personal command.

With oars shipped and, one may imagine, more than a flicker of interest amongst his hard-bitten crew, Magnus enquired through an interpreter where he was and what was going on. Informed of the situation and having considered the options (including the chance of neutralising a substantial slice of mainland opposition) the

History records with evident satisfaction: *". . . King Magnus grew angry. . . ."*

Peeling off three ships from his fleet and leading them personally, he engaged both Anglo-Normans and recreant Irish-Danes alike with his sea-borne bowmen. The History again:

> *". . . the French fell down from upon their horses like fruit from fig trees, some dead some wounded by the arrows from the men from Llychlyn (Norway). And the King, unruffled, from the prow of his ship hit, with an arrow Hugh, Earl of Shrewsbury, in his eye, and he fell a humped-back to the ground, mortally wounded from his armed horse, beating upon his arms. And from that incident the French turned in flight, and presented their backs to the men of Llychlyn. . . "**

With the battle of Anglesey over, Gruffydd's affairs ultimately took a turn for the better. He made his peace with the King and, it is good to record that this Prince of the Cantref of Gwynedd, fiery and cunning, brave and tenacious, lived well into old-age to die with his boots off and in peace, a revered man, respected by all.

Author's Notes and Points for Discussion :

* There is some discrepancy in the evidence however, particularly in the trifling matter of who was actually slain. Whilst the translator of the History of Gruffydd ap Cynan names the Earl of Shrewsbury, Anglo-Norman sources correctly identify Hugo the Stout, Earl of Chester as the victim. Clad in full armour, so these sources tell, he took two shafts point-blank. The first arrow, shot perhaps by the King's personal archer, hit the nose screen of his helmet and bent it. The second, shot by Magnus himself if we are to believe the history, hit him in the eye and killed him.

The Saga of Magnus Barefoot related by Snorre Sturlason tells much the same story, but names Hugo the Brave, as the victim The saga tells us that Hugo (whichever one it was) was fully armoured so that ". . . nothing was bare about him saving one eye. . ." King Magnus and a Haligoland archer shot simultaneously, one shaft hit the nose-screen, whilst the other hit the Earl's eye and went through his head. On inspection the fatal arrow was found to be that of the King.

The saga writer commemorated the event in verse:

> *". . . On the panzers arrows rattle*
> *Where our Norse king stands in battle*
> *From the helmet blood streams flow*
> *Where our Norse King draws his bow;*
> *His bowstring twangs — its biting nail*
> *Rattles against the ring linked mail*
> *Up in the land in deadly strife*
> *Our Norse King took Earl Hugo's life. . . "*

THE BATTLE OF OREWIN BRIDGE, 1282

ALTHOUGH separated by over a century, the battles of Orewin Bridge and Bryn-Glas stand as sentinels to the unsuccessful struggle for Welsh independence. Each small as battles go — the one a defeat and precursor to the loss of national cohesion; the other a victory. Both symptomatic of a greater cause.

Although for a while the Welsh Dragon was quiescent — with Marcher Lords and English Kings able to turn their minds to other pressing matters — political and territorial aspirations still seethed within Welsh hearts; ambitions that coalesced in the person of Llewelyn Mawr (Llewelyn the Great). Whilst he was close to the Anglo-Norman Royal family, through his marriage to King John's daughter, Llewellyn did not let this trifling matter stand in the way of his patriotic goal. The charisma of his presence and his considerable successes against Anglo-Norman opposition brought an uncharacteristic sense of national identity to the Welsh and, although this suffered set-back following his death in 1240, the baton of unity which he left was picked up by his grandson, Llewelyn ap Gruffydd (Llewelyn the Last) and, later still, by that brilliant warrior statesman, Owain ap Gruffydd Fychan (Owain Glyn Dwr).

Orewin Bridge, hard by the town and castle of Builth, was fought in December, 1283, and Bryn Glas, close by the border village of Pilleth in Radnorshire in June, 1402. Common to each, a charismatic leader dedicated to the cause of national unity; common to both an outcome directly affected by treachery.

The events leading to the confrontation at Orewin Bridge are complex. Edward I, determined to deal once and for all with Llewelyn, son of Gruffydd — whose exploits were becoming more and more reminiscent of his grandfather Llewelyn the Great — had mustered a considerable army and had methodically made his way into mid-Wales, there to seek out and destroy this thorn in the Royal flesh and with it all aspirations to Welsh independence.

Edward's Commanders had brought the Welsh to bay close to the confluence of the Rivers Irfon and Wye, near to the town of Builth whose castle Edward strongly held. Although their main force was concentrated upon the higher ground above, the Welsh held the bridge over the Irfon in some strength and were in good defensive position. Llewelyn, for reasons that are unclear but which may relate to an unsuccessful attempt to commit the town more closely to his cause, was in Builth and not with his men.

Numbers at this engagement were seemingly not large on either side, but those of Edward's Commander, Robert de Tiptoft (or Tibotoft), a singularly appropriate name in the circumstances, were unusual in that his bowmen were exclusively from the English shires, an indication of the rise in military favour of English archery. No 'friendly' Welsh were present at all.

During Llewelyn the Last's absence, treachery struck a cruel blow. Tiptoft was

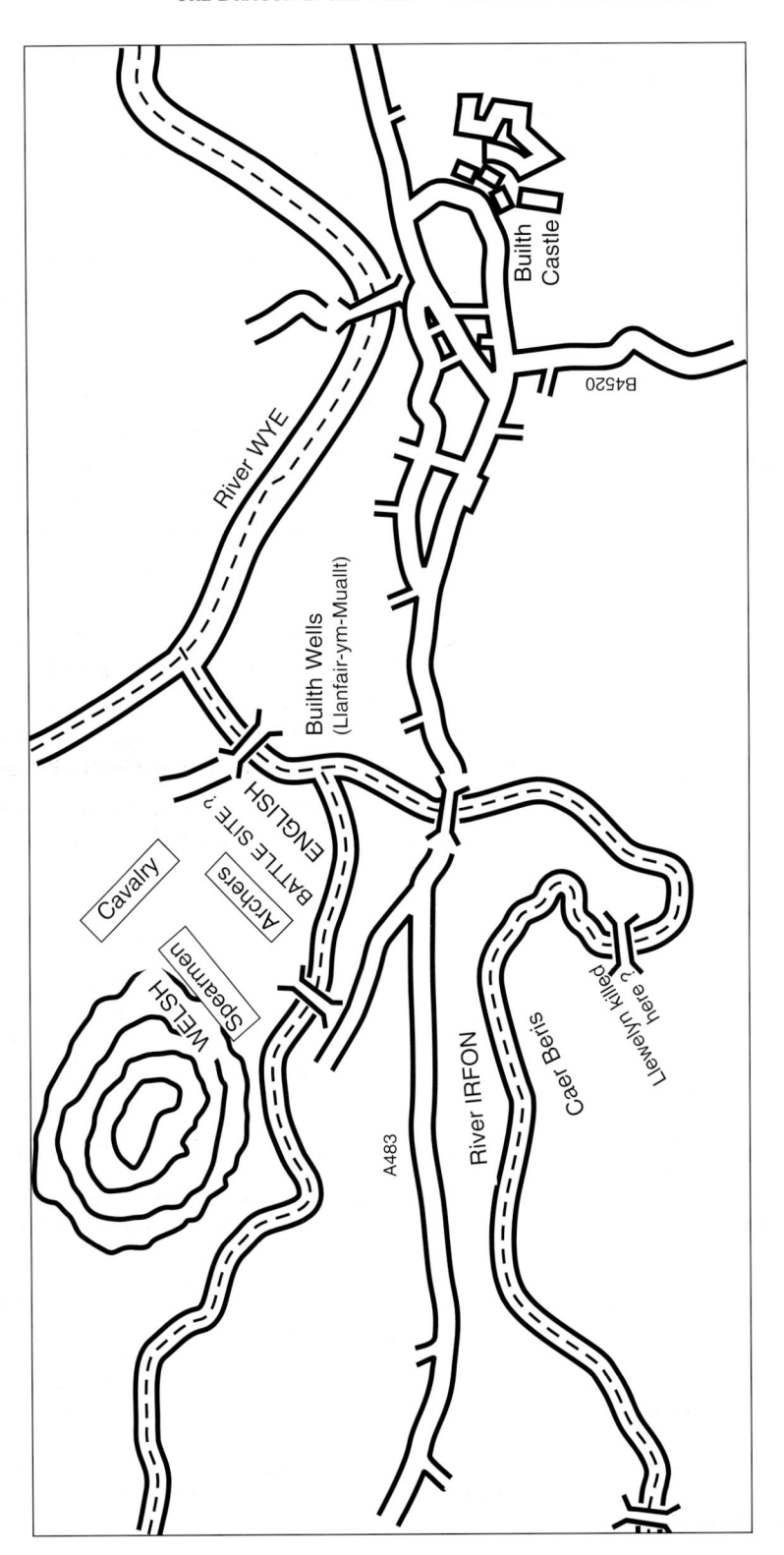

THE BATTLE OF OREWIN BRIDGE — December 3, 1282 A.D.

tipped off — seemingly by a renegade Welshman — about a river crossing-place a little way away and, in a short while, the English were in force on the other side. A foretaste of Blanchetaque, during the Crecy campaign half-a-century later.

Out-flanked, the defenders had hastily to retire to their main force on the higher ground above. Once there, they prepared to make their stand whilst the English, after consolidating their position, moved into the attack. Without their leader, the Welsh spearmen stood their ground bravely but were quickly in disarray. A small contingent of archers shot against the English bowmen — arrow for arrow — but they were finally attacked by mounted men-at-arms on their flank and, with no hope of recovering their position, they dispersed into the surrounding hills and forest.

Llewelyn meanwhile, no doubt hearing the hubbub and the unexpected noise of battle on his side of the Irfon, hurried back unarmed and surprisingly, according to one account[1], seemingly without personal attendants. En route he was waylaid by one Stephen de Frankton (possibly a centenar in command of a Company from Shropshire). De Frankton, although apparently not then knowing who Llewelyn was (although accounts differ in this respect), ran him through with his sword and killed him on the spot.

Politically this was a crushing blow for Welsh thoughts of self-determination. Although Llewellyn's brother, Dafydd, carried the struggle on for nearly a further year, he was not of the same calibre as Llewellyn and was eventually hunted down and betrayed by his fellow Welsh. His sons, Owain and Llewellyn, were taken and sent to Bristol for safe custody; whilst saddest of all, Gwenllian, Llewellyn ap Gruffyd's young daughter, was taken as a baby after her father's death, imprisoned for a time, and then incarcerated in Sempringham Priory[2] until she died in June, 1337 — the last true Princess of Wales.

---

[1] There are at least seven separate versions of Llewelyn's death. I am indebted to a dear friend for drawing my attention to the more important of these. By the account of Walter of Guisborough, de Frankton speared Llewelyn (who was lightly armed) and his servant whilst they were fleeing. Returning later to the corpses, he saw whom he had killed, cut off his head and sent it to King Edward. How, is glossed over.

By the Peterborough Chronicle: Roger l'Estrange, and others, met with Llewelyn and his comrades at 'Gwerthrynion' at eventide and 'confounded him and all his army' so that he was killed there and his head cut off.

By Roger l'Estrange himself: "Know Lord that your good men . . . fought with him (Llewelyn) in the country of Builth, so he is dead."

By a letter of John Peckham to the King: "Lord, know that those who were at the death of Llewelyn . . . he asked for the priest before his death. A treasonable letter signed by false names was found on the body."

By letter of Robert Mannyng: ". . . confess yourself quickly, for you must forfeit your head." In this version, Sir Robert Body, a knight whose sword was sharpest, dismounted and cut off Llewellyn's head.

Folklore tells a different story. Llewelyn had an assignation with a girl, and was treacherously slain. Lastly, although not finally, because there are other variants, a (contemporary) Medieval Welsh poet, Gruffudd ab yr Ynad Coch, in his lament for Llewelyn, mentions a party of 18 who died with him. "A lord of advantage, till 18 were slain." "O heavy swordstroke caused him to stumble." "There indeed was a man, till a foreign hand killed him." And so it goes.

[2] For those whose roots are deep: although the Priory has long gone, the monument to Gwenllian, merch Llywelyn ap Gruffydd, stands for all time in the grounds of the Priory Church, Sempringham, Norfolk, two miles south of Billingborough, off the B1177.

In a well-publicised and politically important ceremony at Caernarvon, Edward I dedicated his son to Wales as its Prince. That much is enshrined in history. However, there is a curious story concerned with the birth and upbringing of this heir to the English throne and one not, perhaps, altogether lacking in authenticity. It may not be generally known that in the year 1312, a young man, named John Tanner, appeared on the scene with the intriguing information that he and not the Prince, was in fact King Edward's son. The CHRONICLE OF LONDON has the tale, and the alleged facts are worth recording:

> "... *he seide thorugh necgligence of his noryce* (nurse) *whil he lay in his cradel a sowe corn in and foule rent hym* (bit him severely) *and the noryce durst not tellen it, but toke a tannere sone* (tanner's son; although another reference names a Carter's son) *and kepte hym in hys stede, and so he was putt to kepyng of another noryce, be whiche he was preved of his rewnie* (deprived of his right): *an for to make this the more certeyne to be beleveyd he shewed the places of the woundes whiche that he seyde the sowe hadde mad. And he seyde Kyng Edward mamers were acordyng with the mamers of hys fadyr for as moche as he loved swyche rude werkes: and for this seyenge moche peple yaf* (gave) *credence to hym and leved* (believed) *hys wordes...*"

Whether there was truth or not in this strange tale it matters little at this late stage. Legitimate prince or charlatan, John Tanner was drawn and hanged and the door of history closed behind him.

Edward IV banned football matches between rival Guilds because he feared football would supersede in popularity, the useful practice of archery.

OF BOWMEN AND BATTLES

PLATE 1

Norman Archer, Hastings, 1066

PLATE 2

GEOFFREY DE CHARGNY
Bearer of the Oriflamme, Poitiers, 1356

OF BOWMEN AND BATTLES

PLATE 3

An English Archer of the Poitiers Campaign, circa 1356

OF BOWMEN AND BATTLES

PLATE 4

Uniform and Equipment of an English Archer, 1375-1435

xviii

OF BOWMEN AND BATTLES

PLATE 5
An English Mounted Archer of the Agincourt Campaign, 1415

OF BOWMEN AND BATTLES

PLATE 6

King Henry V, Agincourt, 1415

OF BOWMEN AND BATTLES

PLATE 7

Guillaume de Martel, Bearer of the Oriflamme, Agincourt, 1415

PLATE 8

SIR THOMAS ERPINGHAM
Captain of Archers at the Battle of Agincourt, 1415

BRYN GLAS (or the BATTLE of PILLETH) 1402

FOR NEARLY 100 years something akin to peace reigned in Wales, until the appearance of one of the most charismatic of all Welsh battle-leaders — Owain ap Gruffydd Fychan, known vernacularly as Owain Glyn Dwr (Owen of the White Water).

Born into a family whose impeccable pedigree included the blood of princes — his birth date a matter of mystery — this forceful man Glendower (for so we English know him) first studied law. The social equal of his peers, he turned quickly from legal matters to the profession of arms, fighting with distinction in the wars of Richard II and proving himself the match in valour of any around him.

It is generally accepted that a feud between Glendower and Lord Grey of Ruthin over disputed land, provided the catalyst for his revolt. Be that as it may, the year 1400 saw his proclamation as Prince of all Wales, his sacking of the town of Ruthin, the settlements at Denbigh, Rhuddlan, Flint, Howarth and Holt and, his capture of Reginald, Lord Grey of Ruthin — a significant political prize.

Despite his popularity, matters went against him initially. Although suffering a crushing defeat at Welshpool by the combined levies of Shropshire, Warwickshire and Staffordshire, he was undeterred. Taking to the hills and forests as his forbears had done, he fanned the flames of widespread rebellion across the length and breadth of the Principality.

Whilst matters were brought more or less under control for a time, Parliament was seriously concerned about the Welsh situation, as well indeed they might be; for Owain was an able and popular leader. The CHRONICLE OF LONDON records:

"... *and in this year* (1400) *began the warre in Walys of Oweyn of Glendore* ..." and, later "... *also this year Kyng Henry rood into Walys be the excitation* (exhortation) *of the Lord Grey of Ruthyn for to destroy Owan of Glondere* (sic)."

In the great English Universities Welsh scholars downed their books and made haste to return to their native land for service under Glyn Dwr's battle flag. Here was a truly subtle choice, for Owen had chosen to rally the Cymry, not under the Red Dragon battle Standard of Cadwallader ('y draig goch') but, beneath the golden war-banner of Uther Pendragon, reputed father of Arthur, war leader of the British and conqueror of the Saxon host at Badon. A clever choice this for, to those who understood, it spelled out his ultimate agenda: nothing less than the recovery of Lloegr (England) the lost lands of ynys prydain (the Isle of Britain).

In Anglesey the Standard of rebellion was raised; whilst on the wild slopes of Plynlimmon, Owain won a signal victory against a superior force gathered for his overthrow. Once again his fortunes were mixed. Confident (over-confident as it appeared) of his strength, he tackled the town and castle of Caernarvon, birth place of the English

THE DRAGON IN THE WEST — BATTLE OF BRYN GLAS

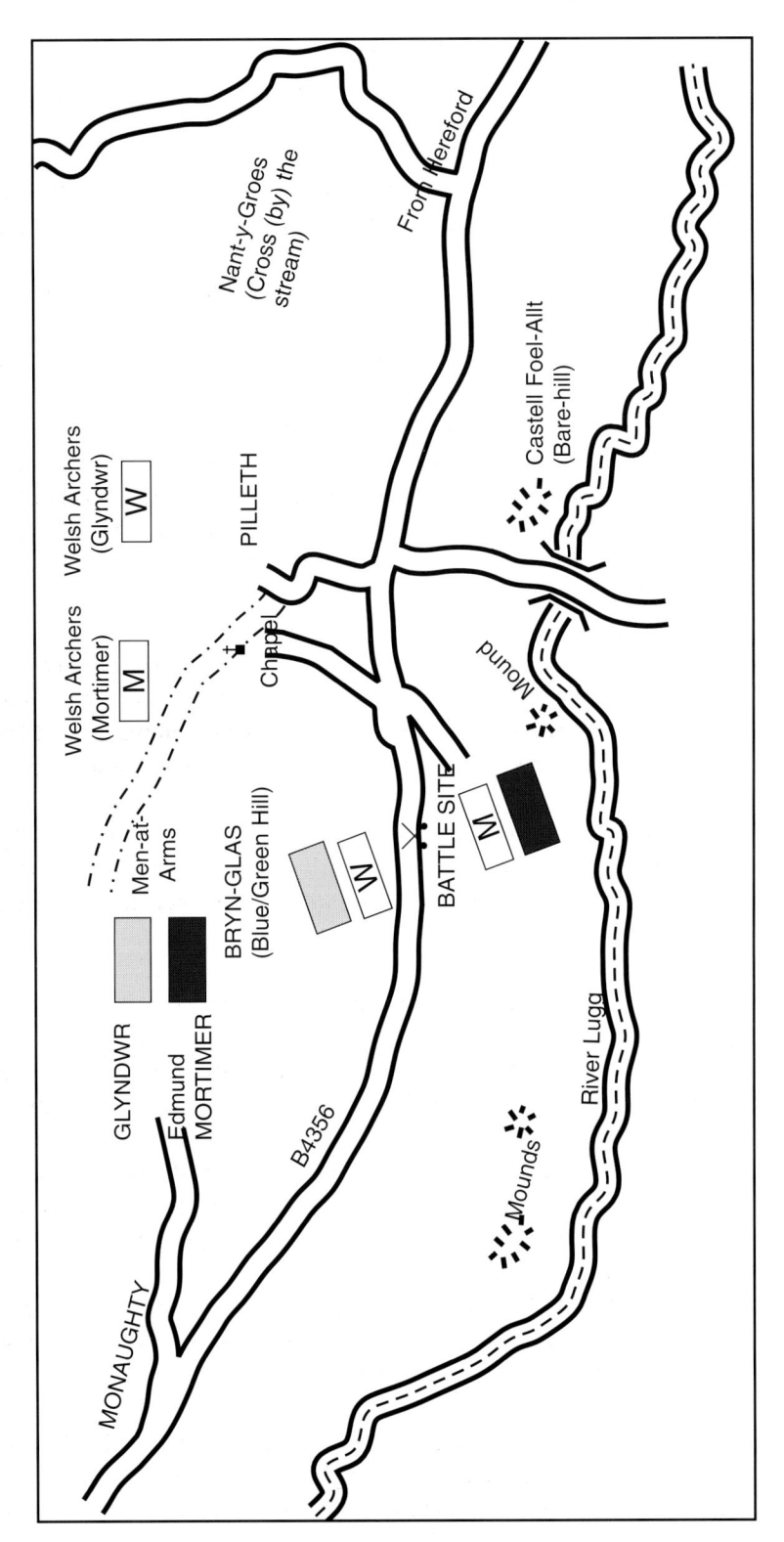

BATTLE OF BRYN GLAS (PILLETH) — June 22nd, 1402 A.D.

'Prince of Wales,' an enterprise which, had it succeeded, would have rallied even more popular supprt to his cause. As it happened however, he failed, losing some 300 of his men.

Unperturbed, Glendower revitalisd his forces and pursuing his policy of striking in new quarters, led his small army across the mountains of Malienydd into the border country of Radnorshire; Marcher territory, controlled for the crown by the ancient house of Mortimer.

Thus it was that in answer to this impudent Welshman, Edmund Mortimer mustered the Herefordshire levy at Ludlow and led them against the intruder. On June 22nd (St. Alban's Day) they joined in battle at Bryn Glas, a hill to the west of the little town of Pilleth.

The traditional site for this battle is on the low ground to the North of the River Lugg, an undulating area falling away gently towards the banks of a shallow river and, from personal observation, an area well suited to the purpose. However, a second and stronger tradition has the battle fought on the steep slopes of the hill immediately facing the present road (B4356) and, if the massacre of which all accounts speak took place, then an ambush by those on the hill top would be entirely in keeping with Glendower's skilful military tactics.

In accordance with the practice of the time, 'friendly' Welsh archers had been called for service with the Herefordshire levy and it was these, infused with sudden enthusiasm for the greater National cause defected to Glendower en masse and from a position of strength on the steep hillside, turned upon their leaders and the following men-at-arms.

We do not know what caused this change of heart; it may be that approaching the hill top the Welsh 'friendlies' became aware of Glendower's archers above them and, to save themselves, turned coat. Or, with that subtlety that has ever distinguished the Celtic mind, it could have been planned thus.

Whatever the reason, the CHRONICLE OF LONDON maintains a dignified silence about the occasion and it has been fashionable to dismiss the action as little more than an ambush. Although not a classical military engagement, it was certainly more than a skirmish however. English losses were considerable and both the military and political outcomes significant. It was reported that for days after, the English dared not approach the field of slaughter to take their dead for burial, which suggests this hill as the battle site. The victims lay exposed to the hot June sun whilst Glendower's men stripped them of their weapons and armour. By tradition, grave pits were dug on the hill-side to accommodate the dead and there is an ancient Chapel close to what may have been the battle site.

Amongst notable casualties, killed along with others, were Robert Whitney, Kinard de la Bere, and Walter Devereux, Knights of the Shire. A particularly important capture was Edmund Mortimer himself. Glendower now had in his possession both Lord Grey of Ruthin, and Mortimer, two considerable prizes.

The King was told the outcome three days after the affair and he resolved to mount an expedition, directing a general muster at Lichfield for July 7th, to deal with Glendower once and for all. In the event however, the campaign, then in its early stage of planning, was postponed sine die; trouble in Scotland and in France proved far more pressing and Glendower was allowed his victory and its consequences.

His advantage was now considerable. He had fought a battle and had won a significant victory; moreover his hold over North and Central Wales had been consolidated. With his Welsh bowmen drawn from the countryside against them, the English were confined to the walled towns and castles; whilst with Edmund Mortimer and Lord Grey of Ruthin in his hands, he had first-class trump cards to play at his discretion. Lord Grey was eventually ransomed for a sum that virtually bankrupted him — and was set free. Mortimer fared rather differently however; on the promise of kingly accession, he joined Glendower's faction and married his daughter, Catherine, to become the great man's son- in-law.

The rebel forces could now be numbered in their thousands; money poured into the Cause, collected by Franciscan Friars who had no love for the House of Lancaster and, were it not for a series of setbacks, not all of which could be foreseen, Welsh history might have taken a different turn. For reasons that are no part of this Chapter, fate chose otherwise and Owain Glyn Dwyr, he of the white water, last claimant to the Princedom of Wales, faded into the mists of time.

Like Arthur before him, his spirit lingers on. In the best of heroic Celtic lore he has no known grave; Hope Hill, Dinmore, Haywood Forest, Callow? Fickle tradition favours each. Monnington Straddell, home of the Scudamores to whom a daughter was wed? Perhaps!! Will we ever know for sure?

Principal References, and further reading:

MEDIEVAL PRINCE OF WALES, The Life of Gruffudd ap Cynan. D. Simon Evans Llanerch Enterprises: Felinfach 1990 ISBN 0947992 47 2.

THE WELSH WARS OF EDWARD I. John E. Morris. (Reprint) Llanerch Publishers: Felinfach 1994 ISBN 1 897853 52 1.

OWEN GLENDOWER (OWAIN GLYNDWR). Sir. J.E. Lloyd (Reprint) Llanerch Publishers: Felinfach 1992: ISBN 0947992 89 8.

THE REVOLT OF OWAIN GLYN DWR. R.R. Davies. Oxford University Press 1995 ISBN 019 285336—8

THE NORSE KING SAGAS. Snorre Sturlason; Ed.: Ernest Rhys. Everymans Library 1930.

THE DRAGON IN THE WEST — BATTLE OF BRYN GLAS

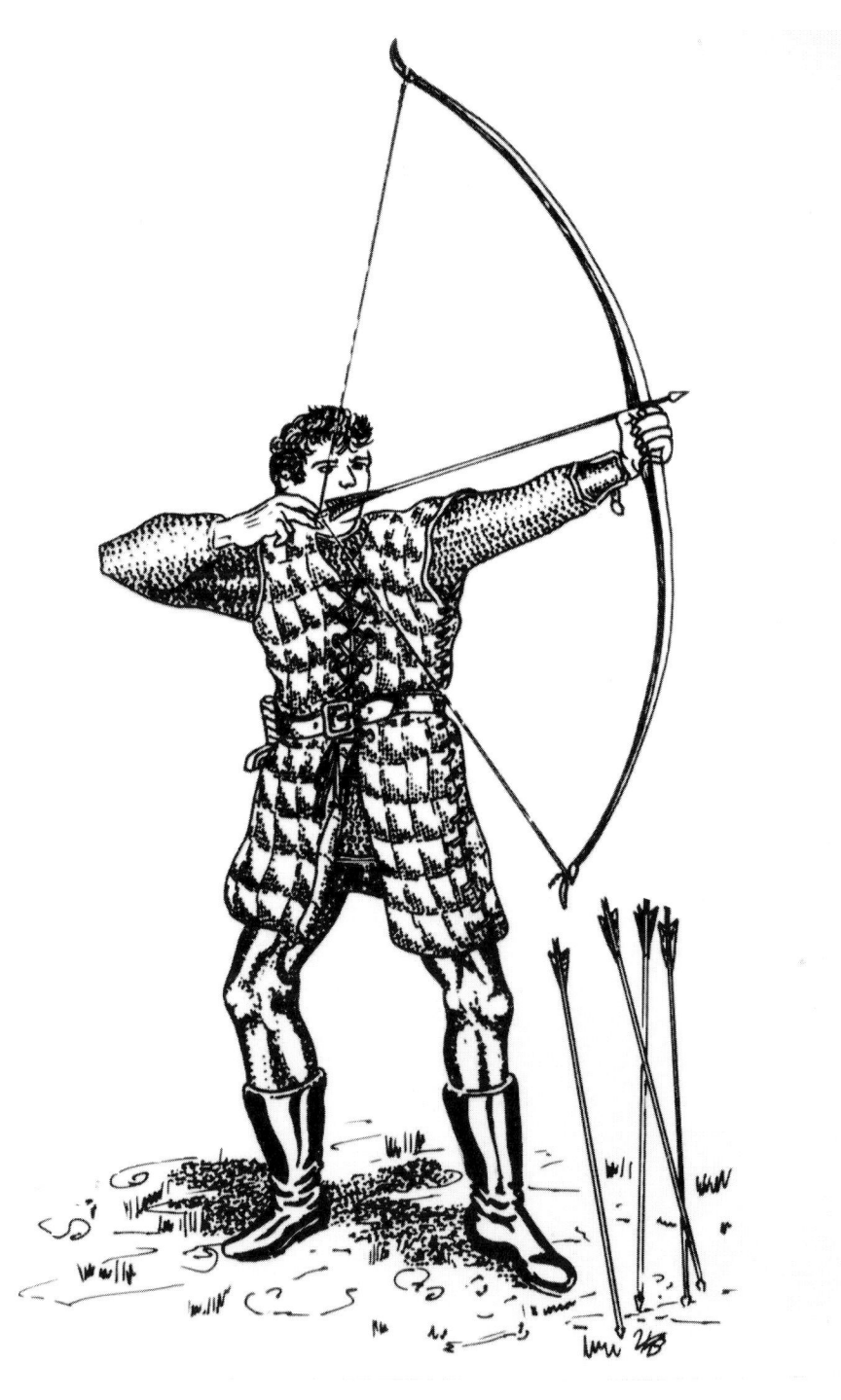

HIS ARROWS PLACED WITHIN EASY REACH THE ARCHER DRAWS BACK TO LOOSE THE FIRST OF HIS BARRAGE

DRAWING THE BOW STRING BACK TO HIS EAR THE LONGBOWMAN IS READY TO LET THE WAR ARROW FLY TO ITS TARGET

Part 4

The Hammer of the North

The Battle of Stirling Bridge
The Battle of Boroughbridge
The Battle of Dupplin Muir
The Battle of Halidon Hill

Part 4

THE HAMMER OF THE NORTH

IT IS A truism perhaps, that a Nation records and celebrates its triumphs and downsizes its failures. So it is with battles. Success is a heady thing and the stuff of which such great films as 'Braveheart' are fashioned, travesty of fact that it may have been. Defeat is remembered only for the lessons which may be learned.

Such was the battle of Stirling Bridge on September 27th, 1297.

One must search deep in English annals for an account of the engagement that September day, for the Chronicle of London, intimate recorder of both the local and the National scene, is silent on the subject. Of the triumph of Scotland over her oppressor, not a word. Of the subsequent battle of Falkirk: Yes! However, that was a victory was it not?

The preamble to Stirling Bridge had been the capture and incarceration of John Balliol, King of Scotland, by English King Edward I, following his success at the battle of Dunbar. With the King gone and many Scottish nobles held in England, the resultant vacuum of power had thrown up a natural leader in the person of William Wallace, a nominal feudal vassal of the Royal house of Scotland.

Brutal fighter and gifted warrior of huge strength and machoistic appeal, it was Wallace's self-imposed and single-minded task to unite the Scottish nation; to rid the country of the hated English and their domination. It was to English military discredit that his worth as a war-leader was not appreciated earlier.

THE FLOWER OF SCOTLAND

A QUICK-TEMPERED man of action, Wallace had been outlawed for killing the son of the English Sheriff of Dundee, together with a number of his retainers, having already made something of a name for himself as a guerilla leader.

Thus it was that in the absence of the blood royal and with the support of a few of the Scottish nobility to guide and counsel caution where this seemed right and proper, Wallace left his forest fastnesses for endeavours new. In June 1297, he raised his battle-flag and, carrying the 'Flower of Scotland's' manhood with him, like fire sweeping through the heather, he led a small army of dedicated clansmen to wreak havoc in the Scottish towns of Aberdeen, Forfar and Brechin, driving the occupying English forces out and away.

Although there can be no real excuses for the outcome of subsequent events at this critical time, King Edward was deeply troubled by political in-fighting over English taxation and other internal matters. Hard-pressed by these, he had perforce to rely upon the Northern forces led by the Earl of Surrey who, comfortably ensconced at Berwick upon Tweed had, it must be said, no immediate plans to leave.

POSSIBLE SITE OF THE BATTLE OF STIRLING BRIDGE, SEPTEMBER 1297

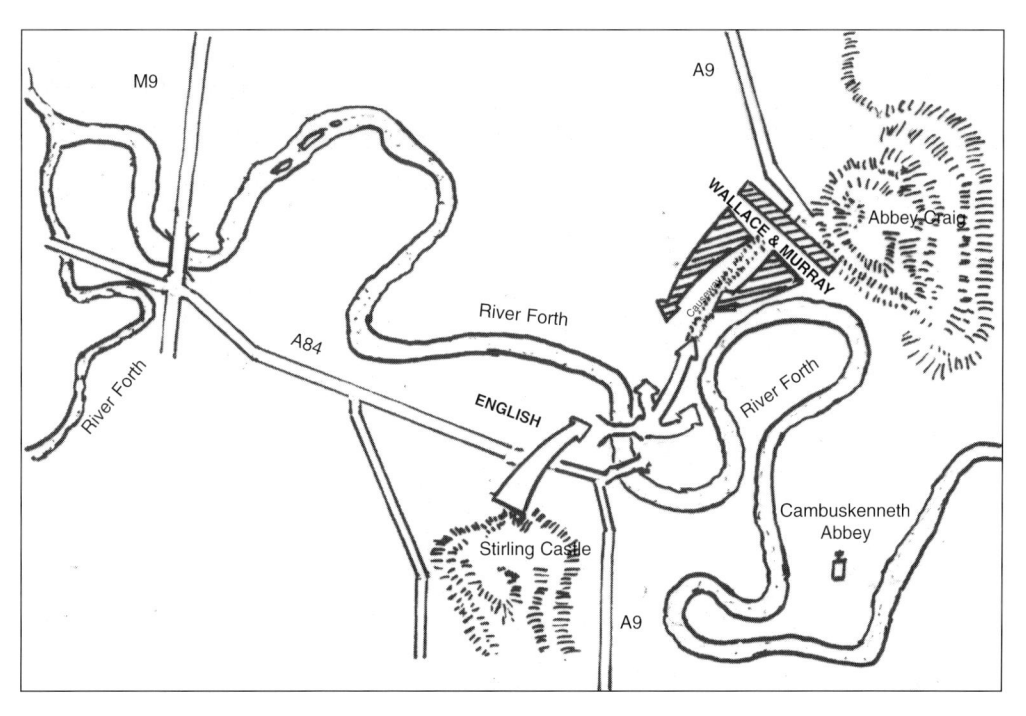

Surrey was a dyed-in-the-wool ditherer who had no great wish to become embroiled in military matters, particularly those involving Willam Wallace. However, he was finally convinced that if anything was to be done about this fire-eating Scot, then it was he who would have to do it. Mustering his forces therefore and accompanied by Edward's penny-pinching Treasurer, the thoroughly unpopular Sir Hugh Cressingham, he crossed the Tweed and, with a supporting baggage train, made his way slowly towards Wallace who, by that time had reached Stirling.

Once at Stirling and, never one to hurry matters, Surrey spent the following three weeks considering what to do next. Meanwhile, across the River Forth, Wallace was encamped with his spearmen in a strong position flanked by a loop in the river, a mile or two to the North-East of Stirling Bridge. To his front a comparatively narrow causeway stretched across wet-lands towards the bridge, at his back the slope below Abbey Craig — rising ground ideal for a withdrawal should one be forced upon him. Here, accompanied by his co-leader Andrew Murray, he waited with mounting impatience for something to happen.

High-powered attempts at peace-making made by clergy and nobility alike proved fruitless. James Stewart (a Guardian of Scotland) and the Earl of Lennox singularly failed to persuade their countrymen against confrontation and, having done so, retired gracefully to sit upon the fence and watch events unfold. Thus it was that with Wallace and Murray obviously prepared for battle, Surrey accepted the inevitable and had perforce to assume the initiative.

It is here that a thoroughly modern circumstance shines like a beacon through the murky medieval scene. The money conscious Hugh Cressingham, in command of the purse strings as he was, had decided that the army was over-manned for the job in hand. Fiscal arguments being as powerful then as they are today, a substantial part of the fighting force was disbanded and sent home

Surrey, who seems to have been as indolent as he was inept, overslept on the day appointed for confrontation, whilst his diminished army and its Commanders waited with fast evaporating forbearance for him to wake up, get dressed and join them.

Since it was increasingly obvious that Wallace was not going to move, it was agreed (and Cressingham had more than just a hand in the decision) that the army should cross the river and assemble on the other side. An eminently sensible proposal by Surrey's Captains to cross by means of a fordable causeway some way downstream was rejected, perhaps by Cressingham on the grounds of cost. The bridge was there; it was of the narrow pack-horse variety certainly, but it was intact and he could see no good reason why it should not be used.

However, the structure was wide enough for only two horsemen to ride abreast and to the incredulous delight of the waiting Scots, the English army advanced like animals into Noah's Ark, two by two.

Thus it was that mounted men-at-arms, accustomed to dismounting and fighting on foot, accompanied by small numbers of Welsh and some English archers and knifemen arrived, assembling as best they might in considerable confusion, partly on and partly off the dry causeway which formed the approach to the bridge.

Waiting until a substantial but manageable portion of Surrey's force was concentrated across the river, Wallace and Murray, with their clansmen struck and, struck hard.

With the English army now effectively cut in two, those on the North bank were quite inadequate to deal with the ferocity of the attack; whilst within bowshot but fearful of hitting their own colleagues, those on the South bank were powerless to help.

Reinforcements could only be got across two by two and proved more than useless, impeding as they did, retreating English men-at-arms and infantry as they desperately sought cover on the Southern side.

Some archers and knifemen, being lightly clad, swam back and saved themselves but, although the Scots by no means had things all their own way (since Andrew Murray seems to have received a wound here from which he died a few weeks later) half of Surrey's army ceased effectively to exist.

Sir Hugh Cressingham it would seem, was singled out for special attention and, although he went down fighting bravely, he could literally not save his skin. Indeed it is recorded that Wallace had his body flayed and a sword belt made of it.

Whilst the Scots had won the battle and won it decisively, they were unable to consolidate their success and Stirling Castle remained in English hands. Surrey, totally traumatised by events, not all of which he could blame on the parsimony of the unlucky Cressingham, handed the keys of the Castle to Sir Marmaduke Twenge and, losing his baggage train to Lennox and Stewart, who were never very far from the action, he hightailed it to Berwick, from which safe retreat he composed a doleful message of failure to his King.

Stirling Bridge was a watershed for English battle tactics in more ways than one. It showed that heavy cavalry was not the invincible force some claimed. It was significantly vulnerable to determined infantry resistance when not acting cohesively and where the pike was involved. It also proved that under a determined leader, the Scots were in deadly earnest and a force to be taken extremely seriously.

Just how seriously was shown a year later when, with internecine squabbles satisfactorily settled, Edward I — conqueror of Llewellyn ap Gruffydd, Pretender to the Princedom of Wales and grandson of the mighty Llewellyn Mawr — focussed his full attention once again on Scotland and William Wallace, now knighted and installed as Scotland's Guardian, in particular.

With 2,500 heavy cavalry and 15,000 infantry, including a substantial number of Welsh archers, 'friendlies' from the Marcher lands and an increasing contingent of English bowmen from the Shire counties, he sought out and engaged the Scottish schiltrons — Wallace's newly created defensive squares of pikemen and cavalry — outside Falkirk and decimated them.

Edward got it right but then he was demonstrably in touch with his Commanders and, moreover, under no pressure from a tight-fisted Treasurer to cut corners.

What of the intrepid Wallace? From being Guardian, and virtual king of his country, he reverted to guerilla captain, harrying where occasion permitted and championing Scotland's cause abroad. Betrayed eventually for the price on his head, he was brought to London's Smithfield and there cruelly butchered. A monument to him, erected belatedly during the 1860's, stands by Abbey Craig, scene of his triumph.

It is not recorded whether Wallace's sword belt was retrieved, or whether its involuntary provider, the unfortunate Sir Hugh Cressingham, was reunited with it in long-awaited Christian burial. In piety we must hope that it was so.

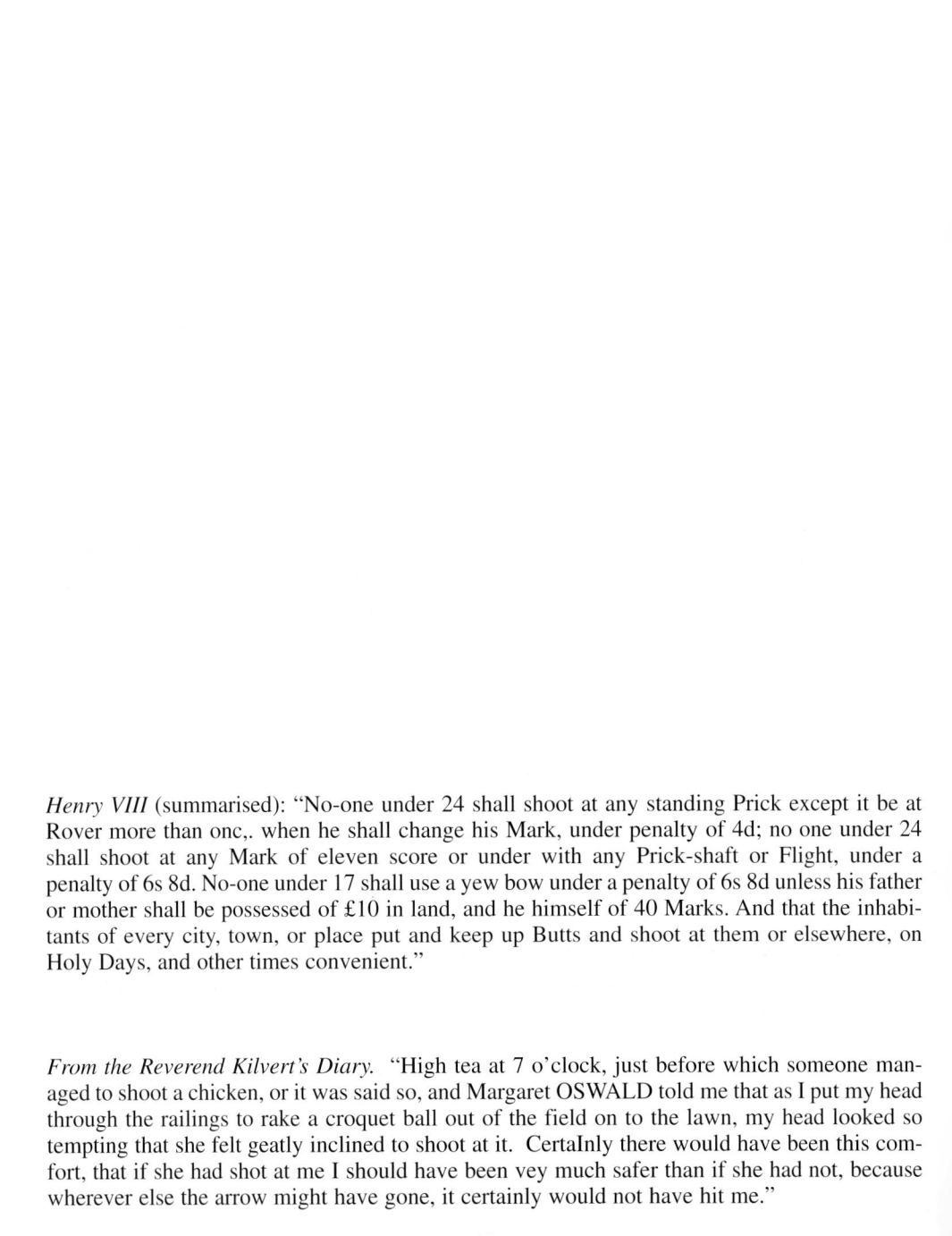

Henry VIII (summarised): "No-one under 24 shall shoot at any standing Prick except it be at Rover more than onc,. when he shall change his Mark, under penalty of 4d; no one under 24 shall shoot at any Mark of eleven score or under with any Prick-shaft or Flight, under a penalty of 6s 8d. No-one under 17 shall use a yew bow under a penalty of 6s 8d unless his father or mother shall be possessed of £10 in land, and he himself of 40 Marks. And that the inhabitants of every city, town, or place put and keep up Butts and shoot at them or elsewhere, on Holy Days, and other times convenient."

From the Reverend Kilvert's Diary. "High tea at 7 o'clock, just before which someone managed to shoot a chicken, or it was said so, and Margaret OSWALD told me that as I put my head through the railings to rake a croquet ball out of the field on to the lawn, my head looked so tempting that she felt geatly inclined to shoot at it. CertaInly there would have been this comfort, that if she had shot at me I should have been vey much safer than if she had not, because wherever else the arrow might have gone, it certainly would not have hit me."

THE BATTLE OF BOROUGHBRIDGE, 1322

TO A GREATER or lesser extent the status quo remained unchanged for a while. Edward II, in whose turbulent reign the Battle of Boroughbridge took place, was not perhaps as other men. Certainly he had not inherited in full measure the strength of his father's character; he was no 'Hammer of the Scots.' Indeed, if one were to believe the script-writer of the film 'Braveheart' — whose interpretation of Scottish history enthusiastically outstripped most known facts — Edward II had, through his mother, a somewhat closer kinship with Scotland than official history records!!

Rather he was a lonely man, seemingly mis-counselled and frustrated in governance by powerful opponents; unduly influenced in matters of State by the handsome Gascon nobleman Piers Gaveston, a dominant friend with whom, it was rumoured (probably correctly) he had the closest possible personal relationship but whose private agenda was designed to feather his own nest.

His father, Edward I, had held the country together by a combination of military acumen and dynamic personality. Cold, calculating and ruthless; by destroying the smouldering warrior Prince of Snowdon, Llewellyn (the Last), he had broken the power of Wales; whilst at Falkirk, in one afternoon, he had decimated the Scottish schiltrons by the power of his arrowstorm, returned Wallace to his woods and glens and tightened the English yoke on a resentful Scotland. His was a hard act to follow.

Edward, his son, had no such flair; although not lacking in bravery and, with some campaign experience behind him, warfare did not come naturally to this young aesthetic man. His instincts were courtly and his inclinations thought unmanly for the time.

Where his father's reign had seen military success arise from initial failure (defeat at Stirling was followed by success at Falkirk and victory at Orewin Bridge expiated the humiliation of Llandeilo) Edward II's reign was to feature the inept tactical disaster of Loudon Hill and, the fiasco of the Bannockburn.

A weak King faced by powerful landed Lords — prime amongst them Thomas, Earl of Lancaster, the King's cousin and Counsellor — was thus the back-drop scenario to an otherwise obscure Northern battle: the military engagement at Boroughbridge.

Edward had no love for Thomas of Lancaster who, with Guy Beauchamp, had abducted his close friend and probable lover, Piers Gaveston, to whom the King had granted free passage overseas. Moreover, Lancaster had followed this calculated snub to regal authority by exiling the powerful Despenser family, Edward's trusted confidantes.

Weak of purpose the King might have been but he could take action when this was needed. Enmity, fuelled by the enforced exile of the Despenser family (including, it should be said, the young and comely fair-headed Hugh, in whom Edward was

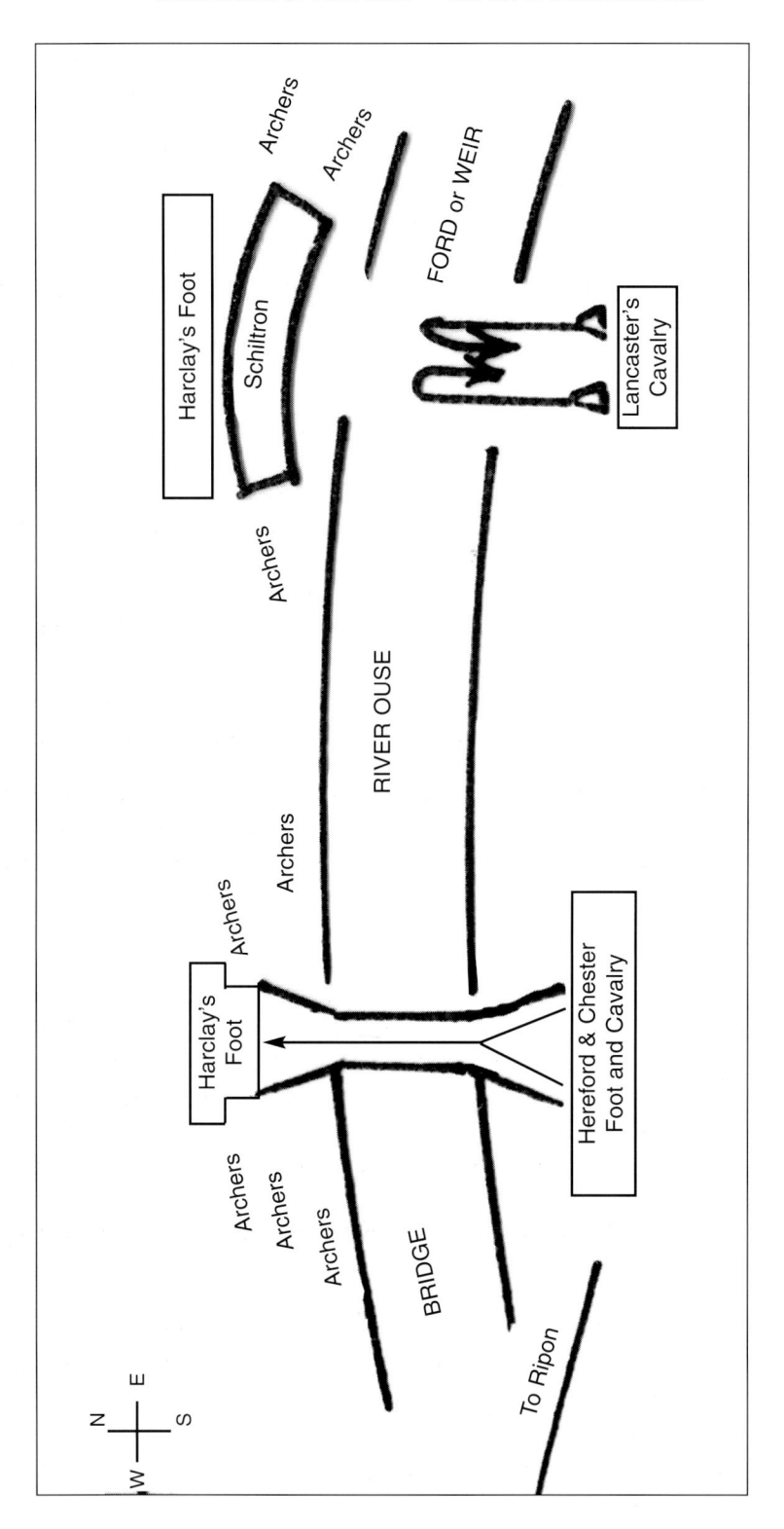

THE HAMMER OF THE NORTH — BATTLE OF BOROUGHBRIDGE

THE BATTLE OF BOROUGHBRIDGE, 1322

developing an interest) compelled action; baronial allegiances, either absent or conspicuously neutral when Lancaster controlled the firm, now consolidated in the King's favour, leaving Lancaster virtually devoid of friends.

Thus it was that on March 16th, 1322, Thomas, Earl of Lancaster, with what friends he had left, his retinue and a rag-tag of an army, were defeated in battle by a brilliantly led force of Northern militia on the banks of the Yorkshire River Ouse.

But, we move too fast. There has been debate as to the reason for Lancaster's withdrawal northwards towards his power base. Initially, it is said, he had wanted to stand his ground and fight the King but the comparative ease with which the Royal force had overwhelmed and defeated a small Lancastrian army (at the town of Burton on the River Trent), perhaps persuaded him that tactical retreat was preferable to a pitched battle in which, as the skirmish at Burton had indicated, he could well have come off worst.

There is also the suggestion (although Lancaster was at pains to publicly deny it) that he was seeking an alliance with Robert Bruce, who understandably had no love for Edward.

An anonymous author records a speech on the subject which he claims was made by Lancaster to his troops. They, if they had heard it, must have wondered exactly what Lancaster and fate had in store for them. For the Earl declared that:

". . . if we go North men will say that we have gone to join the Scots and are traitors. And therefore I say for myself, that I will not go further into the North . . ."

Whether this was patriotic rhetoric forced upon him by circumstance, or reflected his actual intention, we will never know. Sufficient is it that he got no further than the Yorkshire Ouse. The river in early Spring flow was a formidable obstacle and it was in his way.

We are told little of his journey North, beyond the standard record of his despoiling the region through which his army passed. After a forced march to keep ahead of the King, who was rapidly closing on him, his intention had been to halt his soldiers at the town of Boroughbridge to rest the night, prior to crossing by the town's bridge.

His army refreshed, all should have gone smoothly the following day. However, matters were to take a dramatic turn. For when Lancaster's commanders arrived with their forces, ready to make camp and relax, they rapidly became conscious that all was not as it should be. Where there ought to have been an open bridge, facing them was a well-led and exceedingly martial levy; men whose battle experience had been hard-earned against the Scots, troops loyal to the King and men moreover, led by an experienced Commander determined that the rebel Lancaster should proceed no further.

Their leader was Sheriff Andrew de Harclay, a capable leader, warlike and strong in both arm and character. He had been personally commissioned by the King because of his valour and was, in fact, on his way South to join up with the Royal army. Whilst stopped at Ripon he had learned of Lancaster's presence from a spy and, being just a short distance away, he had diverted his small force to Boroughbridge, arriving before Lancaster and securing the bridge.

The rebel Earl was now in something of a dilemma. Although he was still just ahead of the pursuing King's army, the distance between them was not appreciable and was shortening by the hour. In front of him was an unexpected problem but, problems exist to be resolved and this one had to be tackled promptly if he were to have the least chance of success against Edward.

Although hardened in battle, Harclay's opposing troops were comparatively small in number. Estimates vary but a figure of 4,000 in total is mentioned, of which all but 50 were infantry. However, the vast majority were armed with spears or pikes, thrusting weapons ideally suited to a defensive situation such as this. Unusually for the time, Harclay had his men-at-arms dismounted and ready to fight on foot.

After he had sent the horses to the rear, Harclay had deployed his troops, pikemen and men-at-arms, both at the northern side of the bridge and opposite a nearby ford. At the ford he had arranged his pikemen in the form of a 'schiltron' — a 'hedgehog' of pikes facing any of Lancaster's troops foolish enough to try to cross. Harclay also had archers with him and these he placed on each flank — positions carrying some risk it must be said, for, whilst they would be able to harrass any cavalry attack across bridge or ford, they would be immediately vulnerable to Lancaster's own bowmen.

If contemporary chronicles are correct, whilst Lancaster seemingly felt well able to deal with this obstruction to progress, he nevertheless parleyed with Harclay, offering him land and titles if he were to desert the King and join him. Predictably this failed; Lancaster and Harclay returned to their respective positions on either side of the river and the battle began.

Lancaster had decided that his attack would be made by mounted cavalry and it would seem that the assault on the bridge came first, since this was perhaps deemed to be a softer target than the open ford. Led therefore by Sir Humphrey de Bohun, Earl of Hereford and Essex and Lancaster's principal ally, the cavalry gathered in depth and moved forward on to the bridge. For all Lancaster's hopeful anticipation however, once again things did not go as planned.

On the other side of the bridge was no motley local militia to be overawed by the richly blazoned splendour of Sir Humphrey and his fellow knights, rather was it a well-disciplined force of northern pikemen and archers, hardened in the Scottish wars and well able to coldly size up a situation and deal with it expertly and with despatch.

The armour-plated Sir Humphrey, a strong and bellicose leader arrayed in full battle order and mounted on a martial stallion, met the schiltron head-on and suffered the ultimate fate. He was killed outright. His second-in-command, Roger of Clifford, was seriously wounded and what was left of the cavalry retired in some confusion.

Whilst the bridge had not fallen, matters were really no better at the ford. A mounted charge by the cavalry there was met by an arrow-storm from Harclay's northern bowmen before it even reached the water and, although there was some subsequent attempt to move across, news of the fiasco at the bridge quickly reached the commanders and, in the succint phrasing of the Chronicler: "... *their zeal for battle cooled* ..."

His position now almost untenable, Lancaster was forced to negotiate a truce to see to his wounded and to re-group his forces, intending no doubt to resume the struggle on the following day.

Once more, however, matters were not in his favour. He awoke next morning to be greeted by commanders who nervously informed him that a large part of his army had disappeared overnight. His troops had accurately summed up the position as hopeless and were busily engaged in looking after themselves. Now in total disarray, his army melting like snow before his eyes, Lancaster retired with his personal retinue to Ripon.

Once there matters took a positive turn. The resolute Harclay had now been joined by the Sheriff of York, commanding a rather larger force; encouraged by this substantial addition to his strength, Harclay determined to top and tail his success by surprising and capturing Lancaster and his retinue of men-at-arms and esquires at their lodgings. This he did with customary efficiency and consummate success, handing the errant Earl and his crestfallen followers to the Sheriff for incarceration at York to await the arrival of Edward.

Boroughbridge lost the rebellious Thomas, Earl of Lancaster, both his aspiration to power and, subsequently, his head. Of no comfort whatever would it have been for him to know that from the methods used to defeat him, would be forged future fighting tactics of the English infantry; tactics which would prove invincible against French chivalry some 20 years hence. The Battle of Boroughbridge was a victory of infantry, pikemen and archers over mounted cavalry. It consolidated a refreshingly new tactic in English military organisation; for in all succeeding engagements English commanders dismounted their men-at-arms and had them fight as infantry, supported on their flanks by massed bowmen with their devastating arrow-storm.

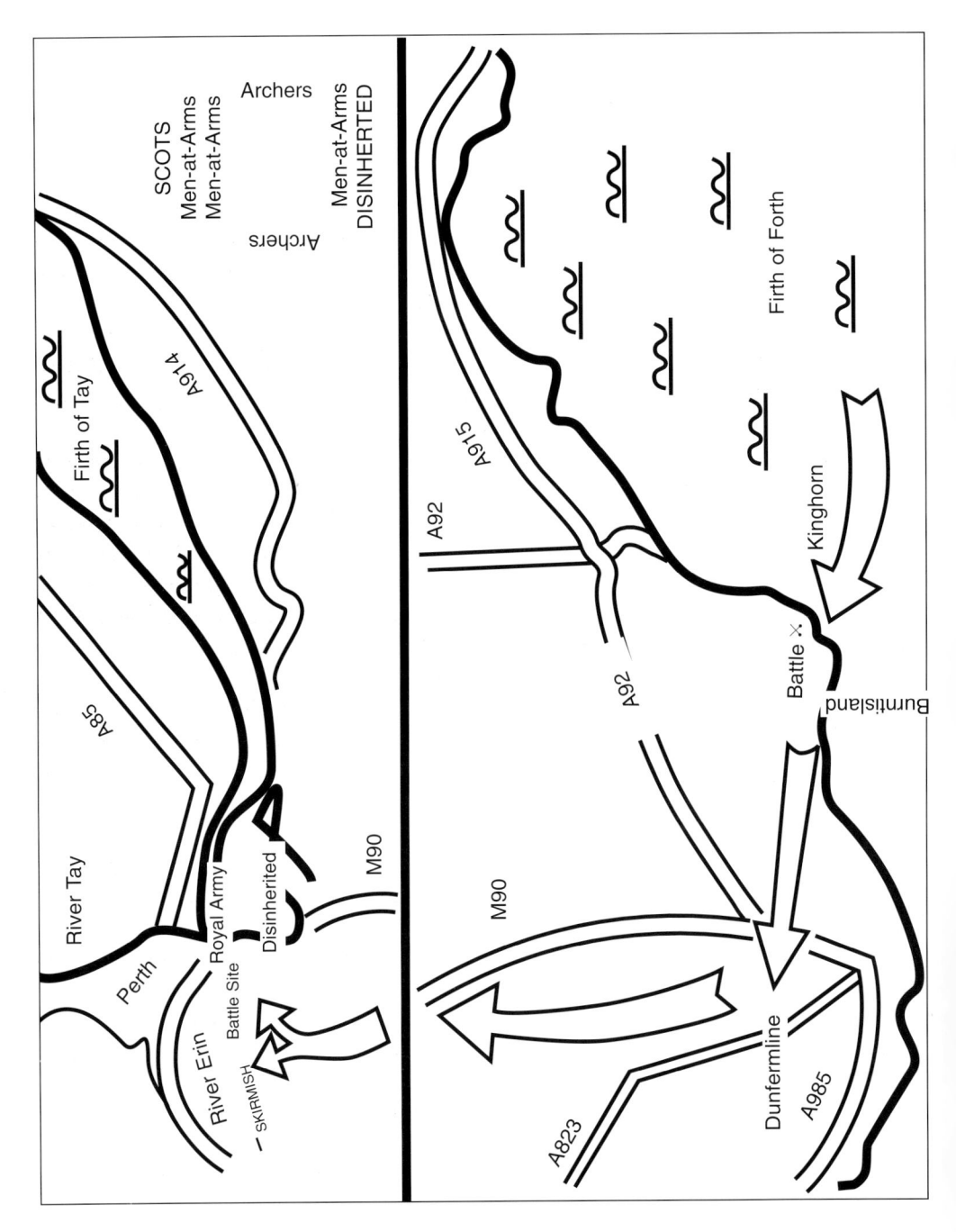

The Two Stages of the **B**ATTLE OF **D**UPPLIN **M**UIR, 1322

THE BATTLE of DUPPLIN MUIR, 1322

ALTHOUGH not the best known of early 14th Century battles, that fought at Dupplin Muir (Dupplin Moor to Anglicise the name), in Scotland, during the winter of 1332, was an important preliminary to the resounding defeat inflicted by the forces of England a year later, on the slopes of Halidon Hill, Berwick.

Politically, England was in some disarray. Edward II had been deposed and was to die horribly at the hands of torturers in Berkeley Castle, Gloucestershire. Succeeded by his teenage son, Edward III, power was nevertheless firmly in the hands of the young Edward's mother Isabella, and her live-in lover, Roger Mortimer.

In Scotland, matters were not a lot better. A Treaty recognising Robert Bruce as effective ruler of that country was now shaky indeed, a situation not helped by Bruce's age and frailty. Unwilling to risk losing his throne under the new English management, the Scottish King decided on desperate action. Observing the old and well-tried maxim that attack is the best form of defence and, gathering his forces, he took the offensive. Crossing the border (significantly on the day of Edward III's Coronation) he entered the Counties of Durham and Northumberland, besieging and taking Norham Castle, South-West of Berwick, ravaged the countryside around.

Goaded into action — for a Scottish army on the loose in the Northern shires was a serious danger — an English force was hastily got together and, led by Mortimer and the young King, despatched Northwards to deal with the matter. The subsequent brief campaign was anything but successful. Although Norham Castle was relieved, this was the only positive outcome. Bruce and his elusive army melted away, pursued by mounted men-at-arms increasingly bogged down by glutinous Northumbrian mud and followed laboriously and, at considerable distance, by a supply train which finally became completely stuck.

It is reported that the bread carried by each knight for food became so contaminated by horse sweat that it was inedible!

Adding to Mortimer's problems, a party of Hainault mercenaries engaged for the occasion to look for Scots, decided that they had had enough of Northumbria and its weather and summarily departed South for food and a good wash.

Not the least of the Hainaulters' worries was their relationship with the English. Never an easy link at the best of times, matters had deteriorated to armed confrontation following a brawl over dice with men from the Bishop of Lincoln's company. Other archers rushed to support their companions — bows were strung and arrows flew. Peace was eventually restored with much difficulty and only after intervention by fully harnessed men-at-arms. Casualties were heavy amongst the lightly-armoured bowmen but for the rest of this abortive campaign, the mercenaries had to watch their backs.

Thus it was that by August, an exasperated Mortimer finally gave a justifiably pleased Bruce best and a weary and bedraggled English army returned home in ignominy. The Weardale Campaign, as it became known, was not of the kind that graces Battle Standards

A year later Isabella and Mortimer negotiated the Treaty of Northampton with Robert Bruce, removing all English claim to Scotland and acknowledging him as rightful heir. Although Bruce survived barely another year, he died knowing that by his audacity he had secured the integrity of his beloved country.

Bruce was succeeded by his young son David and, as had occurred South of the Border, a struggle for power began. Not involved, or at least not overtly so it must be said, were Isabella, guiding the under-age Edward and Mortimer who, with uncharacteristic delicacy of touch had decided that it was politically expedient for them to observe the very recent Treaty of Northampton, the ink of which was, after all, scarcely dry. Thus, therefore, it was that young David at four years of age — scarcely out of nappies — exchanged his potty for the throne without overt English interruption.

Principal contenders for Scottish power were a group of exiled Scots known collectively as the 'Disinherited,' since they had lost their lands on Robert Bruce's usurpation of the throne. Including the Pretender, Edward Balliol and a number of influential lordly landowners, this gathering of disaffected nobles set about plans to seriously upset the Royal Scottish apple-cart.

By 1332 they were ready for action. Their plan: to invade Scotland and secure the throne for Balliol, the spin-off being recovery of their own sequestered lands. Campaigns, however, cost money. No mercenary works for nothing and the army that Balliol and his cronies had in mind was nothing short of the crème de la crème; strong and powerful men-at-arms, coupled with that emergent vital force, the mighty English warbow and the men of independent mind who had its mastery.

With money raised by leasing land, supplemented by an advance provided by the belligerent Archbishop of York (whose personal agenda for Scotland would have given young David nightmares had he known it) the army was raised. Small it may have been — in fact, by some accounts, barely into four figures. However, as someone once said, it's not size that matters but what you do with it, and the 'Disinherited' were soon to prove that true.

On July 31st, 1332, without it should be said, the overt permission of King Edward, the 'Disinherited' set sail, landing at Kinghorn shortly afterwards. Somehow though, the Scots had wind of their intentions and, once ashore, they were met by a force significantly larger than their own led by Duncan, Earl of Fife, determined to deal swiftly with the landless lords.

However, with an ease that boded ill for the Scots, Duncan and his troops were routed and savouring this early victory, Balliol moved west to Dunfermline, to re-stock his supply train with food and weaponry.

Regrouping, and in good spirit, the 'Disinherited' then set out for Perth, skirmishing as they went and expecting to meet the Royal army sooner or later. Their expectations were realised at Dupplin Muir, by the River Earn.

Before engaging King David Bruce's army, the 'Disinherited' had first to cross the Earn. Local fords were unknown and the more obvious crossing points were adequately guarded. However, through fraternal sympathy with the cause of fellow landowners (an endeavour perhaps to save his skin, or just downright treachery) the Lord of Cask, a local nobleman, is said to have pointed out a shallow crossing place where no Scottish night-guards had been posted so men-at-arms and archers were able to cross stealthily by night, in good order and without significant military hindrance.

Numerically, descriptions of the opposing troops are mixed, so often the case in the aftermath of battle. There is no doubt though that the 'Disinherited' had the smaller number; accounts differing between a low of 500 (a figure which seems improbable even allowing for the quality of its composition) and a high of 3,300. It is described however in contemporary documents as consisting of 'strong men'; strong as it proved both in physique and mind, since the sight of the huge force opposing them would surely have frightened lesser mortals.

Besides the men-at-arms, simple infantry and substantial companies of archers from the English shires, a group of some 40 mounted mercenaries provided the only cavalry in the Expedition. Whether these were part of the ill-fated Weardale fiasco is not said.

The 'Disinherited' had perforce to fight on foot. That they had brought horses we know but sea passage for these, even for the short distance involved, would have been expensive and difficult to obtain in those days. Numbers may not have been large; apart from the mounts of the accompanying leaders and whatever it was that hauled the baggage train, it seems that shank's pony was the expected form of transport.

Although surprised by the appearance of the invaders on their side of the River Earn, the Royal army set about preparing for battle. A certain heady confidence prevailed, much whisky was consumed and many boasts born of drink were made. The English would be hung up by their tails (a common belief amongst Scots of the time was that their neighbours were so endowed). Had not the much-vaunted English archers been routed at Bannockburn? What was there to fear from so small an army?

Little did they know what lessons had been grimly learned by English tactical commanders from that most disastrous of defeats; little did they know of the quality of the men who now faced them.

The 'Disinherited' had also made ready for the fray. Three solid lines of spearmen flanked by companies of archers, faced a huge Scottish army drawn up in three Divisions, dismounted to fight as infantry on foot. Drums beat, horns sounded and, stirred by the martial sound of the great war-pipes, the first Division of the Royal army moved slowly forward past the flanking archers, gathering in speed and impetus until it met the English spearmen head-on. This initial clash sent the English men-at-arms reeling back some 30 feet but the line held firm, encouraged by Ralph, Earl of Stafford who shouted:

"... *You English, turn your shoulders not your breasts to the pikes.* ..."

Now, on the flanks, in disciplined files, the archers nocked shafts, bent their bows and at the sound of trumpet and tuck of drum, despatched the arrow-storm. Aiming at the uncovered heads and faces of the Scottish infantry, they seriously disrupted the first Division and thus provided breathing space for the hard-pressed infantry.

The pattern of the conflict then took a turn that was later to become all too familiar to the enemies of England. Galled by accurate shooting from the flanks, the Scots massed together in an undisciplined melée, many dying from suffocation or trampling as they sought to avoid the arrows.

Gradually, the unity of the 'Disinherited' infantry overcame the increasing panic of a rapidly disintegrating opposition and, as afternoon merged with evening the Scottish leaders mounted up and fled the field. Left to themselves and leaderless, the Scottish infantry fought bravely on but the result was no longer in serious doubt. The English spearmen, supported now by archers, began a slow but disciplined advance against the Scottish soldiery and these either ran or were killed.

As was so often the case in contemporary warfare, more were slain during retreat than on the battlefield and the Scottish casualties are said to have numbered thousands. Writers of the time record corpses piled a spear's length high. They were buried in a long deep ditch nearby.

If accounts are to be believed, English losses were small; just two knights and 33 soldiers slain. No archers were killed. It is recorded that the slain were buried at King Edward's personal expense, a tacit acknowledgment, perhaps even approval, of an enterprise which politics dictated he could not openly bless.

Although Dupplin Muir did not place Edward Balliol on the Scottish throne as he had hoped since David Bruce was to reign for another 39 years and the campaign might thus be said to have failed its purpose; however, it was nonetheless important for another reason: it further consolidated a major tactical change in English military strategy. No longer would men-at-arms fight habitually as cavalry, rather would they dismount and stand as heavily armed infantry, four-square and waiting. No longer would archers be regarded as supplementary; their role was now well-defined. Massed on the flanks, they provided the arrow-storm which broke the discipline of the opposition. The way was becoming clear for a partnership of equals.

With his heavy war-bow and his deadly battle-shafts, his iron-headed maul, sword and fighting knife, the freeborn English bowman had come of age. Warfare would never again be the same.

HALIDON HILL, 1333

FOLLOWING from Dupplin Muir and in both a political and military sense arising from it, in 1333 came the far more substantial engagement, in both numbers and result, of Halidon Hill.

The political situation in the 1330's was in delicate balance. Edward III of England, whilst still a minor, had been under the thumb of his dominant mother and her close adviser and lover Roger Mortimer. During Edward's minority, a Treaty with Scotland, to which he was technically a party, had been signed acknowledging Robert Bruce as rightful claimant to the Scottish throne. This to the detriment of Edward Balliol, a perhaps more worthy claimant and his supporting nobles: the 'Disinherited' of Dupplin Muir.

Having by now come of age and the Treaty notwithstanding, Edward III determined to correct matters in a way he knew the Scots would understand — militarily by force of arms. A decision prompted as much by a pressing need to curb unwelcome Scottish incursions into his Northern territories as a wish to see fair-play for Balliol.

The scenario thus opens with rampaging Scots in firm possession of the tactically important border town of Berwick-upon-Tweed and Edward — with its relief just as firmly in mind — mustering a large and powerful army of English archers and men-at-arms. This was no 'stick in the mud' Weardale campaign with sweating cavalry pursuing elusive Scots. Rather it was the tactical manoeuvring of a young, coolly calculating soldier king who, with battle-hardened tactical commanders well versed in the art of war, was out to teach his northern neighbours a short, sharp lesson.

Confident thus of the military, if not the numerical superiority of his forces and the eventual outcome of any battle, Edward made tracks for Berwick where, with the object of drawing Scots to its defence, he besieged the town.

Archibald Douglas, the Scots General, was exceedingly wary of confrontation however and even though Edward obligingly offered him and his army free passage to an appointed spot (emphasing the immediacy of his wish for a close encounter by high profile execution of hostages), the cautious Archibald was too wily, or too wary, to accede.

His answer, in fact, was to besiege Bamburgh Castle in the hope that Edward would himself move to its support — a forlorn wish, since the English King was quite prepared to let Bamburgh take care of itself (something it was well able to do) and continued despatching hostages to their Maker in the belief that Earl Douglas would finally be obliged to fight.

A well-founded belief as it happened, since although still not prepared to meet Edward and the English at Berwick, Douglas moved his huge Scottish army with its mass of infantry to Halidon Hill, some two miles to the North of the town. There, on high ground and positioned by experienced and high-ranking leaders, the Scottish army assembled warily but in good heart and awaited Edward's arrival.

Taking advantage of the interval, Archibald addressed his men enthusiastically and with a confidence that recalled Stirling Bridge and Bannockburn rather than Falkirk and Dupplin Moor, thundered that:

> "... the lords of our enemy are on horseback, so that some of them after being put to flight might more easily arrive at the head of those fleeing ..." Stirred by his own rhetoric, he continued in suitably martial fashion:"... do not allow the English to be ransomed, but let the lords and the infantry be slain equally on this day ..."

One may imagine his flame-headed highlanders preparing for the prospective bloodbath with relish. Claymores, two-handed broadswords, Lochaber axes et al were sharpened to the stirring sound of war-pipe and pibroch; the air thick with usquebaugh-enriched Gaelic gusto.

Meanwhile, Edward, with his commanders and an army which, although substantial, was outnumbered — conservatively by five to one — had arrived on the scene. Forewarned of the Scots approach (they could hardly miss such a huge force) they assembled at the base of the hill in a defensive formation, a substantial number of long-bowmen mustered on each flank, supporting three lines of men-at-arms.

Despite the odds stacked against them, morale in the English camp appears to have been high, particularly amongst the archers. They were well aware, as should any cerebral Scot have also been, of the 'stand-off' advantage given them by their chosen weapon; the effect of needle sharp arrow heads delivered from the heavy war-bow upon masses of unarmoured men.

In keeping with the tradition of the time, Edward also delivered an oration to his troops. Rather more restrained than Earl Douglas in his choice of words, he reminded his men — if any of the Northern levy needed reminding — of the personality of the opposition:

> "... It pains me to remember the subversions and massacres they have borne against the people and the ecclesiastics of our time. God willing, the day of vengeance has come, unless you are frightened by their numbers. For trusting in the leadership of God, we will be of equal strength to them in this battle. ..."

Edward and his Commanders had the result of Dupplin Muir, achieved largely through the power of English archery to support them, a force of whose capability Edward was by now well aware.

At the forenoon of July 19th, 1333, the positions were set.* Two strong and confi-

---

* It is of passing interest that there is apparently disagreement amongst academics as to who was actually where on the hill. Although it seems understandable, if not rather obvious, that Douglas would have taken the higher ground, having in effect chosen the battle site; Bert S. Hall of Toronto University, writing in the 'Medieval City under Siege' and quoting an unpublished B.Lib.MS (Harl. 4690 fol. 82v) has Edward at the top, and Archibald below).

dent armies faced each other, neither wishing to take the first initiative. The Scots had chosen the field in the expectation that the English would advance and were not particularly anxious to open the batting. Equally, Edward held his lines in check. This was to be no repetition of Bannockburn.

Stalemate ruled. The sun beat down, crickets chirped and men grew restless. Finally, according to one account, in an effort to get something going, the Scots commanders challenged the English to single combat between Champions. One may guess at a certain stirring of interest, if not a shuffling of feet, amongst both armies as the challenge was accepted on the English side. Stepping forward down the hill came the Scottish champion, a giant of a man, unnamed, but armed with a variety of weapons and accompanied by a very large black dog.

Striding purposefully towards him from below (after having received blessings and doubtless words of personal encouragement from the King) came Robert Benhale, an equally substantial man-at-arms from Norfolk. History does not record much about the encounter, just the outcome, for after some basic preliminaries, Sir Robert met the dog, which he despatched promptly with his sword, following this by first slaying and then decapitating its owner.

One may now fairly assume a certain restlessness in the Scottish camp; a development that Edward must have noted with some satisfaction, since meeting and dealing with a disorderly charge would be his key to a successful outcome.

He hadn't long to wait. Enraged by the summary despatch of their Champion, with bloodcurdling Gaelic war-cries, those soldiers forming the first Scottish line merged into one huge mass and, waving their weapons, sought retribution below, whilst attempting to reach and deal terminally with Edward Balliol, whose presence behind the English lines as an interested observer had more than just rankled with their leadership.

Although reeling from the shock of this attack, the English line held, whilst from the flanks archers poured volley after volley of arrows into the crush, creating carnage and disorder in the ranks. The chronicler of the battle recorded:

> "... Now the Scots approaching in the first Division were so grieviously wounded in their face and blinded by the host of English archery, just as they had formerly been at Glendenmore (Dupplin Moor) that they were helpless, and quickly began to turn away their faces from the arrow flights and to fall ..."

Other accounts suggest that the archers aimed high on the body and this implies point blank shooting at perhaps no more than just 50 yards.

Although the second and the third Scottish lines now advanced, the English line, supported by the activities of the archers, still held firm; gradually it became apparent that Edward was winning the day. Although many brave men remained embroiled in the fighting, more and more Scottish troops deserted the field. As in the aftermath of so many battles, both before and later, casualties were enhanced by the treatment meted out to those fleeing. They were pursued by the remounted English men-at-arms, who mercilessly hacked down and killed them as they ran.

By their own historians, Scottish losses were put at some 10,000 men, including several of their principal leaders, notably Archibald, Earl Douglas. The English death rate was miniscule in comparison (under 20 men was reported, although one tongue-in-cheek account puts the figure at seven!). Low death rates amongst victorious armies are not unusual in historical accounts of battles, in contrast to the losses of the defeated who were cut down without mercy as they fled.

The CHRONICLE OF LONDON, laconic as ever, records the battle thus:

"... *Kyng Edward beseged the castell of Berwvk and upon seynt Margaretes even*(ing) *the Scottes in wondyr* (wondrous) *grete noumbre comen to remove the sege, with whom the kyng faughte and discomfyted them; and there were sclayn of the Scottes viii erles and a m and ccc knyghtes and squyers, and of footefolk mo than xxv m; and of Englysshemen there were dede a knyght and a squyere and xii foot-folke. ...*"

It would be satisfactory to record that following this engagement every-day life in the Borders became that much easier but, sadly, this was not to be. Despite the overwhelming victories of both Dupplin Muir and Halidon Hill, politics being what they were (and indeed even are today), peace was a transient thing and before long, militant Scot and Englishman (and Welshman) were once more locked in mortal combat. It was ever thus.

After the English rout at Bannockburn, the three battles fought at Boroughbridge, Dupplin Muir and Halidon Hill represented a major re-shaping of English military thinking: the use of dismounted knights in frontal formation, with massed archery in close support.

Forced upon local commanders at Boroughbridge by geography and circumstance, the result must have caused much stroking of beards and nodding of heads at the subsequent cold wash-up. There is nothing like defeat — ignominious defeat at that — to concentrate the military mind and, if Bannockburn had done nothing else it had caused a good, hard look at tactics.

Although the livery bows and their battle-shafts armed with forked and swallow-tailed horse-heads and mail-piercing needle bodkins (if those were indeed the names then in vernacular use*) were undeniably effective as killing machines — given conditions in which they could be accurately aimed — history suggests that the carnage traditionally associated with these weapons exists largely in the minds of those who would have it so.

The bow was primarily a disorienting weapon, designed to disrupt enemy cavalry formations and, through them, advancing infantry; concentrating them rather as a herd of deer was concentrated and bringing them forward for slaughter by men-at-arms awaiting their disordered arrival. This is not to denigrate the bowmen or their bows however, for we must not forget that once their initial task was done they moved in as powerful, lightly armed infantry, with sword, dagger and maul, to help their armoured colleagues and, in that capacity undoubtedly proved their worth once more.

Today we archers, who are familiar with the traditional English bow, its vagaries and its strengths, are better placed than many to know the value of their contribution.

---

* Contemporary descriptions included 'duck-bills,' 'bykers,' 'speareheads' and 'hooked broadheads.'

Principal References consulted, and further reading:

THE WELSH WARS OF EDWARD I. John E. Morris 1901. Facsimile Reprint Llanerch Publishers 1994; ISBN 1 897853 52 1.

INFANTRY WARFARE IN THE EARLY 14TH CENTURY. Kelly Defries: Boydell Press 1996 ISBN 0 85115 567 7.

MILITARY OBLIGATIONS IN MEDIEVAL ENGLAND. Michael Powicke: Clarendon Press 1996: ISBN 0 19 820695 X.

THE ART OF WAR IN THE MIDDLE AGES. C.W.C. Oman (Ed.: J.H. Beeles) Cornell Univ. Press New York 1953.

THE WARS OF EDWARD III C. Roger. Boydell Press 1999. ISBN 0 85115 664 0.

ON BOARD SHIP AN ARCHER PREPARES FOR A BATTLE AT SEA, circa 1340

Part 5

Sea and Shore

The Sea-Battle of Sluys
The Battle of Morlaix
The Affair at Auberoche
The Affair at Blanchetaque

Part 5

SEA AND SHORE

THOSE campaigns which began in 1337 with the successful attack by Sir Walter Manny on the Flemish island of Cadzand, and which ended in 1453 with the humiliating English defeat at Castillon, are called conveniently the Hundred Years War. During that period many battles were fought at which the power of archery was prominent and decisive. Others are recorded in which that was not so.

In this Part are outlined four engagements which took place during the 14th Century, each one different to the last; each displaying the bravery we couple with the private soldier. Important threads within the political tapestry hanging in English and Continental halls of power. They are, in the order in which they happened, the sea-battle at Sluys (1340) the battle of Morlaix (1342) the ambush at Auberoche (1345) and the affair at Blanchetache (1346). In Part Six we will dig more deeply and look at some engagements which took place during the 15th Century campaigns.

THE SEA-BATTLE AT SLUYS, 1340

OF THE numerous naval battles, both large and small, fought in medieval times and employing archers, that at Sluys in 1340, on what is now the Belgian coast, is perhaps the best known. One of the principal preliminary engagements of the French Wars, success gave Edward III a much needed naval dominance in the Channel, greatly influencing the outcome in 1346 of what, in recognition of the concluding battle, has become known as the 'Crecy' campaign.

Medieval sea-battles were very much close range affairs. Broadside 'men of war' were unheard of and the King's Navy consisted largely of imprest ships taken from the Southern Cinque ports and the East coast, diverted — sometimes with a less than enthusiastic crew — from their legal (and illegal) activities. A practice continued in modern times. One has only to look to the 1982 Falklands Campaign for a contemporary parallel. 'S.T.U.F.T' — the acronym for 'ships taken up from trade' —formed a significant part of the British battle-fleet.

Although matters changed as the wars rolled on, the Royal House maintained just a small number of 'King's ships' in peace time.

It has been said, with questionable accuracy perhaps, that Edward's entire navy may have mustered just one purpose-made gun: firing quarrels and lead pellets. Sea warfare was very much a hands-on affair. Ships engaged each other by grappling or, no doubt after carefully gauging the opposition, by ramming; locking together to provide a more or less stable platform from which archers on fore and after-castles might shoot. After softening the opposition, subsequently fully-armed and armoured men-at-arms boarded and engaged in hand-to-hand combat, to conduct, in effect, a land battle fought at sea.

No-one can be exact about the relative sizes of either Edward's fleet or that of the French. However, a detailed contemporary list indicates some 200 vessels on the French side, including the 'Christopher' — recently acquired and flaunted as a captured Prize — and another, the evocatively named 'Edward,' together with 28 other 'Royal' vessels.

Included also were a number of huge barges of the 'Norse' type, with two decks, cabins and fore and aft castles. A number of large-oared Genoese galleys, eight of which exceeded 200 men in complement, completed the opposition. A formidable force by any standards.

The French Fleet was moored in four lines, the first three roped and chained together to form one huge floating platform. To their front were four of their largest ships; particularly noticed was the 'Christopher,' loaded to the gunwhales with a substantial number (records say 400) of mercenary Genoese crossbowmen.

All French vessels had been made fully ready for battle. Shooting positions were

Sea and Shore

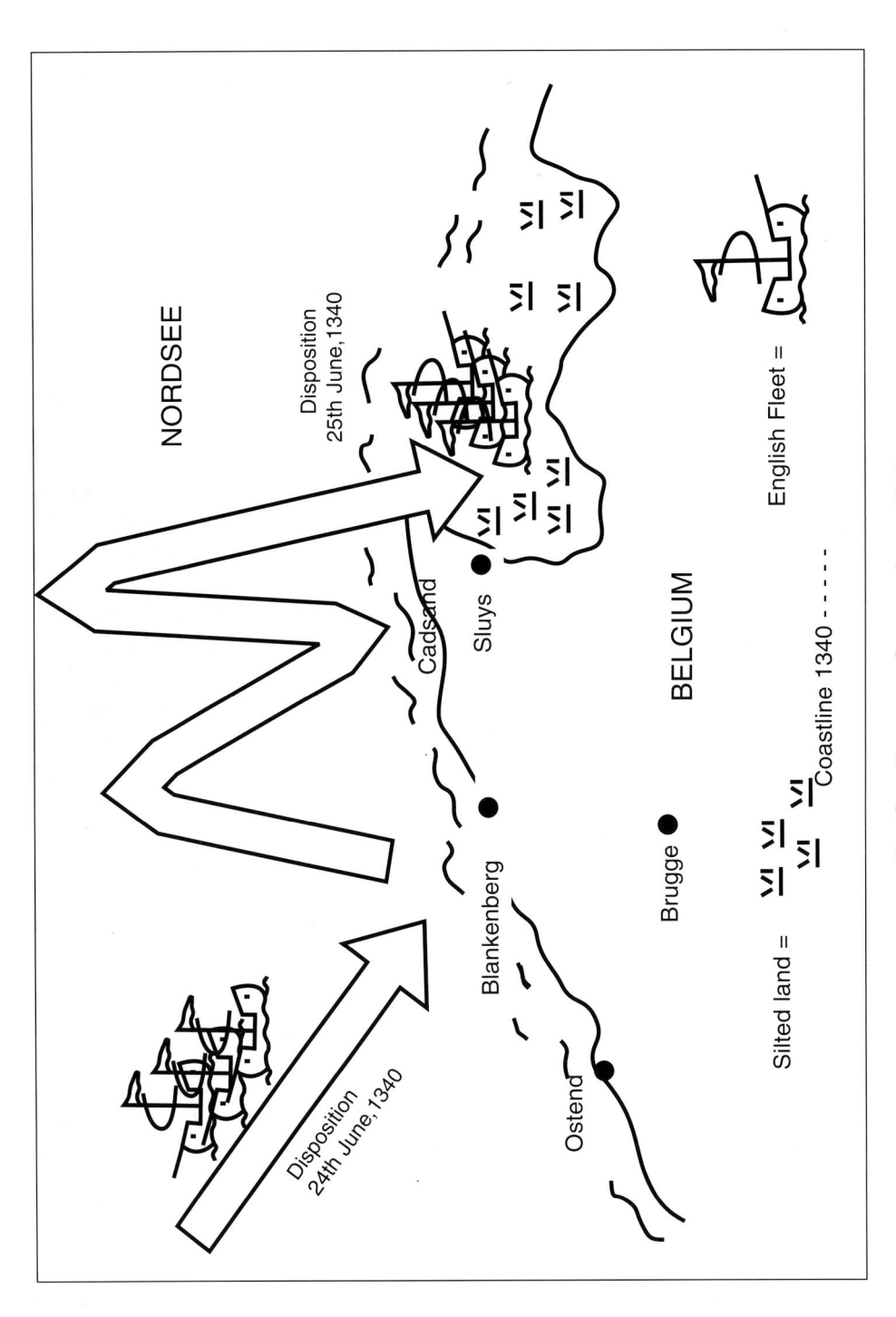

The Sea-Battle at Sluys - June 1340

fully manned and stone-throwers, with the occasional crossbowman in support, filled not only the fighting tops but also the ship's boats which were hoisted to the mastheads.

Against this very substantial navy, Edward may have mustered around 120 armed ships, although individually his ships were rather smaller in size. An able Commander in his own right and advised by, amongst others, the already almost legendary Sir Walter Manny, victor of Cadzand five years before, he positioned his fleet carefully and to best advantage, taking due note of tide, wind and weather. Placing his best vessels in the front line, he alternated archers and men-at-arms ship by ship, much as he would have done were he on land.

The English fleet anchored at Blankenburgh, some 10 miles to the west of the mouth of the river Zwyn: the French fleet being just visible in the bay (today now totally silted). After anchoring, King Edward landed a small force of men-at-arms to reconnoitre the French coast whilst, at the same time passing, a request to his Flemish allies for back-up help.

At sunrise the English fleet weighed anchor and by six o'clock it was ready to sail. However, with the morning sun in the East shining in their eyes, the current running strongly against them and high water some time off, conditions were unpropitious for battle. The fleet therefore tacked about and stood away until it was to windward of the French and the tidal stream had turned.

About noon, half-an-hour after full tide, the English ships downed sail and closed with the enemy. Inevitably there were casualties. Edward by no means had matters his own way against such a formidable and well-prepared enemy. An early loss, with all hands, was a 'nef' (a small vessel) overpowered and sunk whilst optimistically engaging the huge and well fortified French 'La Riche.' (One is reminded of the Royal Navy Corvette, 'H.M.S Glow-worm,' 600 years later at the Battle of the River Plate, gallantly endeavouring to ram the German battleship 'Graf Spee' before being blown out of the water by her broadside guns.)

Things were rather different though when Sir Robert Morley mounted his attack on the 'Christopher.' Honour was at stake here, and his enthusiastic archers put down a comprehensive arrow storm as the vessels closed. The decks cleared as though by magic and, in Froissart's words:

> *"the English archers firing* (sic) *strongly and all together soon showed these Genoese that they were their lords and masters, and entering the ship, conquered them.. . ."*

That business being satisfactorily settled, with Genoese blood clogging her scuppers, the freed 'Christopher' was re-crewed and sailing once more under the banner of Saint George with English bowmen aboard, rejoined the fray on the other side.

After fighting bravely for some eight hours, with the approach of sunset the French first Division finally gave way and the English advanced to the second which quickly succumbed. At about sunset, the Flemings arrived from Bruges, Damme and Sluys to engage the Third Division. The battle continued through the night, 24 French vessels escaping on the morning tide, amongst them the 'St James.' The Master of this vessel, having successfully grappled an English ship from Sandwich, was taking her to France as captive until engaged and dealt with by the Earl of Huntingdon.

The contemporary Royal despatch succinctly summarises the battle and its outcome thus:

> "... *We sailed all day and the night following and on Friday, about the hour of noon we arrived upon the coast of Flanders, before Blankenburg, where we had a sight of the enemy's fleet who were all crowded together in the port of Sluys. And seeing that the tide did not serve us to close with them we lay to all that night. On Saturday, St John's Day* (June 24th) *soon after the hour of noon at high tide* (the time has been computed as 11.23 precisely) *in the name of God and confident in our just quarrel we entered the said port upon our enemies who had assembled their ships in very strong array and made most noble defence all that day and the night following* ...."

Losses on the French side were almost incalculable, some seven-eighths of their fleet was sunk or captured and in and around them, many thousands of Genoese crossbowmen and French sailors and infantry died. Flemish estimates of the English losses put these between 4,000, and 9,000, an indication of the fierce nature of the opposition and the confusion which surrounded the fighting.

The often quoted conclusion to this most bloody of sea-battles is the reaction of those whose task it was to report the outcome to the French King. Legend says that it was finally decided to send in the Court Jester who, appearing in full costume with bells and whistles, waved his mandatory pig's bladder on a stick, and with some trepidation posed a riddle to his King:

> *"Do you know, sire, why the English are such cowards?"* One may imagine the jaundiced eye with which he was regarded. *"Pourquoi, imbecile?!" "Why, Sire, because unlike our brave Frenchmen they dare not jump into the sea!"*

History does not record what King Philip VI did with either the bladder or the stick.

In addition to the many qualities required of him as an archer, the seafaring medieval bowman needed the ability to remain upright and in good aggressive condition when Nature dictated otherwise. A lineal successor to the Anglo-Saxon 'butescarl,' whose task it was to guard the sea-ways, he was often recruited from coastal counties where he would have a more or less intimate knowledge of the sea.

In later times we know that prior to her final refit, archers serving on the Tudor warship 'Mary-Rose' were drawn from Norfolk and, indeed, it is not perhaps improbable that some of those who went down with her in 1545 came from the area as well.

Rapidly gaining one's sea-legs was an obvious necessity for all who served afloat. This fact is neatly illustrated in the un-likely source of a late Robin Hood ballad.

Whilst under the pseudonym of Simon of the Lee, our forest hero takes to the sea as a fisherman. His singular inability to stay upright invites derision fom his shipmates and a threat by the Master to throw him overboard if his stability doesn't rapidly improve.

Danger appears however in the form of a predatory French pirate, to the dismay of all except Robin/Simon who, coming into his own, deals expertly with the entire French crew. Keeping upright is still initially a problem however.

> "...*Come tie me to the mast, he cried,*
> *Against my object fair.*
> *And give me my bend bow in my hand,*
> *Then I'll no Frenchman spare . . ."*

Although this delightful story is transparently fictional, it does high-light what was surely a major problem for muster-masters seeking competent sea-faring bowmen.

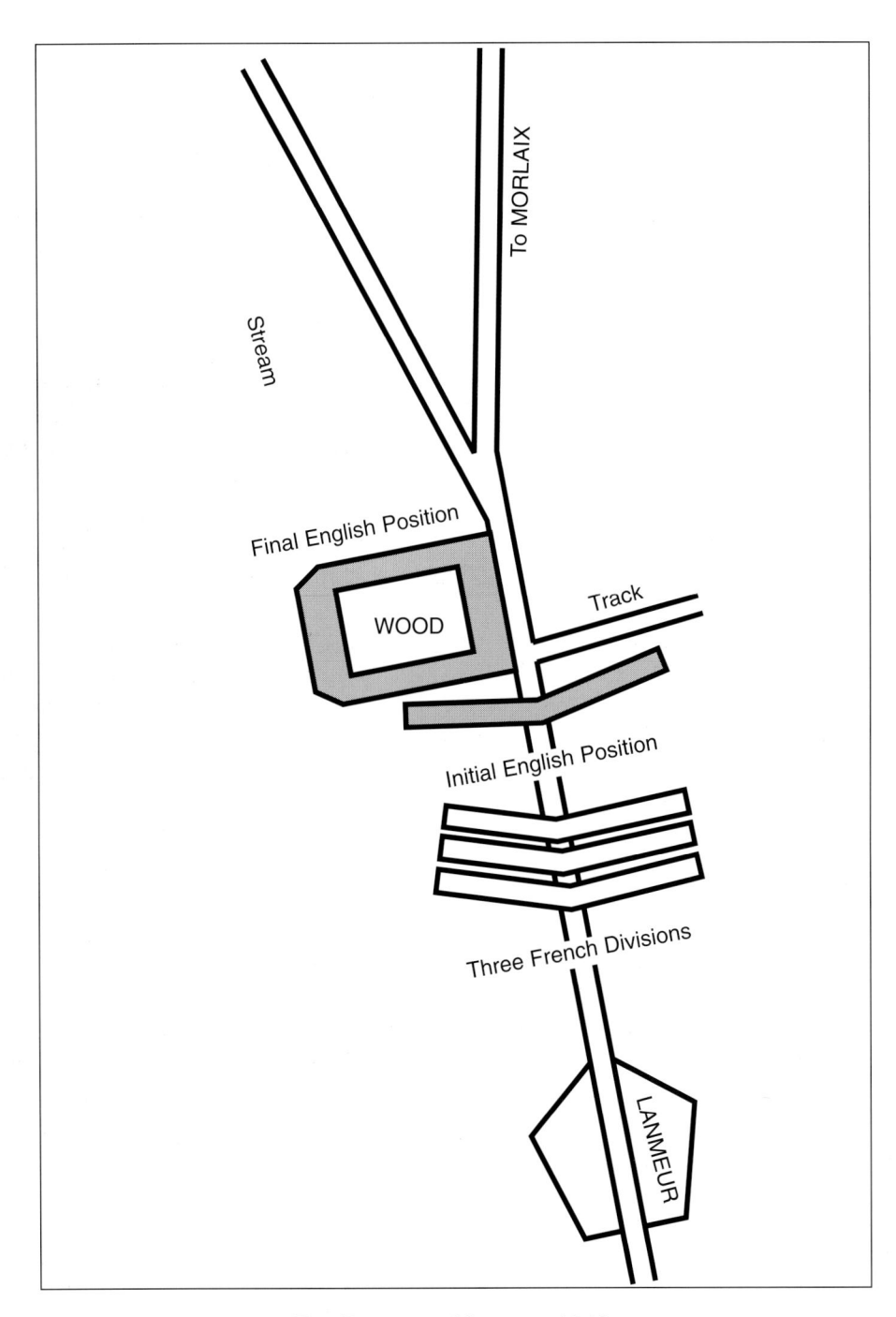

THE BATTLE OF MORLAIX, 1342

MORLAIX, 1342

THE BATTLE that took place just outside the town of Morlaix in the early Autumn of 1342 deserves a good deal more attention than it is sometimes afforded. Not only was it a prelude to the successful campaign which culminated at Crecy, but it so nearly ended in ignominious defeat; a defeat which would have radically affected the course of Edward III's French adventures.

Circumstances which, in the matter of a few brief days, brought an army — scarcely as yet a cohesive force — from its aggressive siege of a well-fortified town to a last-ditch action of defence against very considerable odds, bear telling in some detail.

The political scenario concerns two contenders for power in Brittanny. On the one hand John de Montfort, whose claim was recognised by Edward III; on the other Charles, Comte du Blois, nephew of Philip VI of France whom, understandably, the French King favoured.

Unable to match his antagonist numerically, matters had rather gone against John, who had asked Edward for help. The English King, ready as ever to further his own cause by embarrassing Royal France, was not slow to offer practical assistance and so it was that, in August of 1342, a small army, certainly no more than 3,000 strong and probably fewer, comprising men-at-arms supported by mounted and foot archers, sailed towards Brittany and the Port of Brest.

After four days of fine weather they arrived in good order and in strong heart. Commanded by William de Bohun, Earl of Northampton, assisted by the Earls of Derby and Oxford, with Robert of Artois (a loyal French subject whose martial abilities had impressed Edward in the earlier Flanders campaign) the little army landed close to the port and rapidly established a beachhead.

Garrisoned by English soldiery, the City and Port of Brest was at that time under attack by Charles du Blois, an able if a sometimes injudicious Commander, whose armies had by then occupied much of the adjacent Breton countryside, to the evident dismay of the peasant population. A prime task for Northampton was relief of the city. On the arrival of the English soldiery however, du Blois, being unwilling to risk a major engagement against fresh troops, abandoned the siege and withdrew to the East of the Region to prepare a new war-plan and to obtain much-needed reinforcement.

Brest having now been relieved without undue trouble and, encouraged by the rapid departure of his potential adversary, Northampton moved across the peninsular towards the French occupied, well-fortified and stoutly defended town of Morlaix; his clear intention, to take it promptly and thus consolidate his position before the inevitable confrontation with a major French field army.

There is a significant difference though between design and fulfilment. Conscious of his opponent's potential military muscle and the size of his own small force, Northampton decided upon an immediate assault. His attempt to storm the town's defences was thwarted however; although his fierce attack lasted for the whole of September 3rd, nothing came of it. Whilst keeping both eyes open for the wily Charles, he resorted therefore to his only other option, methodical siege.

Meanwhile, du Blois had fallen back to Guingamp, a village some 40 miles distant, and was actively planning his counter-offensive. Knowing full well the quality of the force opposing him, he had quickly enlisted both trained soldiers and local levies. Estimates of numbers vary, as they do so often in records of early confrontations (an unlikely 30,000 has been suggested) but whatever the total, we may be sure from subsequent events that Charles had very considerable numerical superiority, outnumbering Northampton by at least four to one.

Size however, is not everything. As September 29th dawned, Charles, Comte du Blois, pretender to the throne of Brittany, with his huge and almost certainly unwieldy army at his back, set off ponderously for Morlaix, Northampton and fate.

The English Commander, warned of the advance by his scouts, hastily called off the siege. Rapidly putting his troops and baggage train into marching order, he struck camp and moved off on the road towards the village of Lanmuir, seven miles to the northeast, there to choose a place suited to the defensive battle which he now knew was inevitable.

By dawn the next day he had found a suitable position: his back to a substantial wood, to his front a gentle slope. Here he would await le Comte and his advancing horde.

The little English army, further depleted perhaps by troops left at Morlaix, occupied a position some 600 yards long, the archers stationed in depth on each flank, dismounted men-at arms in the centre of the line. The baggage train, or that part of it which had by then arrived, being carefully placed to the rear, under cover of the forest trees.

September 30th had dawned bright and clear. Under Northampton's directions, archers and others were busily deployed to prepare a trench across their front, some 100 yards from the line. Covered with grass and sticks and protected from immediate view by a small rise in the ground beyond, this would have been invisible to the French whose columns could now be seen manoevring slowly into position.

The English returned to their stations and waited quietly. Men-at-arms adjusted harness and added last minute edges to weapons; archers chose their stands with care, fingering bodkin points and broadheads, or honing swords, falchions and fighting knives in readiness for the hand-to-hand combat they knew would surely come. Arrow stocks were depleted and men had little more than the two sheaves which each habitually carried. Baggage trains move slowly at best, and the small detachment left at Morlaix needed stocks as well. The Morlaix garrison's reaction to the aborted assault was a wild card in the pack and Northampton had to be ready for eventualities.

Through the noon heat haze of a fine September day and, barely moving in the calm air, the limp flags and pennants of Charles' huge army were now in full view.

Eventually, all being ready at 3 o'clock, the French advance began. Charles had divided his army into three Divisions, one behind the other, each separated by a considerable gap. The first Division, sent in to estimate the character of Northampton's force, consisted of the local Breton levies, ill-armed and with no real heart for fighting. Moving forward with some trepidation, they reached the crest of the intervening slope and, coming within bow-shot, took the full brunt of the arrow-storm. Disintegrating almost at once, they reeled back down the hill and into the path of the next Division, to take no further part in subsequent events.

There was turmoil in the French camp. Charles had not expected quite such a swift end to his opening assault and debated with his Captains as to the next move. He decided, upon best available advice, to launch his second Division, a far more formidable force of mounted men-at-arms in a cavalry charge. The plan being for the third Division to arrive to mop up what was left of the defeated English. Such was the intention.

He did not, and could not know, what awaited his horsemen. Northampton's ditch proved more than adequate for its purpose; the levies had not reached it and could thus not have revealed its presence. Horses and men plunged into it in a writhing mass, their plight made worse by the attentions of the archers who shot virtually at point-blank range and, although a small number did get through, they were quickly surrounded and made hostage.

Two Divisions had now come and gone in confusion and, with many casualties. However, there was a third, as yet untouched Division, prepared and ready for battle. Northampton knew its size full well — larger than his own small beleaguered force. Moreover, the trench was now full and no longer a significant obstacle.

With his archers short of arrows and little time to replenish stocks (even had they been available) and, with nothing to impede advance and the distinct possibility of an outflanking move by du Blois, Northampton showed the flair for innovation that was later to become an English brand of warfare.

He ordered a tactical withdrawal into the wood, 100 yards behind his lines. There, with his archers now secure amidst the trees and facing in each direction, he awaited the ponderous approach of Charles' third Division with what patience he could muster. Five hundred years before the affair at Waterloo, an English defensive square had formed to await the arrival of the French!

Charles was puzzled. His Commanders at a loss. Although, following advice, the men-at-arms of his third Division were dismounted, they could not approach closely enough to penetrate the wood. Individually aimed English battle-shafts were rapidly taking their toll. His mercenary crossbowmen, always singled out by English archers for special attention, had broken and fled the field. The flower of Breton cavalry had been decimated, night was rapidly approaching and Northampton had patently neither wish, nor need to surrender.

The option to besiege, even to burn out his enemies, must have occurred to du Blois and his Commanders and, there is some belief that a half-hearted siege was in fact maintained for a day or two. Although stalemate had been reached, with hindsight it is puzzling to know why Charle du Blois gave up his initiative when he did. Whilst numerically stronger on the ground however, he was faced by an aggressively led and, demonstrably formidable force, the extent of which he could not see. Moreover a force still in obvious good heart and probably capable of inflicting considerable further damage on his already exposed and demoralised troops.

As darkness drew on, Charles decided to abandon the contest and, slowly at first but with increasing despatch — helped along by English arrows — his troops made ready to depart the battlefield.

Meanwhile, unaware of his opponent's intention, Northampton had his own problems. Although he could scarcely claim victory, he had fought a vastly superior force to a standstill and, moreover, his own army, although hungry, was still in good heart and virtually intact. He was, however, to all intents and purposes, trapped.

As du Blois was making up his mind to quit the fight, Northampton and his commanders made up theirs. He gave the order to charge and, roaring their lusty battle-cries, English 'goddams' and men-at-arms alike, with swords, falchions and fighting knives, bills and battle axes, launched themselves at the departing enemy, cutting their way furiously through the astonished French lines to reach the other side and freedom.

An observer, if such there had been, would then have been treated to a most unusual spectacle. A large column of French troops was moving away from the field of conflict in reasonably good fettle towards Guingamp, whilst equally-sized columns of English soldiery, in full battle order, were moving in the opposite direction towards Morlaix, and resumption of the siege.*

The engagement outside Morlaix on September 30th, 1342, was the first pitched battle of what was to become known as the Hundred Years War. It was neither a French victory, nor an English defeat. However, if it was decisive in nothing else, it demonstrated to the French the deadly stand-off capability of the English and the English longbow, a lesson to be pressed home later in full and ample measure.

---

* There is some doubt as to the exact number of troops accompanying Northampton on his expedition. Although Edward III's arrival later that year brought some 4,500 men, Northampton may have had an absolute maximum of 2,000, including engineers and civilians, and perhaps as few as 1,000 with him at Morlaix. There is even doubt as to his Commanders. Lt Col: Burne, author of 'The Crecy War,' mentions the Earls of Derby, and Oxford; whilst Andrew Ayton, in 'Knights and War Horses,' writes of the Earl of Devon accompanied by Lord Stafford. Colonel Burne suggests that the almost legendary Sir Walter de Mauny (Sir Walter Manny) with a company of 340 men was present, although other evidence suggests that he had left for England earlier.

All very uncertain; we can only surmise that the odds were well stacked against Northampton on that September day.

THE AFFAIR AT AUBEROCHE, 1345

THE MILITARY campaign in France between 1337 and 1360 has been popularly dominated by two major battles: Crecy and Poitiers. Each catches the imagination, since the English armies were numerically inferior, and might be thought to have been at a disadvantage. As events subsequently proved, this wasn't the case. Albeit with its back pressed firmly against the wall, a largely professional army, well led and with morale boosting victories under its belt, took on huge and over-confident adversaries and beat them into the ground.

Important as these titanic clashes were, there have been other confrontations equally as eye-catching in their way but which have had far less prominence. The battle which took place on October 21st, 1345, a year before Crecy, was one such.

The little hamlet of Auberoche, hard by the River Auvezere, was dominated by its castle. Within these austere walls a small English force was besieged by an excessively unfriendly French commander, le Comte d'Isle. No respecter of dignity or protocol, it is recorded by the chronicler Froissart, that a messenger despatched by Sir Frank Halle, the castle commander, with an urgent need for help, was taken by the Comte and catapulted back inside, to his lasting detriment and the dismay of the Governor.

Happily, however, Sir Frank was eventually able to get word of his plight to the Earl of Derby at Bordeaux and, with the minimum of delay a small army of 400 men-at-arms and 800 archers was raised.

Concerned quite naturally about the size of the opposition — for d'Isle had with him some 7,000 troops — Derby thought it prudent to enlarge his force so sent word to the Earl of Pembroke for a contribution towards the exercise. For reasons best known to himself — doubts perhaps about the wisdom of the venture — Pembroke failed to show up at the agreed rendezvous and Derby, with his tiny army, had perforce to set off for battle alone.

The castle at Auberoche is built upon a rocky outcrop which overlooks the River Auvezere. It lies some nine miles east of Perigueux in Gascony and, in 1345, it dominated the area strategically. Its commanding position made it a natural and essential target for the French and preparations for its reduction were approaching completion.

The French army had been divided into two unequal parts. The larger was encamped in a meadow about a bow-shot in width, placed geographically to the West of the river. The smaller lay in a narrower valley and to the North of the castle.

The noble Comte was fully conscious of his superiority in numbers, the garrison was stubborn but small and, although the task would not be too easy (for the castle was difficult to approach), the result could not be in serious doubt. The days were still long and the weather conducive to idleness; he had no great reason to hurry the inevitable.

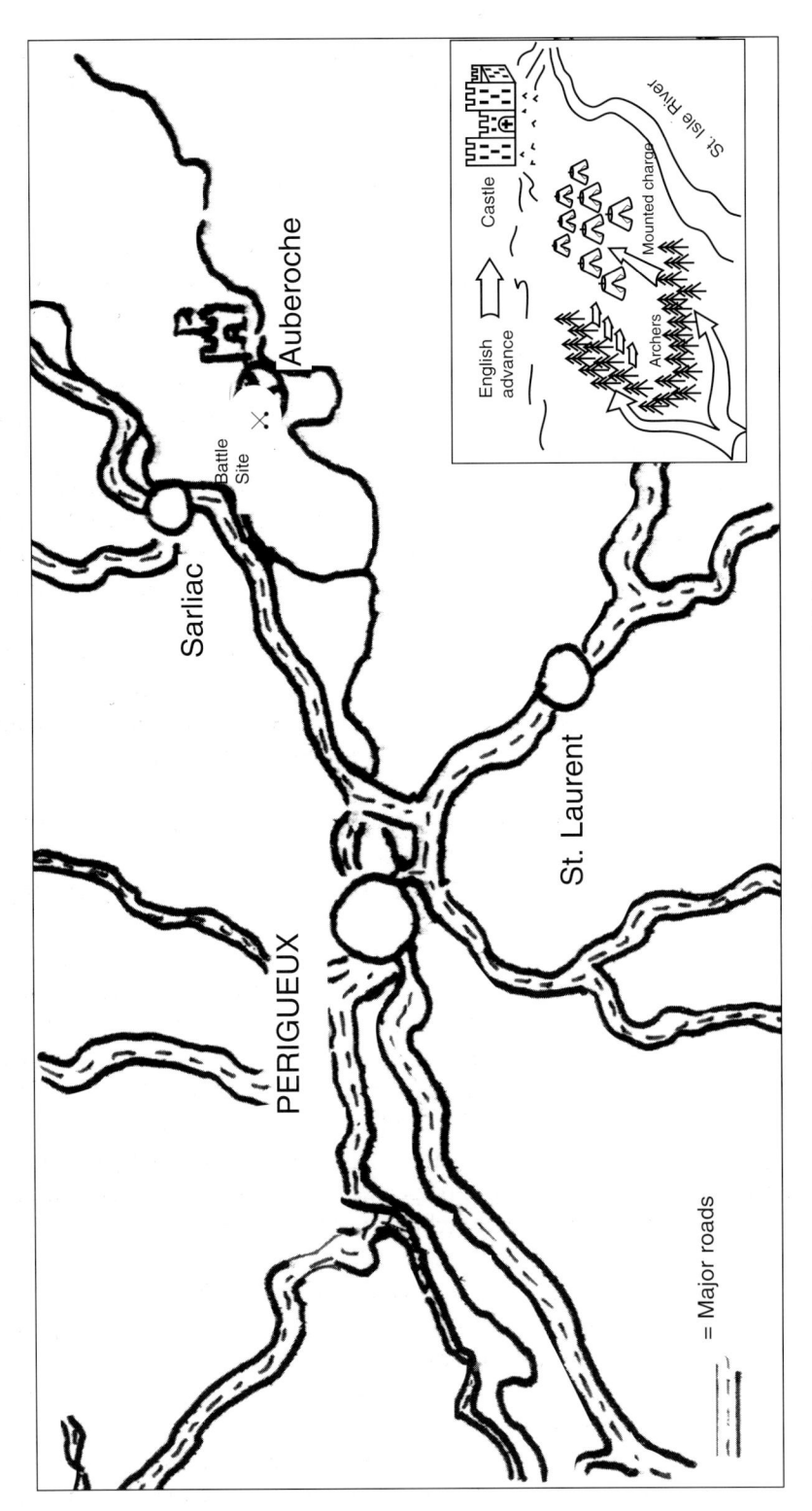

THE BATTLE OF AUBEROCHE 1344

But, he had not reckoned with the Earl of Derby and 1,200 English fighting men.

Having arrived in the vicinity on the evening of October 20th, Derby's men settled down for the night in their tents and bivouacs on the edge of a small forest, beyond which, some 800 yards away, were the French lines.

Discipline was absolute but Derby was a worried man. He had again sent word to Pembroke but still there was no sign of reinforcing soldiery.

Dawn broke on the morning of the 21st; the men had brought food with them and they breakfasted on this. Foraging for supplies had been expressly forbidden and the horses had been quietly grazed amongst the bivouacs.

If Derby was worried, then this was as nothing compared to the concerns of his commanders. They believed the French force to exceed 10,000; enormous odds for this small, albeit battle-hardened and highly-motivated professional battalion but, a dilemma called for an ingenious solution.

A Council of War was called and it was at this (if the French chronicler Froissart is to be believed) that Derby's Chief of Staff, Sir Walter Manny, a charismatic leader whose exploits during the Crecy campaign were to become legendary, proposed that Derby move his force through the forest to the meadow's edge, to take the French by surprise.

A plan breath-takingly unchivalric but bold as need decreed, for there was little virtue and no possible advantage in precipitating conventional conflict.

If accounts are true, then Derby himself reconnoitred the ground, moving stealthily through the wood until in sight of the French camp. He could scarcely believe what he saw.

All was peace and tranquility. Crickets chirped contentedly in the lush meadow grass, coils of smoke rose slowly heavenwards, a hint of garlic lay on the early evening air. Divested of armour and weaponry, the French were unhurriedly preparing for dinner.

Silently Derby crept away. Consulting with his commanders, he sought how best to turn this interesting situation to advantage. It was agreed that the archers should take up position on the forest edge adjacent to the main encampment, whilst his 400 men-at-arms, with their mounts, should assemble to the South. On command, the archers were to deliver volleys of arrows and, under cover of this confusion, the cavalry would charge over the intervening 300 yards of ground and cause mayhem.

One can picture the scene. One moment all is sweetness and light. Dinner is finished; Francois has allowed himself to be persuaded into that second bouteil du vin; the dice are out and with hands clasped lightly over full bellies, sentries are drowsily enjoying the pleasant country air.

Then, from the forest edge, the sudden sound of trumpets. A lusty roar: "Derby, and Guyenne" from 800 English throats and shower upon shower of needle-sharp bodkin-pointed English battle shafts are raining from the sky.

Before the French had fully grasped the situation, they became aware of a force of 400 horsed men-at-arms, in full armour, bearing down upon them from the South.

Surprise was complete. As the cavalry created havoc amongst the tents, French knights struggled to find and strap on armour. Banners were quickly raised and men began to assemble in the meadow beyond the camp. The archers, who had of necessity to withold their shots whilst the men-at-arms were amongst the French, now again came into their own as enemy captains endeavoured to create order out of chaos. They poured their shafts at medium range into the assembling groups.

But, even as the French tried desperately to counter the unexpected attack, a fresh force joined in with gusto. Sir Frank Halle had watched incredulously from the castle battlements as this tiny relieving army turned the tables before his eyes.

Not one to let opportunity pass untaken, he had no difficulty in persuading his own small force to join in and, without more ado, they donned armour in readiness.

Whilst the small French contingent, left to watch the castle gate, were gawping with amazement at developments unfolding below, Sir Frank and his gallant band had opened the gates and, with every available horseman, had burst through the cordon to take part in the fray from his side.

No-one knows quite how long this increasingly one-sided conflict went on before victory was declared but the outcome is a matter of history. Seven thousand French soldiers, well-armed, under one of their most able commanders, fled the field in total disarray; Derby, with Manny and his other officers, was able to formally declare the Castle of Auberoche well and truly relieved.

But, what of the tardy Earl of Pembroke? Excusing his non-appearance at the critical time, this gentleman arrived during the evening to witness a jovial Lord Derby entertaining his captive generals to a belated meal.

With the largesse of one rather pleased with himself, the victor greeted his laggard brother-in-arms with an invitation to help him finish off a venison pasty instead! And this is just what he did.

DEFENDING AUBEROCHE CASTLE

THE AFFAIR AT BLANCHETAQUE, 1346

WHEN Edward III, with the 15-year-old Black Prince, left England for France in July, 1346, it was in response to a plea for assistance by the Earl of Derby, victor of Auberoche who, with Sir Walter Manny amongst other captains, was now besieged at Aiguillon. The Earl was under heavy military pressure and seriously concerned at the course matters were taking.

Whilst subsequent events were to prevent Edward's direct intervention, his 12,000-strong army was thus embarked with Bordeaux and Lord Derby firmly in mind. Wind and weather were against him however and, although he maintained his original intention almost to the last, he was eventually persuaded to use the wind to make for Normandy; effectively leaving Derby and Sir Walter Manny to their own devices.

The King's landing on the Cherbourg Peninsula was therefore by chance rather than design; thus it was that on July 12th, the astonished inhabitants of St. Vaast-la-Houque awoke to an invasion fleet so huge that it dominated the horizon — shades of 1944 and the Normandy landings!

Edward assembled his three battalions without interference during the next six days. The element of surprise was in his favour and it was not until July 19th that he turned his attentions to Harfleur, which, although the castle made a token show of defence, bowed to the inevitable and surrendered without a fight.

The campaign then began in earnest. Valognes, St Marie-Eglise and Montebourg were each ransacked and burnt; Carentan resisted but the English strength was such that defeat was a foregone conclusion and both town and castle quickly gave in.

On and on Edward's army swept; it had rapidly become a cohesive and confident force and was anxious to show its mettle.

This would not be long in coming, for the troops — satiated with plunder after a fortnight of looting and general pillage — were now to be faced with their first real test: the subjugation of Caen, an important centre of commerce strategically placed to guard the River Orme and, after Rouen, the largest fortress between the King and Paris.

In the town, secure behind stout walls, everyone was making merry, confident of victory against this impudent English King. The next day they would leave the ramparts, assemble outside the walls in all their martial glory and annihilate these upstarts in a well-executed battle. Was it not planned so?

Planned it may have been but when dawn broke on July 27th and the bellicose Norman soldiery left for the business of the day, they came face to face for the first time with English and Welsh bowmen — the formidable 'Goddams.'

Banners to the fore, pennants streaming in the wind, Edward's disciplined troops were assembling at their battle stations, tightly ranked and ready for the fray. Order and precision were maintained by tuck of drum and blast of trumpet as wheeling and manoeuvring into position, they calmly awaited their Centenar's instructions to engage.

Taking in the sight, the French, bewildered by this professionalism, stood and watched, confidence evaporating by the minute as, with precision born of long practice at village butt, the archers braced their great war-bows, readied their arrow sheaves and took up position.

Drums rolled, broadheaded battle-shafts were nocked and on command, the first arrow-storm rose and fell as a cloud amongst the French. Massed archery was new to the defenders of Caen; understandably they panicked and many departed in disorder from the field. After a lengthy engagement, at which the English men-at-arms were eventually successful, the remaining defenders broke and ran.

The English followed, over bridges and through gates, killing as they went. In the town the desperate townsfolk defended themselves as best they could from house tops, slaying some 500 English soldiers in the process. Learning of this, a furious Edward turned on the remaining inhabitants, ordering their massacre and the complete destruction of the town — an order reluctantly rescinded only after direct intervention by Geoffrey d'Harcourt, the King's close adviser and counsellor.

Booty and plunder in plenty followed the sacking of Caen and, on Edward's direction, this was returned to England. Due however to an ambiguity of orders (and here one leans over backwards to be objective), not just the treasure ships but the entire fleet then set sail for home Whilst just 17 days had passed, with much of Normandy reduced and a serious engagement fought and won, Edward was now left in an uncomfortable predicament — his retreat cut off and no ready means of return.

Faced with the situation, he had little choice. He would need to march to Calais many miles distant for the closest opportunity to return home. Grasping the nettle firmly but conscious now of stirrings amongst the French, Edward set out for the port and safety. Louviers on the River Eure fell without a fight, although with concern for its potential, Edward's rearguard fired the town.

Matters were now taking a different and grimmer turn. Ahead lay the River Seine whose bridges had been destroyed. That at Poissy was still partially intact however, although five precious days were spent as Edward's carpenters repaired and reconstructed it.

By August 15th, Edward and his army had crossed the Seine.

Meanwhile, Phillip VI of France had not been idle. Eventually convinced that battle was inevitable and, that matters were slowly turning his way, he was busily assembling the military might of France and at St Denis, on the outskirts of Paris, he raised the Oriflamme* and set off in pursuit.

Cut off from England and now deep in increasingly hostile territory, a grim-faced Edward was in no doubt of the potential danger of his position. The major obstacle of the Somme River lay ahead and his mounted spies had told him that Phillip was not far away. In imminent danger of being trapped, by his order the army doubled its pace, achieving an incredible twenty or so kilometres a day. Skirmishes though, were now

---

* THE ORIFLAMME: the French battle standard denoting that no quarter was to be given and that the troops under it were expected to fight to the death,

more frequent and gathering in intensity, as townsfolk sensed a change in fortune; that at Beauvais giving the vanguard some very stiff opposition.

Matters were grave indeed. Intelligence was that all the Somme bridges had been burned whilst Phillip was at Amiens, just one day's march behind.

Time was most certainly against Edward now. He had three choices, each unpalatable, each dangerous. He could storm Abbeville where the bridge was intact but, from reconnaissance, he knew to be stoutly defended. He could try for St. Valery at the mouth of the river and fight a Dunkirk-style rearguard action, or he could ford the Somme and make for Calais and safety.

He chose the last. There was a ford between Abbeville and the sea; Edward had been brought up in the area and knew this — but where was it? He could not risk a lengthy and perhaps a futile search. Equally, he could not risk being trapped with his back to the river by Phillip who was now uncomfortably close at hand.

Surrounded by his anxious tactical commanders, Edward sought the whereabouts of this ford from prisoner knights. But they, true to their concept of honour, claimed not to know of it. In desperation he turned to the lesser ranks and here to his relief he was more successful. For the King's proffered reward of 100 gold nobles (a substantial fortune) a good horse and the custody (for ransom) of six prisoners, a cow-herd named Gobin Agache was prepared to lead the way.

He knew the ford well he said; it was called Blanchetaque. He explained that because it was of white marl, it would take 12 men abreast at low tide, when water was no higher than their knees.

Edward gave orders at once. The camp would rise at midnight. There would be three muted trumpet calls. At the first the troops would arm themselves. At the second they would commence loading the wagons and make ready to move. At the third they would move off.

The men, nerves strung, ate sparingly and lay down to rest. By day-break the army was well under way with Gobin in the lead. English and Welsh archers with bows ready braced and sheaf arrows uncovered; men-at-arms in full battle order; Irish, Welsh and Cornish pikemen and the lumbering, slow-moving baggage train. By 5 a.m. they had reached Blanchetaque, the ford and frustration. The tide was full and the water too deep.

The position was critical. In front of him an uncrossable river. Behind him a huge and steadily advancing French army now less than a day's march away. To compound matters further, a mile or so away, on the further bank, a considerable defending force commanded by the Bailiff of Vermandois, one Godemars du Fay, awaited him.

It was now 8 o'clock on August 28th. An impatient Edward ordered his Marshals, Sir Hugh Despenser, Sir Reginald Cobham and the Earl of Northampton, to take the van-ward across. With the tide still running high but steadily receding, the mounted men-at-arms, accompanied by a strong force of archers, pressed forward.

On the North bank, impetuous French knights, anxious to get at the enemy, charged into the water, watched by foot soldiers on the bank. The English, backs to the river, fought like tigers, eventually gaining firm ground and establishing a beachhead. Behind them came the archers, bows held above their heads to keep strings dry. Grim-faced but ready, they took their stances and poured their shafts at near point-blank range into the opposition. This melted like snow in summer and Edward was in control of the Somme's north bank.

The gamble had been successful. Although Phillip's forces caught the last of the rear-ward and the stragglers of the baggage train, the English army, once more a cohesive fighting force, was again on the move, banners unfurled, tired but in good heart. Whilst, his work done, Gobin Agache rode away into historical obscurity, jingling his new wealth in his pocket.

Since his crossing of the Seine, in one week Edward had successfully survived five intensive skirmishes and, by the skin of his teeth, a major obstacle in the River Somme. He could not know that the following day, at the little village of Crecy-en-Ponthieu, his resolve, with that of his young son the Black Prince and his men, would be put to the supreme test.

POSTSCRIPT

THE BLACK ARMY OF LIANTRISANT. Called a myth by pedantic historians but firmly embedded in the fabric of Welsh folk-lore and archery legend, is the story of a small force of bowmen mustered for the Crecy campaign and who are said to have accompanied the Black Prince as part of his personal retinue. The story goes that in the battle, the Prince was struck down and lay on the ground. Whilst he was recovering, the men of Llantrisant formed a protective shield around him, and held his attackers at bay. For their bravery, they were awarded a piece of ground in the village, to be held by them and their ancestors in perpetuity. To this day the descendants of this gallant band — those who can trace direct ancestry through 600 years — proudly claim the right of tenure to this ground. Perhaps they no longer shoot in the old longbow; perhaps they no longer tell of past glories. But to these Black Bowmen and their Company — lineal descendants of the Welsh archers who forded at Blanchetaque and at Crecy — must go the proud title of the oldest Association of Archers in the land. Those who are of their lineage salute them.

Principal sources referenced, and further reading.

THE CRECY WAR. Alfred H. Burne, D.S.O. F.R. Hist.S. 1991. Greenhill Books, London ISBN 1 85367 081 2.

ARMS, ARMOUR AND FORTIFICATIONS IN THE HUNDRED YEARS WAR: Ed. Anne Curry & Michael Hughes, 1994. Boydell & Brewer: ISBN 085115 365 8.

CONTEMPORARY CHRONICLES OF THE HUNDRED YEARS WAR. 1966. Folio Society:

EDWARD, PRINCE OF WALES AND AQUITAINE. Richard Barber: 1978 Penguin Books. ISBN 0 7139 0861 0.

THE WARS OF EDWARD III. Clifford J. Rogers. 1999 Boydell & Brewer: ISSN 1358-779X

PLATE 9

A French Knight, circa 1370 - 1400

PLATE 10

English Archer, circa 1400-1435

OF BOWMEN AND BATTLES

PLATE 11

'To harry the King's foes from the seas.'
Tudor Archer of the Reign of Henry VIII, The 'Mary Rose, 1545

OF BOWMEN AND BATTLES

PLATE 12
A Bowman of the Duke of Somerset's Retinue, circa 1470

OF BOWMEN AND BATTLES

PLATE 13

'COMPANIONS'
English Archers on the March, circa 1400-1425

PLATE 14

John, Lord of Aumont ('The Brawler'), 1415

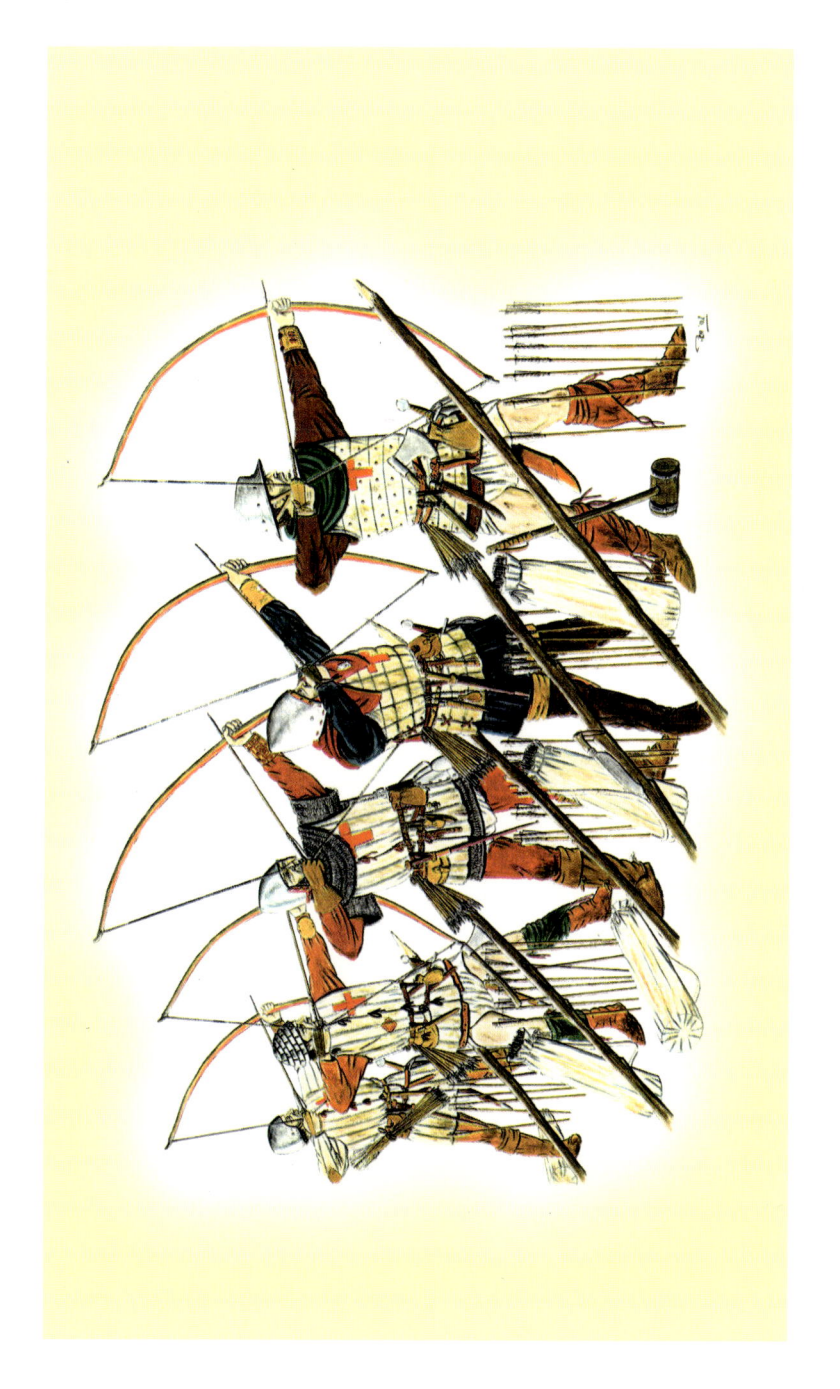

PLATE 15

English Archers in Defensive Position, circa 1400-1430

PLATE 16

SKELETON 16
Interpreted from the reconstruction of a skeleton recovered in a grave pit at Towton and wearing the livery of the Earl of Clifford

Part 6

The Sun Sets on France

The Siege of Harfleur, 1415
The Sieges of Caen & Rouen
The Battle of Verneuil, 1424
The Experience at Orleans
The Siege of Patay

DEFENDING THE RAMPARTS

Part 6

THE SUN SETS ON FRANCE

ET US move on, for we have much to cover. Whilst the 1346 campaign was a military success, in spite of its rather unpromising start and the subsequent traumas of Blanquetaque and the fight at Crecy, the years that followed were, despite the glory of Agincourt, harbingers of destiny for England.

The four engagements that will be described in this chapter include a 'set piece' battle, and three sieges. The successful taking by siege of the cities of Harfleur in 1415; Caen, and Rouen in 1417; the battle of Verneuil in 1424 (where English archer met Scottish billman in a clash of titans) and, in 1429, the decisive defeat of English soldiery by Jean d'Arc at Orleans, with the brave but unsuccessful defensive rearguard action at Patay that followed from it.

THE SIEGE OF HARFLEUR, 1415

THE FLEET that departed England on its two-day journey to France was led by the Royal Flagship, the clinker-built 'Trinitee Riall,' a two-masted vessel of some 540 tuns and the King's 'Great Ship,' the proud Master chosen to carry his King being one Stephen Thomas. The flagship was accompanied by a motley collection of others, various in type and size; amongst them the 'Grand Marie,' single-masted, and of 126 tuns burthen; the 'Petit Trinity, 120 tuns; the 'Petit Marie,' 80 tuns; the 'Philip,' 130 tuns; the 'Katherine,' 210 tuns (later sold for £5!); the 'Nicholas,' a 120-tun Ballinger, steered by sculls and, a Cogship, the 'Redcogge,' of 120 tuns — formerly the French Flaward de Geraint.

The armament of these vessels makes interesting reading. During her de-storing, the 'Grande Marie' returned "... *two duzen dartes... sixteen bowes*..." but, just "... *two sheaves of arrowes*..." One imagines that the remaining sheaves were used to good effect somewhere.

The evening of August 14th saw this patchwork fleet anchored at the mouth of the River Seine, a mile or two distant from the Port and City of Harfleur.

Ever methodical, Henry V took three days to unload and set up camp — a period that was not wasted by the French who despatched a very welcome reinforcing company of 300 men-at-arms to aid the defending garrison. After some skirmishing, Harfleur was surrounded — with the English fleet safeguarding the river entrance.

Henry had now to decide his course of action. A direct assault would be difficult because the city was well defended with stout high walls; whilst starvation would be lengthy, digging beneath the walls would be economical of man-power and, prospectively safer. Accordingly Henry brought up his miners and they set to work. Despite their best endeavours however, French counter-mining successfully put paid to the work and, with his immediate plans thwarted, Henry turned to his artillery pieces. Named 'London,' 'Messenger,' and 'King's Daughter,' by all accounts these were sizeable weapons and did much damage to walls and towers. The garrison was equal to the problem though and what was knocked down by day was promptly rebuilt by night.

It was during this spell of damage and repair that the English soldiery — with nothing to do, and all day to do it — occupied their time by eating. Their choice fell to largely unripe fruit and, with lack of exercise and inadequate sanitation this had predictably disastrous consequences — dysentry became rife and many died.

Clearly something had to be done to end this stand-off. Following a brave and partially successful sortie by the French from the South-West gate, which caught the English off-guard, the Earl of Huntingdon, with Royal approval, launched a counter-attack. Opening with an artillery barrage of incendiary cannon-balls, he set fire to the wooden bulwark which stood before the town. With this ablaze, the defenders retired hurriedly into their houses to await fate. This was not long in coming. Henry delivered an ultimatum. Either immediate and complete surrender, or an all-out assault with the massacre that this implied.

Offered this choice between a rock and a hard place, the garrison accepted the inevitable and peaceable terms were negotiated. After keeping the city fathers waiting for a considerable time to underline the superiority of his position, Henry received the surrender of the town from them. Lord de Gaucourt and his 76 burghers were duly ushered into the King's presence with ropes symbolically strung around their necks.

Matters being settled to his satisfaction and with the ropes now off, the King treated them all to a good supper and, at least for a time, Harfleur became an English town.

With Harfleur secured, Henry had a decision to make. Should he march on Paris, with the prospect of an inland battle against what might prove insuperable odds? Should he settle for Harfleur and sail for home? Or should he march to Calais, a chevauchée in the manner of his grandfather? For, assuming a safe crossing of the Somme at Blanchetaque, he would be there in some 16 days. He held a Council of War with his commanders and, after much debate, decided on the latter. History records his choice — and his dilemma, for Blanchetaque was denied him. On October 25th, the day of St. Crispin, 17 days after leaving Harfleur, his destiny and that of France was to be decided on the outskirts of the little village of Agincourt.

Impressions of England, by an Italian visitor, November 1497: "Of London. Some of the men are exceptionally tall. All exercise themselves in a marvellous way with great bows made of yew wood, with which they practice continually outside the walls. They also fight with them on foot in such a way as to show that they have been enthusIastically trained in this from their earliest youth."

From the 'Brokerage Book' (Trades of Southampton, 1439 -1440). Thursday 8th October. From William LOMBE, carting towards Salisbury with 1½ cwt of bowstaves of Henry BARON, customs 1½d. brokerage with pontage (?) 2½d. Sum 4d.).

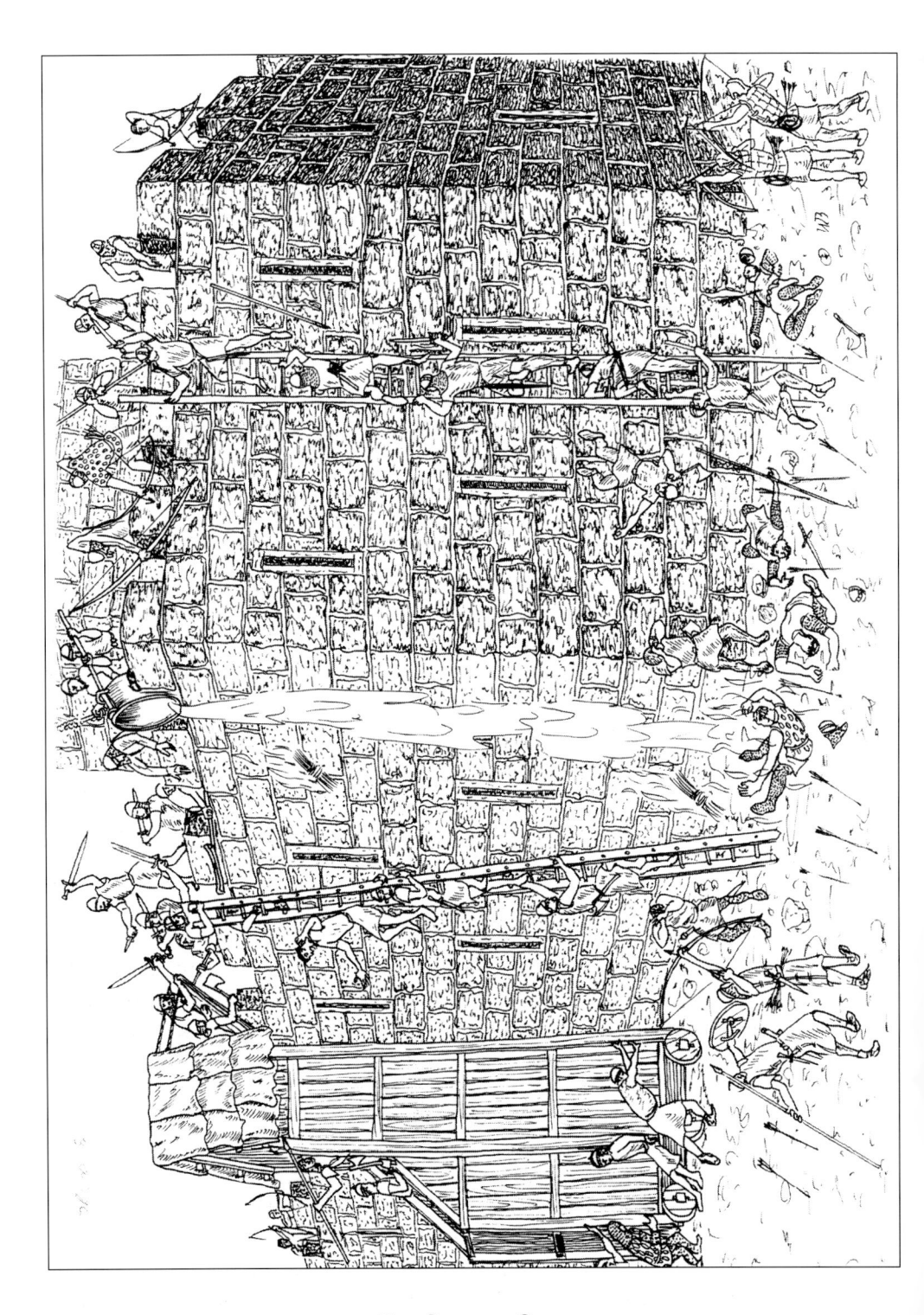

The Sun Sets on France — The Sieges of Caen and Rouen

The Siege of Caen

CAEN AND ROUEN

SPLENDID and decisive a victory that it was, the Battle at Agincourt (renamed Azincourt by the French after the conflict) by no means ended the problems that King Henry had with the Continent. In the summer of 1417, a decisive sea-battle took place in the Channel between ships under the command of the Earl of Huntingdon and nine huge Genoese Carracks, described by contemporary sources as the greatest ever seen near English coast.

Three of the Carracks were taken and brought to port, together with their Masters and a large amount of treasure. As an aside, although a welcome addition to Henry's sea-power, their huge size put refit beyond the capability of many English boatyards and (a curious reflection on protocol at that time), advice and assistance from the Genoese was subsequently sought to ensure their satisfactory upkeep.

Whilst having the immediate and useful effect of safeguarding the Channel ports from raiders, thereby easing the minds of the local fishermen and on-shore inhabitants in general, victory also secured Henry's mastery of the sea. An essential preliminary to schemes he was hatching for an even larger and more ambitious Continental campaign that year and one for which he was actively planning.

His targets: the great cities of the Normandy Peninsula. Ever meticulous, his arrangements involved the acquisition of substantial quantities of material for siege purposes and included — besides the usual quantities of bows, arrows and other personal military equipment — guns, both heavy and light. Trebuchets, huge siege engines, sows (a covering shield for miners digging to collapse city walls), leather boats, leather bridges and scaling ladders, as well as the more mundane spades, shovels, picks and pavises without which no self-respecting commander would move an inch. All were painstakingly put aboard.

Thus, fully equipped, he and his fleet of ships set sail, landing this time at Deauville, a small town on the Normandy coast. Having quickly consolidated his position and secured his flanks and rear, Henry then moved his army with its large attendant siege train towards Caen, provincial capital of Western Normandy and the first major objective.

Caen stands on an arm of the River Orme, the 'old' town with its castle on a hill, the 'new' town on the Ile de St Jean; land surrounded by the waters of the river. It was a formidable obstacle to the King's progress, and of this he was well aware.

Once there, Henry lost no time in preparation for his attack. He personally occupied the Abbaye aux Hommes to the east of the city walls, whilst his brother Thomas, Duke of Clarence, stationed his men at the Abbaye des Dames to the west. The Earls of Salisbury and Gloucester, with others of his commanders, ringed the Ile and prepared for the assault. One of Henry's collapsible leather bridges was placed across the river to give him access to Salisbury. With his guns established on the roof of the Abbaye aux Hommes, the stage was set for attack.

Since the garrison was not prepared to surrender, Henry made ready to storm the old town. However, the walls of Caen were thick and powerful and built to last, they were not designed to yield easily and, for a time, it was touch and go as to whether they might be scaled. Henry's scaling ladders were too short (a common problem) and were the cause of many deaths — not always through the actions of the opposition.

A crowd of enthusiastic men-at-arms, each in armour, often proved more than wooden rungs could stand, with inevitable results once gravity had taken over. A notable victim was the unfortunate Sir Edmund Springhouse, whose ladder let him down at a crucial moment and who fell into the surrounding dry ditch. Whilst there and incapacitated, unsympathetic defenders dropped burning straw on him from above and, with bones broken and unable to move, the unlucky Sir Edmund was quite literally cooked.

Eventually, despite increasingly desperate opposition, both Henry and Thomas were successful and advanced to meet each other in the town's market square. Since the city had been taken by force, the Rules of War permitted butchery of the inhabitants. English archers and Welsh knifemen alike were thus let loose and casualties were enormous. Contemporary records suggests that more than 2,000 French townsfolk were killed within minutes. The castle held out well after the town surrendered and successfully negotiated separate and, more humane terms for its submission.

With Caen in his hands, Henry stood poised and ready to move further into Normandy. Falaise gave him some trouble but finally fell after a grim winter siege. The captain of the castle, who turned out to be a Welshman working for the other side, was summarily hanged, drawn and quartered as a traitor. An uncompromising message to others in authority who might be persuaded that the European product was better than the green, green grass of home. Henry was as efficient as he was merciless.

With Cherbourg also in his hands and Western Normandy now effectively under his control, Henry turned his attention to the East — and Rouen. Conscious of the likelihood of aid reaching the city from the hinterland, he turned his ever-willing Welsh knifemen loose in the vicinity with instructions to intimidate the inhabitants. One may presume that they were effective, since no sustenance or support came subsequently from that quarter.

Henry, though, was not one to take on a task lightly. He realised the strength of Rouen full well. Considered at that time to be second only to Paris in its importance, its defences included five miles of walls, supported by great earthen banks, interspersed by 60 towers and gates, each with bastions. Every tower had guns and each gate was well defended. In addition, the bridge across the River Seine had been cleverly doctored so that it could be removed in a crisis.

Caen may have fallen with no appreciable delay but, Rouen was not Caen. Conscious of the task ahead, the king sent for additional supplies and, despite the ineffectual protestations of merchants, these duly arrived. London sent 500 additional archers and the substantial gift of £1,500, as well as butts of wine, pipes of ale and, thoughtfully to complete the picture, 2,500 cups with which to down it all.

His army suitably re-invigorated and ready for the expected prolonged siege, Henry arranged for a ditch to be dug surrounding the walls, hedged with pitfalls and other traps as an assurance that the besiegers could not be caught off-guard. Wooden towers were built and equipped with guns and detachments of archers to guard them, each tower with three large guns below and seven smaller ones above.

The siege was lengthy, as Henry had expected, although by October the effectiveness of the blockade was evident, with the townsfolk virtually at famine point. However, the garrison, backed up by the city Governors, was not about to give up easily, despite the obvious privations of the poor — invariable sufferers in every similar siege. The desperate state of these ordinary citizens has been described in a curious poem, more or less contemporary with events and startlingly evocative of the conditions obtaining within the city walls.

> *"Meat and drink and other victual*
> *In that city began to fail.*
> *Save clean water in plenty too,*
> *And vinegar to put thereto."*

Bread was practically non-existent; the only flesh left was horse meat and not a great deal of that either.

> *"For a horse's quarter, lean or fat,*
> *One hundred shillings it was at,*
> *A horse's head for half a Pound,*
> *A dog for the same money round."*

The horse meat would have succoured the rich; the less fortunate had to make do with rats at 30 pence, cats at two nobles and mice at sixpence. Vegetables there were for a time, with onions and leeks fetching one shilling a small piece. Eggs were ninepence (until the hens that laid them were killed) and apples were tenpence each.

As winter came, mortality increased. With little food with which to build resistance against the cold, deaths were daily occurrences; more dying than could be coped with by those still strong enough to dig their graves. The starkness of the situation in those last days of siege is exemplified by the poem.

> *"Even if a child would otherwise be dead,*
> *The mother would not give it bread.*
> *Nor would a child to its mother give,*
> *Each one tried himself to live.*
> *As long as he could last,*
> *Love and kindness both were past."*

With a callous disregard for their welfare, the garrison soldiers drove the poor outside the city walls, hoping apparently that the English would succour them out of humanity. They had misjudged Henry however. This was the man who had ordered the massacre of the French prisoners at Agincourt three years previously and who had directly countenanced the slaughter of the citizens of Caen. He had no intention of taking Rouen's problems upon himself. Unlike Edward III at Calais during the opening campaign of the French wars, he refused permission for them to pass through his lines. They were allowed no further than the boundary ditch.

> *"There men might see a great pity,*
> *A child of two years or of three,*
> *Go about and beg his bread,*
> *For mother and father both were dead."*

Here they stayed, to take what shelter they could amongst the pits and stakes. Only at Christmas did Henry relent a little, sending them food and succour.

Meanwhile, the governors of the city waited desperately for relieving forces to be sent to engage the English King and, hope against hope, defeat his archers in battle. In fact, a Burgundian force was marshalled and this got to within 20 miles of Rouen before wisdom prevailed and the attempt was abandoned. Another larger army raised by the Dauphin Charles, who had bravely unfurled the Oriflamme, was subsequently disbanded and Rouen, with its unhappy burghers, was left finally to its fate.

Although Henry had shown uncharacteristic consideration for the poor at Christmas, he resumed the siege with the fullest vigour on New Year's Day, despite entreaties from the Roueners who, vainly hoping to conjure a mite more Christmas spirit from the besiegers, called out of each of the gates to beg for pity upon the poor in the ditches.

Their appeal was duly conveyed to the King. Henry's response was terse and to the point. It was not he who had turned out the poor, he saw no reason why he should take over the problems of the city. The governors knew full well what was expected of them and he was waiting as patiently as he might for them to recognise the situation.

With what little chance there had been of relief by their countrymen now gone, the Roueners began at last to accept the inevitable. At the Port du Ponte, the bridge over the Seine, Sir Gilbert Umfraville, as the King's emissary, met with 12 of the leading citizens and conveyed them to the King's presence. After a deliberate delay, Henry met with them. He was in no mood to compromise, neither had he the need. He left the miserable 12 in no doubt that he considered Rouen his by right and that he was not going to leave until it surrendered to him. The citizens returned home dejected and the poor continued to die like flies.

At last, after terms had been discussed and agreed, the city accepted its fate and, in January of 1419, Rouen finally gave in. Henry rode through the main gate in State, a regal figure clad in black and gold astride a huge black horse. A true warrior, he was as magnanimous in victory as he was cold-hearted in battle. He gave food, drink and clothing to those few starving inhabitants who were left, whilst they and the garrison were searched meticulously for valuables. Since, unlike Caen, the city had surrendered, the citizens were left relatively unmolested.

The CHRONICLE OF LONDON for that year records Henry's victory with customary brevity:

the *"kyng of Engelond with his lordes beseged the city of roen, the whiche sege dured half a yere and more; but at the laste through the grace of God, it was yolden* (yielded) *to hym upon the day of seynt Woistan . . . it was seyde their deyde withinne the towne . . . mo thanne xxxm* (30 thousand) *durynge the sege . . ."*

With that out of the way, it then dealt with the local news:

". . . John Bryan, scirreve (sheriff) *of London feile in the water of Thamyse at Seint Katherine's mille as he went to ease himself, the whiche was cause of his deth, and dyed on the X day of Octobre. . . ."*

From 'The Institution of a Gentleman' 1555. 'Shooting in the Long-bow.' "It shall become all gentlemen to use this, our English pastime of shootIng for their greatest game and disport. This pastime hath in it two singular points which in no other game as yet could ever be found; that is, it serveth both for a pastime, and a defence in the wars. . . ."

On 5th July, 1531, Richard Slak of Arnold (Nottinghamshire) estimated by jurors to be 12 years of age, assaulted another boy named John Banes of Arnold, 'gent', estimated by the jurors to be 13 years old. Richard forcibly snatched John's bow from his hand, and struck him with it. John then drew his knife to defend hImself, and Richard seeing John do this took him in his arms. Thus wrestling they fell to the ground and by misadventure Richard fell upon the knife which gave him a wound or the right side $1/4$ in. wide, $1/2$ in. long and 2in. deep of which he died at Arnold about midnight that night, John was outlawed on 28th October, 1531 because he had fled.

THE SUN SETS ON FRANCE — THE BATTLE OF VERNEUIL

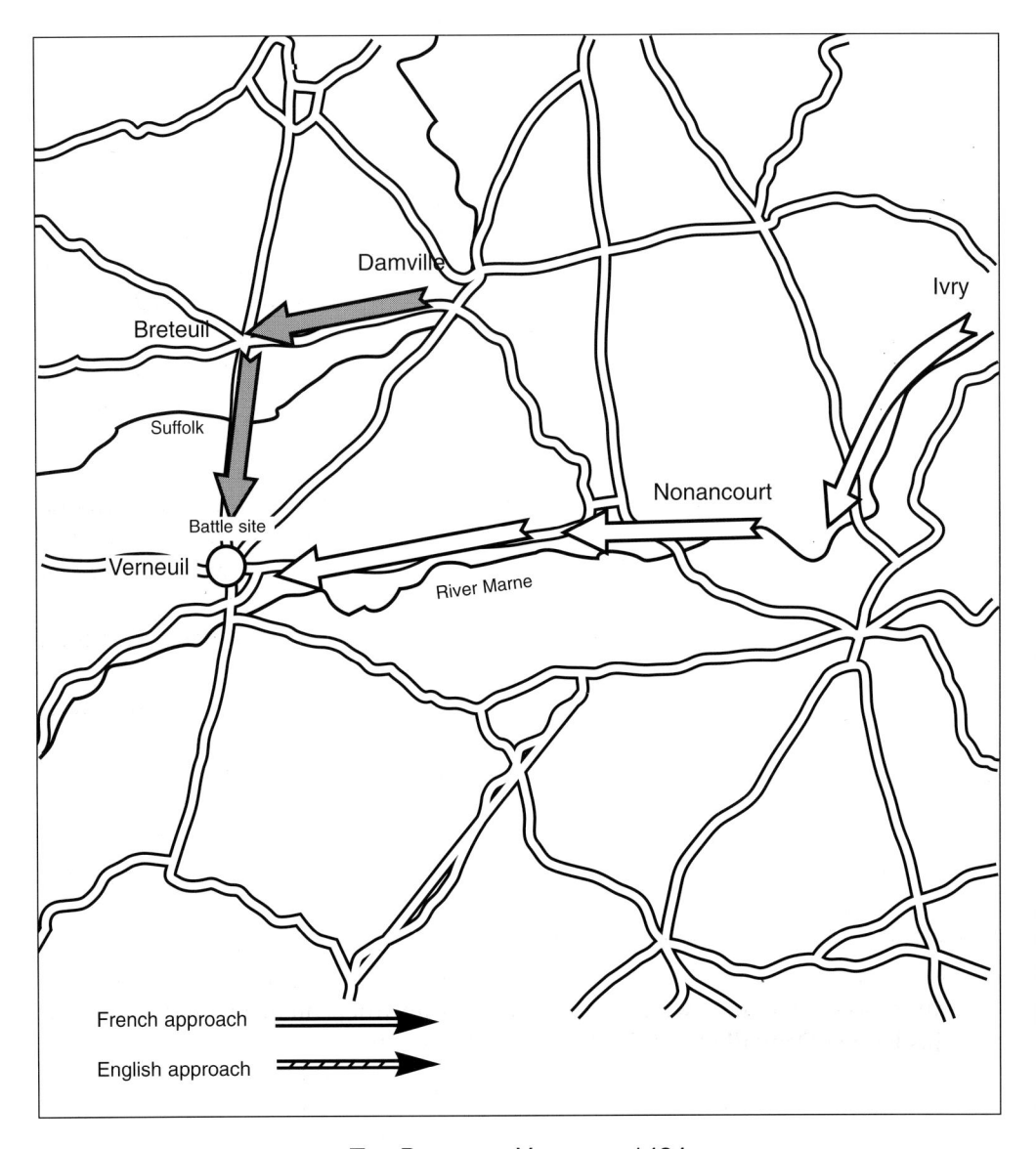

THE BATTLE OF VERNEUIL, 1434

VERNEUIL (1424). The second Agincourt

"...and in this yere the xvii (17th) *day of August was the bataill of Vernill in Perche, betven the Duke of Bedford, Regent of Fraunce, and the Armynakes, with the Scottes: but thinkyd be God the victorve fell to the Englysshe partye: for there were scleyn of ower adversarves the erle of Boughan* (Buchan), *the erle Doyglas, the erle of Almar, the erle of Tonnar, the erle of Cauntdore, and the viscount Nerbon that traytourly sclewe the Duke of Bourgoyne knelyng before the dolphin* (Dauphin) *at Motereil, and many mo to the nombre of x m* (10,000) *and mo: but the moste vengeaunce fell upon the proude Scottes; for there wente to schep wassh (?!?) of them the same day mo thanne xvij.c* (36 hundred) *of cote armes be a countynge of herowdes* (heralds) *..."*

THUS, in the language of the 15th Century did the CHRONICLE OF LONDON describe the battle of Verneuil, a major English success of the French wars, a bowman's battle par excellence and one which has been likened to Agincourt in both style and savagery.

In 1424, Ivry, a small town some 30 miles to the West of Paris, had been taken from the English garrison by French troops in a surprise raid. Whilst the town was re-taken easily enough, the new French garrison stayed firmly put behind strong defensive walls and, knowing this, a large French force had been assembled to relieve it

Fate chose otherwise however, since the garrison conveniently surrendered before the French army arrived. Seemingly not wanting to provoke matters further, the army continued its march, coming eventually to the walled town of Verneuil. Although the small English garrison fought bravely for a while, they had little chance against the huge odds and Verneuil fell.

Hearing of this and not wishing to lose a strategically important place to the Opposition, John, Duke of Bedford and Regent for the young Henry VI in France, determined to re-take the town and so, assembling his troops in battle order, he set off from his base at Damville towards Verneuil and retribution.

The confronting armies were unequally matched in size, as was generally the case during the French wars, although size in the context of French armies was often more inhibiting than useful. The English mustered about 9,000 men, the French twice that number.

On a hot day in August, Bedford's force emerged from a march through thickly forested land on to a dry and dusty plain some little way from the town to see, to its front and massed on the crest of a slight rise in the ground, the ranks of the rival army.

On its right flank they saw some 900 mounted crossbowmen, paid mercenaries from Lombardy whose exploits the English archers knew full well. These men guarded the large Scottish contingent of archers, billmen and men-at-arms, some 6,500 strong and virtually an army within an army.

The left wing consisted of 1,000 French chivalry, each man-at-arms in full armour, with lance and battle-axe and mounted on a 'barded' horse. The bulk of the army, including a large contingent of that ill-trained and poorly equipped local peasant militia without which no French army was ever considered complete, formed the centre.

The English deployed on the lower part of the slope, just outside the range of bow-shot and facing the French centre. All were dismounted as was English custom then. The front was in two separate portions of broadly equal size; one commanded by Lord Salisbury, the other by Bedford himself. In keeping with the tactical plans of the time, archers were positioned on each flank, a substantial reserve of 2,000 being held in readiness but stationed as guard to the baggage train located some 1,200 yards away.

Although, as it proved, one particular and important factor had been miscalculated, all was deemed to be ready. Bedford having given the traditional signal "Advance Banner" and, receiving in reply a great shout from his men of "Saint George and Bedford," the armies moved slowly and cautiously toward each other — the French down and the English up the slope.

There was then much activity on the English flanks; sharpened stakes which in normal circumstances could have been easily hammered into the earth would not penetrate the rock-hard soil; because of this they were not ready with the customary arrow-storm as the French left wing of mounted cavalry charged. Half erected stakes were brushed aside as the horsemen drove through, riding down the archers who, gathered together for mutual protection, defended themselves as best they could with swords, mauls and arming knives.

The cavalry however did not delay to consolidate their unexpected success. They made haste towards the baggage train and booty.

Bedford's men-at-arms were by now fiercely engaged with their French opponents and although outnumbered two-to-one, were slowly forcing the enemy back up the slope towards the town. However, on the other flank, Salisbury's men were being given a hard time by Alexander Douglas's Scottish troops who, wielding sword, mace and battle-axe kept the conflict in this quarter in serious doubt for over an hour, even after their French allies had fled and the mounted crossbowmen had left the field for the baggage train.

Here events were unfolding fast. The 2,000 archers of the Reserve Division, observing the approaching cavalry were well prepared for its arrival; they had let fly the arrow-storm with its inevitable disruptive result and were now dealing effectively in hand-to-hand combat with the men-at-arms, many of whom had either dismounted or had lost their horses.

Having quickly and totally routed the opposition and exhilarated by their success, the archers then turned their attentions to the freebooting arbalesters from Lombardy who, with only lightly armed pages and varlets to deal with in the baggage train, were pillaging at will. Faced now by 2,000 fired-up English 'Goddams' however, flushed with victory and seeking even greater glory, the crossbowmen stood small chance and offering little real opposition were driven pell-mell from the field.

Having amazingly disposed of two well-armed and seriously large bodies of mounted men, armoured cavalry and well-armed mounted crossbowmen, the archers, whose fighting blood was now fully roused, looked around for new conquests and seeing the fight developing on their left determined to join in the fray.

Pausing only to secure the baggage train and tend the wounded as best they could, these redoubtable fellows formed quickly into their companies and, with battle-cries advertising their imminent presence, wheeled in a great swathe to thunder into the right flank of the Scottish Division.

Fighting like demons and helped now by Salisbury's men-at-arms who, having chased the French centre up to the town ditch, were slowly straggling back; they decimated the Scots. These men, brave as they were, could not withstand the combination of determined English chivalry and elite bowmen. Scarcely one remained standing and as an effective force the Scottish army virtually ceased to exist.

The success of this quite extraordinary battle was in very large part due to the aggressive spirit of the 2,000 archers in the Reserve Division and one can imagine that they held their heads as high as their front-line comrades for many years to come. Well did Froissart later describe these men as "Milices redoubtables, la fleur des arciers du monde."*

* Formidable soldiers, the flower of the world's archers.

POSTSCRIPT TO THIS BATTLE.

Whilst there is much evidence for close association between France and Scotland for many years before Verneuil, a significant aftermath was the formal creation of the 'Ecossais Francaise,' the Scottish Archer Guard of the French Kings.

Twenty-four of this distinguished Body of hand-picked Scottish chivalry provided the King with personal protection. They held the keys to his bedchamber, and to the chapel where he prayed. They guarded his boat when he went by sea and stood by his throne on ceremonial occasions.

A good description of this Guard is contained in 'Quentin Durward,' the classic adventure tale written by Sir Walter Scott. Their weapons had by then become highly decorated, as had their uniform. Each was allowed a squire and two yeomen, one of whom was a coutelier (we would say a cutler) so-called from the long knife he carried to despatch those whom his master had thrown to the ground. Members of the Guard were ranked as 'gentlemen' in chivalric terms and, titled families in Scotland vied with each other to be represented, if only amongst these 'menials.'

Although not all historians agree, it has been said that what residual fighting strength remained of this Guard was incorporated within the British Army in 1662 as the First Regiment of Foot — the Royal Scots. If this were indeed so, then it was by curious twist of history, though surely right and proper, that a regiment whose forbears were dedicated to preserving 'le royaume Francaise' should have been instrumental at Waterloo, four centuries later, in bringing to heel the followers of those who overthrew it.

THE ORLEANS EXPERIENCE, 1429

*I*T IS sometimes said of the English at war that they lose every battle except the last. Romantic nonsense of course and, moreover, inaccurate when one thinks about the last years of the medieval Anglo/French wars. True, Crecy, Agincourt, Poitiers and many other were resounding victories gained against formidable odds but, as time passed, matters by no means always went the English way.

The aborted siege of the City of Orleans is intimately tied to the meteoric rise of the warrior woman whom we have Anglicised as 'Joan of Arc.' In fact, it might be better and more accurate had we literally translated her name, for she was born in the village of Domremy, to Jacques d'Arc, whose name quite literally meant 'of the bow.' It was Joan Archer, daughter of Jack, whom the English bowmen had reason to fear and hate.

Joan's persuasive oratory is well documented; the charisma which she undoubtedly possessed in full measure and which surrounded her brief appearance on the European stage, stood France and Dauphin Charles in good stead at a time when French morale was faltering.

In 1429, following a Council of War at which the Dauphin, his Marshal le Duc d'Alençon and other important captains were present, it had been decided to attempt the relief of Orleans, a strategically important city on the River Loire, by then besieged for some time by a comparatively small and barely adequate English force.

An army was to be raised and Joan pleaded to be allowed to accompany it. Permission grudgingly granted, Joan, decked out in full armour as a captain with troops under her command, raised her personal Standard at Blois, focal point for the relieving force.

The English, meanwhile, had now besieged the city for some seven months with (it should be said) only modest success; although their construction of siege towers and other fortifications, from which they had launched artillery attacks, had aleady done some damage to the city and its defences.

The close proximity of the River Loire offered the city a ready-made life-line for vital stores and, since the English had insufficient troops to properly encircle the place, it was reasonably supplied with both food and water.

Notwithstanding their apparent ability to hold out against out-right attack, the City fathers had sent to Charles for help and it was his relieving army, some 7,000 strong, of which Joan was a part.

Gaining access to the city by the river, the fresh French troops rapidly consolidated their position. The die was cast and matters moved swiftly. Determined to lose no time, Joan gained the attention of several fellow captains and men-at-arms and, by sheer force of personality, persuaded them to make an initial sortie outside the perimeter to attack a particularly strongly defended fortification some way from the walls. Known as the 'Bastille Saint Loup' and situated to the east of the city, this tower, with its defences, was the sole significant fortification on that side and was manned by some 300 or 400 English archers and men-at-arms.

After a fiercely-fought battle in which both sides suffered many casualties, Joan and her fellow captains triumphed and the tower was demolished and burnt.

The attack seems to have taken Lord Talbot, the English Commander, totally by surprise. Reinforcements hastily got together had barely left their encampment at the Western fortress of Saint Laurent in support of their embattled comrades, when smoke and flames told them it was too late.

Meanwhile, morale inside the City had lifted significantly at this unexpected victory and not one to let grass grow under her feet, Joan followed this with another sortie against a second English fortification on the following day. This time the prize was the weakest of the English manned forts, at St. Jean-le-Blanc, south and east of the city but across the river.

With St. Loup gone and the East now free of English troops, the French prepared a bridge of boats across the Loire and made ready for attack. This time, the English were prepared. Seeing what was evidently planned, they had abandoned the fort and moved to far stronger positions in a ruined Augustinian monastery nearby.

Under sustained attack from Talbot's longbowmen, who had caught their troops in deadly crossfire and, with seemingly little chance of success, the French were in course of calling off the attack. Joan appeared at this point and, rallying the French, turned them from retreat to attack. Talbot quickly withdrew his men to the shelter of the monastery; with fresh troops marshalled against them and subject now to heavy cannon fire from artillery manhandled across the bridge of boats, the stronghold finally fell. English forces were routed with heavy casualties and Joan once again returned in triumph.

As a woman, Joan was at first the butt for many English jokes and insults. Nicknamed 'la Pucille' (the flea) it is suggested, from the French account of the battle for St. Augustines, that it was her personal reaction to raucous bawling from the archers that turned her original plan for an organised defensive return across the river into a full scale and eventually successful frontal assault.

Whatever her fellow captains thought of her in private — and a dominatrix can attract covert disloyalty as modern politics have demonstrated — understandably the 'Maid of Orleans' was now a cause celebré within the city; flushed with victory the defending troops were not slow to volunteer for service in her next venture.

However, this was to be a far more dangerous undertaking and, although victory was claimed since the English withdrew, there are conflicting views even by the French about the result. Had it failed in its purpose, Joan's flame would undoubtedly have burned more dimly and she might have returned to obscurity but, this was not to be.

For, on Saturday, May 7th, Joan accompanied a strong force which attacked the well defended 'Tourelles' Tower at the further end of the bridge across the Loire. The tower was particularly strongly constructed and was defended by some 800 well-prepared English men-at-arms and archers, led by Sir William Glasdale. The battle was exceptionally fierce and, initially at least, the defenders had the upper hand. Men-at-arms and

The Sun Sets on France — The Siege of Orleans

archers each fought hand-to-hand, archers with sword, maul and knife, the men-at-arms and gunners with axe and sword, pike and gun.

Joan suffered her first injury in this battle. Always a target for archers, since she often appeared without a helmet in order to be recognised, she was hit by an arrow whilst involved in an attack against the walls. This penetrated above the collar-bone, emerging from behind her shoulder and weak from loss of blood, she was forced to leave the battlefield for a time. However, the arrow head was broken off and the shaft pulled out — some say by Joan herself — the wound was dressed and Joan returned to the fray.

Matters were not going well for the city troops at this juncture and all might have ended quite differently had Joan not come back. With her presence to encourage them however, the French managed to set fire to the drawbridge leading into the Tower. Withdrawing over this weakened structure, Glasdale and his fighting rearguard of men-at-arms fell through and, heavily weighted as they were with armour, drowned in the moat. Although their captain was lost, those within fought to a standstill and whilst losses were heavy, the Tower seems not to have been finally taken.

However, very considerable damage had been done and losses had been substantial enough to convince the English commanders — at a hastily convened Council of War — that things were not likely to take a turn for the better. On Sunday therefore, realising that their force, never really adequate for the task, was now even less able to hold the siege intact and, very conscious of the surge in French morale and a mounting toll of casualties, the Earl of Suffolk, Lord Scales and Lord John Talbot decided that enough was enough.

Marshalling their remaining troops in full battle-order in front of the city, they first defiantly invited the French to a pitched battle to decide the issue and waited for the challenge to be accepted.

A full-frontal confrontation with an English army, although reduced in number, would not have been the option of most French captains and, to her credit, Joan was no different. On her advice (so we are told) the French stayed put; a prudent choice perhaps, although given the French successes of the preceding few days, an English victory would have been by no means a certainty.

So it was that after an abortive seven months siege, the remnants of the besieging army, never large, made its way from Orleans in good order towards those strongpoints along the River Loire, established at the beginning of the campaign and which included the small town of Jargeau, some 10 miles away to the West.

Despite their judicious rejection of the pitched battle option, the French of Orleans had not been idle. A large force, commanded by the French Captain Dunois and, including Joan and her fellows, was on its way, determined to recapture all the English controlled Loire towns and, at Jargeau, defended by the Earl of Suffolk and the brothers Sir John and Sir Alexander de la Pole, fortifications were hastily thrown up against attack.

This was not long in coming. The small number of men invested in the town (numbers vary between 400 and 2,000) were quickly surrounded. After an abortive attempt at truce by Suffolk, the French opened their attack and although the English fought as fiercely as ever, the result was never in much doubt. After many casualties the town was taken and the few survivors (some say just 60 were left alive) were taken captive.

In the thick of things as usual, Joan had been hurt again. This time by a stone which hit her on the head as she climbed a ladder. The wound was slight and she was quickly back in action.

Jargeau's fate also befell Meunt, 10 miles to the east; although some say this town was never taken and the garrison was allowed to leave in full marching order. During a skirmish there, Joan, having been wounded for a third time (on this occasion in her leg) fell into a ditch where with her charmed life, she lay until rescued.

The English garrison within Beaugency, last of the Loire towns to fall, managed to negotiate a truce and was allowed to leave unscathed.

Before losing Jargean, the Earl of Suffolk had been able to despatch messages to the Duke of Bedford in Paris, telling him in no uncertain terms of his position and reminding him of his own vulnerability if the country between Orleans and Paris should fall to the Dauphin. Grudgingly accepting this unwelcome news, Bedford gathered together an army of men of "various nations"; very much a scratch force and, with little time to exercise as a cohesive unit, this set off towards the Loire to meet the combined remnants of the battered Orlean besiegers and the troops from Meunt.

About 2 p.m. on 28th July, 1537, when William Bayswood, late of Hardwick was at Hardwick, he shot an arrow called a mattrez (a mattross, quarrel, or bolt) at a bird called a robynett (robin) with a cross-bow which he held in both hands and by chance and without any malice aforethought or felonious intent he unknowingly, by misadventure and against his will struck John Doughy with the arrow on his right side as John was lying hidden behind a hedge. William was pardoned.

THE BATTLE OF PATAY, 1429

THIS raggle-taggle force met together outside the large village of Patay, where arrangements for defence had rapidly to be made, for a feature of the 'Orleans' campaign, once Joan became involved, was the speed at which things happened. Patay was fought on the same day that Beaugency fell. Indecision, so often a trait of French commanders, had been replaced by enthusiasm in full measure and, with Joan in front, they were now lusting for English blood.

It had been decided that the French vanguard should be led by the Constable, Marshal de Boussac, with Captains la Hire, Pothon, and others. It would proceed with cautious despatch, closely followed by the main army of some 8,000 or 9,000 men. Ahead of the vanguard a mounted scouting party about 80 strong would set off, with responsibility for seeking out the English positions.

Meanwhile, Lord John Talbot and Sir John Fastolf were considering the disposition of their men in a defensive formation. Numerically inferior (the English army may not have much exceeded 3,000) with many having no recent battle experience and, as events were to show, indifferent discipline, the task was difficult. The topography was in Talbot's favour and he made what use he could of it; the countryside was covered with hedges and small clumps of trees, whilst a forest boundary offered a secure place for the baggage train and his artillery pieces. Some 500 of his archers he placed strategically behind hedges in a low valley, intending that they spring an ambush on the hopefully unsuspecting French.

And so it might well have happened, for the French scouts had by now reached the area and were searching, so far without success, for signs of Talbot and his men. As they rode cautiously forward, a startled stag suddenly burst from cover and careered up the track. With this, raucous shouts came from behind the hedges; some English bowmen, discipline forgotten and ever-ready to take venison on the hoof, leapt out enthusiastically and shot at it.

The scouting party reined in swiftly and back-tracked to report.

Their position now known, the archers were turned and moved from their original placings amidst undergrowth and hedges, to what seemed a defensible position in open country, some six or seven hundred yards to their rear and suited to a massed arrow-storm against the expected cavalry attack.

What happened next is not entirely clear. However, after breasting a slight rise in the ground it would seem that the French vanguard, a well-led mounted force of experienced men-at-arms, saw the English archers busily hammering in their stakes against a frontal assault— but not yet in battle-order. In one account, the cavalry charged the archers down before they could hammer in their stakes — as was done at Verneuil — and this seems a likely scenario. In another, they dismounted and fought

The Sun Sets on France — The Battle of Patay

A startled stag suddenly burst from cover; ever-ready to take venison on the hoof and with discipline forgotten, some English bowmen leapt out enthusiastically and shot at it!

on foot. Of the two, the cavalry charge seems the more probable but, by whichever means the French chose, the English were soon fighting hand-to-hand for their very lives.

The battle was over in short order. Lord John Talbot was captured, together with some of his men. Casualties were heavy in what was an uneven struggle between lightly-armed archers (many of whom were not battle-hardened) and highly-motivated and well-led French heavy cavalry. The small party guarding the baggage train and guns, seeing the hopelessness of their position melted into the forest at their back; the field was left to a victorious Duc d'Alençon.

Although Talbot had been taken captive, John Fastolf had not dismounted and, with a small force of his personal retainers, perhaps including the erstwhile defenders of the baggage train, managed a fighting withdrawal.

Marching an incredible 60 miles in one day and a night, his archers beat off constant attacks, first with their bows and arrows and then, when sheaves were exhausted, in hand-to-hand combat with sword, maul and fighting knife.

On his exhausted arrival in Paris, Fastolf's troubles were by no means over. To say that Bedford was displeased would be to understate. In his initial opinion Fastolf had deserted his men. Whilst his fellow commander, Talbot had done the right thing and fought to a finish, he — Fastolf — had fled the field, or so it seemed. He was

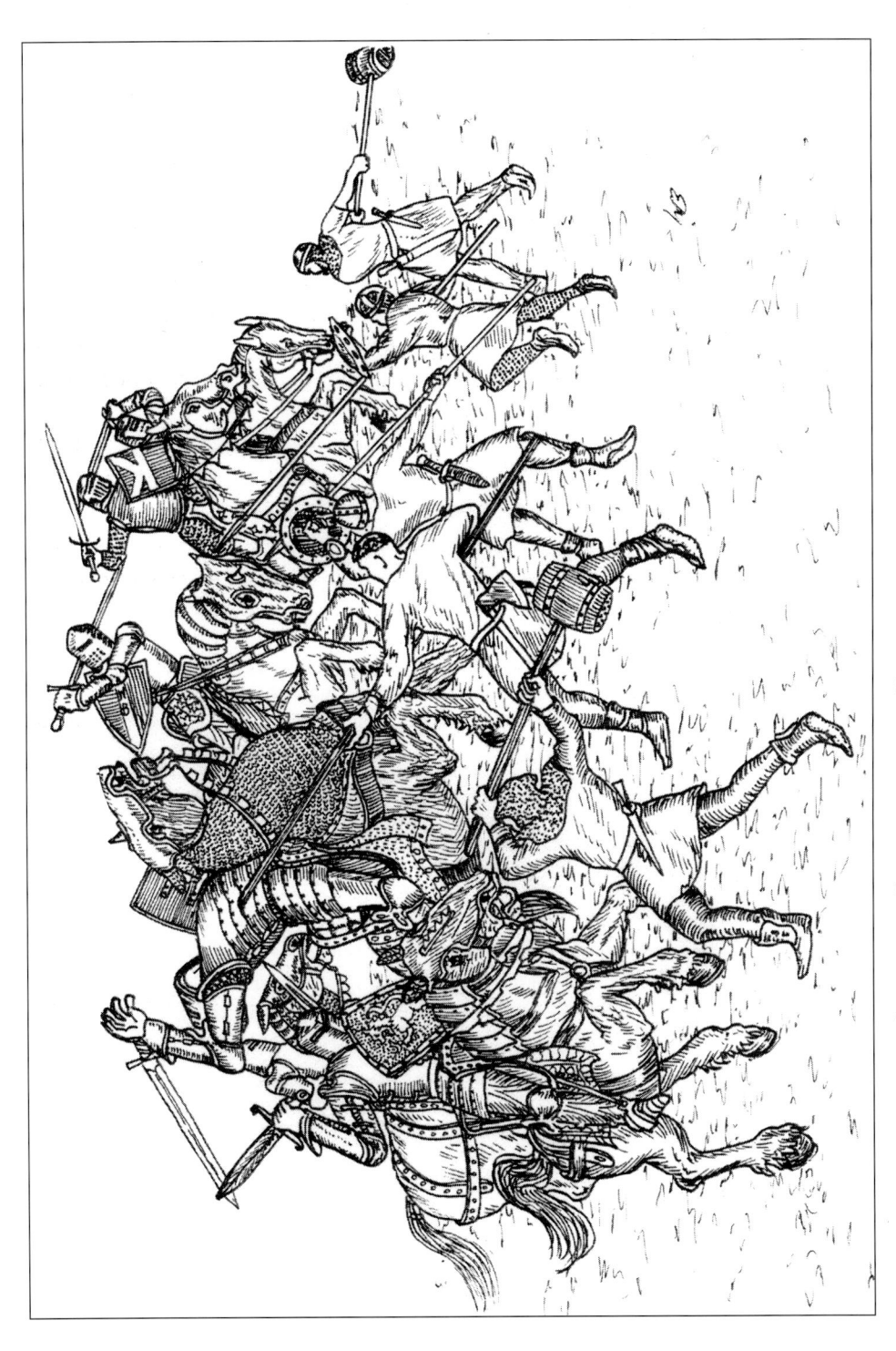

The Sun Sets on France — The Battle of Patay

Attacked by French cavalry, the English archers fight for their lives

summarily divested of the Order of the Garter for these seeming sins and practically accused of cowardice in the face of the foe.

It took a while indeed before his explanation of events was accepted; he remained for some time both out of favour and Garter-less. It is said that despite his eventual return to grace, there remained much bad feeling between himself and John Talbot when that worthy warrior finally returned from captivity. Perhaps, understandably, since to see the backside of one's erstwhile companion-in-arms disappear into the middle distance whilst one is being led away in chains, is hardly conducive to subsequent good relations

Although Joan d'Arc may not have been actively engaged in the battle at Patay, it was her undoubted charisma that had fuelled the fervent French attack. She had, however, a greater prize in store, for in the city of Rheims on July 17th, 1429, her promise to the Dauphin Charles in March of that year came true. She had said that there, with God's help, she would see him crowned King of France.

It is arguable that, if this were indeed her mission, it was complete and she might return to her village and obscurity. But, as history records, fate decreed otherwise for, just one year later as the CHRONICLE OF LONDON briefly records:

". . . the xxiij day of May after noon ayens nyght, before the town of Compigne, there was a woman taken armed in the feld with manye othere capitaynes, the whiche was culled la pucelle de Dieu, (God's flea) *a fals wyche . . ."*

On May 30th, 1431, in the market square of Rouen, Joan, daughter of Jack the Archer, was sacrificed to her faith. On July 7th, 1456, the judgement upon her was declared invalid and posthumously annulled. Beatified in 1909, she was entered in the Catalogue of Saints in 1920.

Principal References consulted, and further reading:
THE AGINCOURT WAR. Alfred H. Burne, D.S.O. F.R.Hist.S., 1956. Eyre and Spottiswoode.
THE BOWMEN OF ENGLAND. Donald Featherstone, 1967. Jarrolds Publishers (London) Ltd. '
JOAN OF ARC. Jay Williams, 1963. Cassell
THE MEDIEVAL SIEGE. Jim Bradbury, 1992. Boydell Press. ISBN 85115 312 7
THE MEDIEVAL CITY UNDER SIEGE. Ed:Corfis & Wolfe, 1995. Boydell Press. ISBN 85115 561 8

AN ARROW IS DRAWN FROM THE BACK QUIVER . . . !

Part 7

Skirmish and Ambuscade

The Ambush of Nibley Green
The Western Rebellion
The Battle of Fenny Bridges
The Eastern Rebellion. Battle of Mount Surry
The Skirmish at Blatchington Hill
Rebellion of Sir Thomas Wyatt

PART 7

SKIRMISH AND AMBUSCADE

BATTLES, the dictionary has it, are combats fought between large organised forces, whilst skirmishes are irregular engagements between two small bodies of troops.

It would be difficult to define any of this Chapter's events as battles, since by comparison with the set-piece affairs upon which military historians are weaned, numbers engaged were few. Each had an effect disproportionate to its size however, and it is with a mite of reluctance that we must call them skirmishes; yet since there is no other term available, skirmishes they must perforce be.

That which took place in 1469 at Nibley Green, in South Gloucestershire, might better be described as a private war, whilst the slopes of Blatchington Hill saw a spirited defence of home and hearth against marauding French. The fight at Fenny Bridge, in 1549, has been called the 'Prayer Book Rebellion' and the skirmish in London 'Wyatt's War.' Each will be described, beginning with that fought on March 20th, 1469.

NIBLEY GREEN, 1469

THE engagement at Nibley Green was the last between private armies on English soil. The culmination of a long-standing land dispute between the great Houses of Fitzharding and Talbot, it took place in Gloucestershire on the Eastern boundaries of the Hundreds of Berkeley and Wootton, lands held respectively by each family.

It had all begun with the death of Thomas Fitzharding (Lord of Berkeley) and the subsequent division of his properties. The Berkeley and Talbot families were related — as were many of the great families of the day. The grandmother of Thomas Talbot (the Lord Lisle) was Thomas Berkeley's granddaughter and therein lay the problem.

Whilst the Lisles claimed Berkeley Castle, power-base of the Fitzhardings, they in turn claimed the Manor and the substantial lands of Wotton, residence of the 21-year-old Thomas Talbot and his young and very pregnant wife.

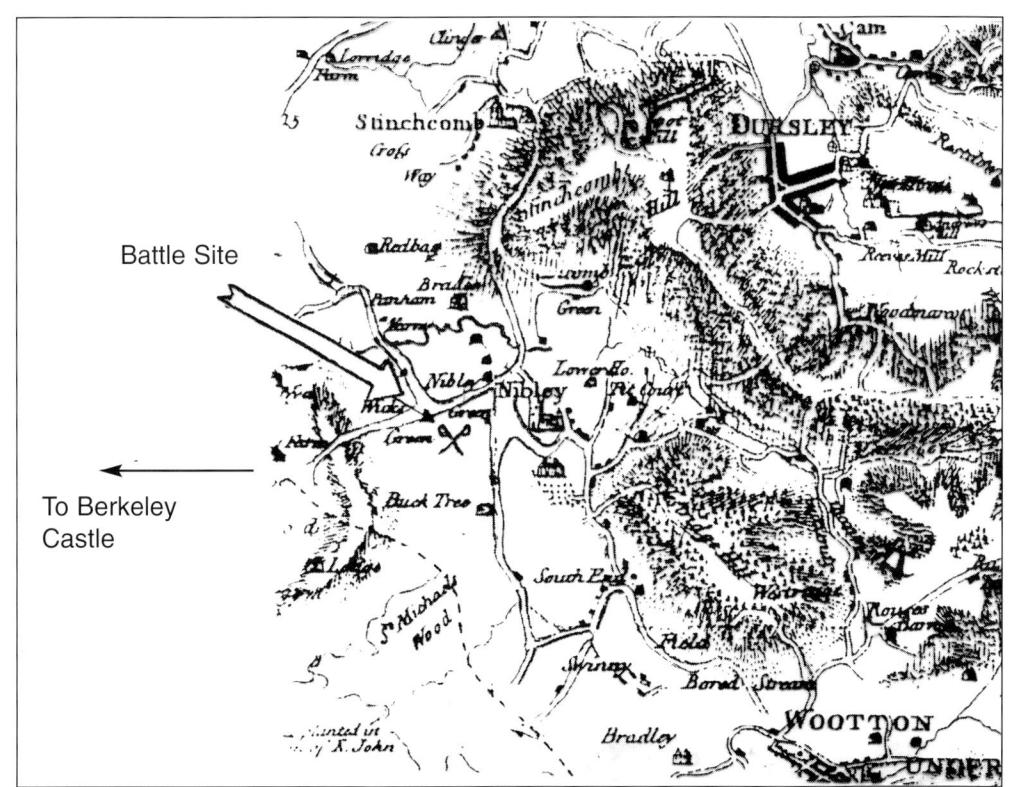

THE BATTLE OF NIBLEY GREEN, March 20th, 1469

Thomas Talbot's grandmother, Margaret, had a fixation bordering on paranoia about her title to the disputed lands and earlier in 1451, had had a serious clash with the Berkeley's in which she came out on top! She and her husband had first bribed the Steward and Porter of the Castle and had then taken it by force of arms, capturing some of the Berkeley family in residence, including William's mother who afterwards died in Gloucester gaol. To say that the matter rankled with the present Earl would be an understatement.

William, Lord Berkeley, was a single-minded man of enormous influence and unpleasant habit. A bachelor until his forties, his character and personality did little to endear him to those whom he disliked. Amongst his titles in 1469 were Great Mareschal of England; Earl Marshal of Nottingham; Lord of Mowbray and Segrave and, Marquess of Berkeley. With a brief that included, inter alia, keeping the South Welsh in South Wales, when William Fitzharding, Lord of Berkeley, Earl Mareschal of England spoke, those with sense stopped what they were doing and listened.

If we are to believe Berkeley and there is no great reason not to, it was the Welsh question that sparked the matter. He believed, or let it be thought he believed, that Lisle was inciting the South Welsh to rebellion. Whether or not this was so, in ordinary circumstances a 21-year-old upstart (albeit a Lisle with the warrior House of Talbot at his back) would have been beyond the notice of the mighty Fitzharding. An irritant to be disposed of by underlings. But Thomas Talbot represented something more; he was of the family who had caused the imprisonment of William's father and the death of his mother and, Willliam was not one to let that matter pass.

Things came to a sudden head when Lord Lisle tried, foolishly, to emulate his grandmother's success at Berkeley Castle. All went sadly adrift however with his attempt at stealth. William had a better grip on domestic matters than had his father and Thomas's plans came to a sudden and precipitate end.

From then on, events moved rapidly. It is certain that William would have spoken with his brother Maurice Fitzharding at Thornbury and William would not have been William if contingency plans had not been discussed. None too soon as it transpired.

With incriminating letters bearing his Seal of Arms in Berkeley's possession, young Lord Lisle was in a highly vulnerable position. He acted swiftly and with the impetuosity of youth. Although it is reasonable to suppose that he had some sort of a force at hand — since he had been preparing a coup and Berkeley was a well-defended castle — on March 19th he chose, instead, to challenge Earl Berkeley to single combat, adding, significantly as it happened, that should the challenge be rejected, the Earl should bring *". . . the uttermost of thy power . . ."* when he, Thomas Talbot, would meet him to decide the issue.

Lord William had other ideas though. The response to the challenge came by return of post and, over 500 years later, the menace is both real and evident.

". . . Thomas Talbot, otherwise called Viscount Lisle, not long continued in that name, but a new found thing brought out of strange countryes: I marveill gready at thy strange and lewd writinge. . . . As for the determynyng betwyxt our two hands of thy untrue clayme, and my title and right of land, and inheritance, thou wottest right

well there is no such deter-minacon of land in this Relme used if it were soe that this matter might be determined by they hands and myne thou should not so long desire but I would as soone answere thee in every poynt that belongeth to a knight: for thou art, God I take to record, in a false quarrell, and I in true defence and title. . . .

". . . And where thou desirest and requirest mee of knighthood to appoynt a day, and that I should be there with all the power that I could make, and that thou would mete mee haff-way, I will thou understand I will not bring the tenth part that I can make, and I will appoynt a short day to ease thy malitious hart.. . . .

". . . Fail not tomorrow to be at Niblyes Green at eight or nine of the clock, and I will not fail with God's might and grace to meete thee at the same place ready to answer thee in all things. . . ."

William Fitzharding, the Viscount Berkeley 19th March,1469

In terms of strategy the initiative should have lain with Lisle, since he was, or should have been, prepared. Even allowing for surprise he would still have needed a substantial force to take and afterwards maintain his hold on Berkeley Castle. He drew, as he had said, upon his own retainers and his neighbours' bowmen and billmen, a total perhaps, of some 500 fighting men.

From the nature of Lisle's plotting we can guess that he had not intended to fight a set-piece battle and his challenge to single combat was, perhaps, a last hope to avoid confrontation. Despite the foolhardy bravado with which he dared Berkeley to meet him with the *'uttermost of his power,'* he must have known that he would be outnumbered and probably his soldiers did as well.

Although saying that he would not bring one tenth of the troops at his command, Berkeley cast around for forces. These came forward quickly and in some number. Whilst admittedly the day of battle was of his choosing, circumstances had given him less that 12 hours to gather an army and, if the subsequent ambush was already on his mind, he had to position his men well before eight o'clock on the following day.

One can imagine the speed with which he despatched trusted messengers; one to his brother Maurice at Thornbury and the other across the River Severn to the Constable of St. Briavels Castle.

His brother Maurice, rather than William, seems to have called upon the Bristol men to help out. Two merchants indebted to him led a band of honest Bristolians spoiling for a fight, adding perhaps a few Kingswood Arrow-men (legalised ruffians who kept order in the Royal Forest) to make up numbers; whilst from St. Briavels came a contingent of Dean Forest bowmen — cold-eyed battle-hardened miners dedicated to holding the Welsh in check — under their formidable leader 'Black Will' Long.

In total therefore, Lisle's force of some 500 bucolic Sunday soldiers was opposed by one of about 1,000 strong, including moreover, a significant leavening of professional archers, forest dwellers for whom the 'crooked stick' and the 'grey goose wing' were no mere Sunday weapons — but a way of life.

Lord Berkeley's army moved quietly through Michaelwood Forest during the evening and night of March 19th, stopping at the outskirts but keeping under cover.

Skirmish and Ambuscade — Nibley Green

Ambush and assassination of Lord Lisle by Black Will at Nibley Green

BLACK WILL LONG, LEADER OF THE DEAN FORESTERS AND REPUTED ASSASSIN.

Sitting amongst the branches of trees at a respectable distance from the action, local youths — so we are told — waited expectantly for something to happen.

At sunrise on the 19th, Lord Lisle's troops could be seen moving down the hill from North Nibley Church towards the open Green, which at that time extended to the forest edge. At their head, the fiery young Thomas Talbot. With the forest so close and with foresters practised at merging with their surroundings, he could perhaps be forgiven for thinking that he was first upon the scene.

The ambush, for that is what it was, took place before he could properly position his men and is a measure of Berkeley's disregard for military convention. His archers delivered their shafts from forest cover to deadly effect, bow-raking Lisle's men with battle-shafts at almost point-blank range. Talbot was killed early in the affair, struck in the left temple through his open vizor by an arrow from 'Black Will's bow and finished off with either ballock knife or rondel dagger.

In the words of the 'Ballad of Nibley Green:

"... *Of their arrow shot:*
Oh, call it not
A battle; it was then,
A screaming shout, a rush, a rout,
And a heap of mangled men ..."

The part of Black Will in all this is interesting. That he killed Lisle is beyond doubt; that he was commissioned by Lord William Berkeley to do so is guesswork but, if he were a medieval 'hitman' under contract, then Berkeley could not have chosen better.

Looked at objectively, whoever took Lisle's life was at the right place at the right time. To put a shaft through an open vizor implies a point-blank bow shot of perhaps 50 yards or even less. Black Will was leader of the Dean Foresters and more than just a competent archer; it would have been consistent with his standing that he should have been in a commanding position opposite the entry of the track along which Lisle was moving and, even more so if he were, in fact, under contract!!

Indeed, with hindsight, one thing is crystal clear. Black Will Long was not where he was by accident.

A contemporary poem has him saying in reponse to a question.:

"I reck not, he replied, and careless laughed,
Of Briton, Saxon, Norman or of Dane,
If I compacted be: so I my craft,
Well know, nor ever do dismiss in vain.
Drawn to my ear, the unerring clothyard shaft.
"He too, the Lord of Lisle, who dare to prance,
At his life's cost, in an ill-omened day,
Joining with Berkeley's Earl in deadly fray.
'Twas I that drew the bow, the shaft that sent,
And planted deep its steel point in the brain
of that proud Lord . . ."

That then is the tale of Nibley Green. Legend says that Michaelwood is haunted and that on March 20th each year the noise of archers and men-at-arms can be heard through what was the former wood. The clash of armour and the twang of bowstrings in the early light merging with the ghostly form of the brave but, foolhardy Thomas Talbot, the young Lord Lisle, as he clutches frantically at the bodkin point driven deep into his brain.

Perhaps ! But it is a sad memorial to an unhappy affair; the last great Baronial fight in England — and we must leave it so.

OF BOWMEN AND BATTLES

PLATE 17

GWYNN ZUCCA

Dressed in the livery of Lord Ferrers (Sir Walter Deveraux), this archer, complete with kit, prepares to leave for Towton and the battle

PLATE 18

PAUL HITCHEN
Dressed in the costume of Agincourt the archer draws his warbow to send a battle shaft towards the enemy

OF BOWMEN AND BATTLES

PLATE 19

ALAN EDWARDS and JEZ HARTLEY
In the livery of Lord Fauconberg (William Neville), these two archers
meet and make their way to join the force going to war

OF BOWMEN AND BATTLES

PLATE 20

'TOGETHER!'
Archers serving two different Lords come together and wait for the action to begin

OF BOWMEN AND BATTLES

PLATE 21

MARK STRETTON
At Agincourt, having hammered the protective stakes into the ground,
the ends are brought to a point with the aid of a battleaxe

Of Bowmen and Battles

PLATE 22

'LOOSE!'

From behind their protective stakes the English archers prepare to loose the Arrowstorm

PLATE 23

'DRAW!'
With 120lb on his fingers, Gwynn Zucca demonstrates that heavy
bows could be drawn with just two fingers

OF BOWMEN AND BATTLES

PLATE 24

MOVE IN FOR HAND-TO-HAND FIGHTING!
Having used all their arrows the archers prepare to use their hand-to-hand weapons of maul, sword, battle-axe, etc.

THE WESTERN REBELLION, 1549

ARCHERS who use the longbow and many who don't, know of Agincourt, Crecy, and the 'arrow-storm' which preceded these homeric confrontations. Few will know of the many lesser conflicts and skirmishes which punctuated the long history of the war-bow and, fewer still of the Western Rebellion which took place in 1549.

Although the bow was still a formidable weapon, military strategists in England, led by Continental tacticians, had turned more and more to the hand-gun, despite problems with it in bad weather and its relatively slow rate of fire. Whilst the battle of Pinkie Cleugh two years before had involved archers on both sides and, English longbowmen had played their part manfully in breaking the Scottish schiltrons, this is often regarded as the last major engagement in which archery played a principal role.

True, it featured as an auxiliary English weapon in the Civil War a century later and James Graham used it to effect in his thrashing of the Covenanting armies but, the day of 'England's Martial Glory' had passed. No more would men say with truth: "... *The might of England resteth upon her archers*. . . ."

But, the bow remained the weapon of the common man. With this, his quarter staff and arming dagger (ballock knife for those untroubled by political correctness) he felt the equal of any matched against him. Strong in back and arm, he was well equipped — when the cause was there — to take on all-comers, be they Scots, French or the hated foreign mercenaries brought in to subdue him.

The Western and the Eastern rebellions in the England of 1549 were just such causes. The boy-King, Edward VI, had yet to reach the age of Royal competence, so England was effectively governed by the Protector, Edward Seymour, Duke of Somerset, a man of disagreeable habit, whose personal insensitivity was matched only by his unbridled avarice.

Three simmering factors dominated the West-Country scene: The land reforms which heavily favoured the great land-owners to the disadvantage of the peasants; the secularising of the monastic institutions, again to the disadvantage of many of the poor, who depended upon them for relief in hard times and who found the new tenants a good deal less charitably inclined and; the third factor involving obligatory changes in Church ritual, including the enforced use of English instead of Latin.

This last bore most heavily in rural Cornwall, where their own Cornish language was still strong and English was at best a second tongue.

Loss of the Latin ritual with which they were familiar and the imposition of an alien tongue, which many did not understand, was anathema to the folk of Cornwall. They felt treated with contempt by arrogant attenders to the King's business and, at Helston on April 5th, 1548, their rage boiled over.

William Body, King's Commissioner, had arrived in State with his bodyguard (an unfortunate mis-nomer as it happened) to strip the Church of statues and symbols of 'Popery.' The Cornishmen saw red; Commissioner Body was hauled backwards out of the Church and summarily knifed by William Kylter, a local priest, whilst his 'bodyguard' looked on.

The Duchy was at flash-point. Three thousand stalwarts mustered in the town as matters got rapidly out of hand. Appeasement came quickly in the form of a general pardon but, ominously, with significant exceptions. Rather a lot of exceptions as it happened, since 10 of those involved were subsequently hanged, drawn and quartered.

The Cornish seethed and, on June 6th at Bodmin, the die was cast. Cornwall rose in full revolt against the Protector Somerset and the Crown Royal. Three days later the Devon men joined in and, with a full head of steam the Western Rebellion was under way. Scythes became swords, bills were sharpened and the war-bows with their long Cornish battle-shafts were made ready.

At first things went well. Humphrey Arundell, their leader, took St. Michael's Mount without loss. Trematon Castle, defended by Sir Richard Grenville, fell after a short siege, the loyal Sir Richard ending up in Dunheved gaol. Strategically important Plymouth yielded promptly and Arundell's little army of archers and billmen moved on.

A lengthy siege of Exeter proved unsuccessful and after considerable prompting by Lord Russell (to whom inter alia the defence of Exeter fell) the eventual despatch of a significant portion of the Royal army inevitably turned the tide. Arundell's soldiers, brave and fearless though they were, had no real chance against a professional force, largely of trained and disciplined Italian mercenaries, with cavalry backing. Falling back from Exeter, towards the end of July, battle was joined at Fenny Bridges.

Although the rebel bow and billmen fought hard, they were forced back by cavalry attack and the hand-guns, bills and pikes in the hands of Russell's Italian soldiers. However, whilst this swarthy crew were engaged in their slitting of throats and the taking of booty, they failed to see Cornish reinforcements peering at them though the hedge. Suddenly a storm of arrows rained amongst them and, with swords and falchions unsheathed, the archers rushed them. Surprise was complete and Russell's men fled in panic, leaving the Cornish in possession of the field. Sadly, however, the outcome was predictable. They were counter-attacked by superior forces and the original 250 bowmen left many dead before fighting their way out of danger.

Whilst there is little doubt that in the minds of those concerned, their cause was just, the Western Rebellion was doomed. A second and final battle at Clyst St Mary, in which the Cornish tinners and the men of Devon played their valiant parts, saw the defeat of Arundell's ill-equipped but dedicated little force.[1] Authority exacted its full toll of life and limb and, in the West Country, religious discontent smouldered on.

In the East disgruntlement took a different path. Robert Ket, a Tanner from

---

[1] vide Sir John Smythe 'Certeyn Discourses Military': ". . . the Archers of the Rebells did so behave themselves with their volees of arrowes against divers olfd bands Harquebuziers that they drave them from all their strengths as from bancks, ditches, hedges, and other advauntages of Ground to the great mischiefe of manie of those Strangers."

Windham, raised the Norfolk peasantry in full revolt against land reforms. After some local successes — including the notable occasion when with a force of archers and bill-men he summarily disposed of William Parr, Marquis of Northampton and his harque-busiers — he came within an ace of total victory when the rebel encampment on Mount Surrey was engaged by a professionally led army headed by the Earl of Warwick, John Dudley.

Protector Somerset had deputed the noble Earl to deal with the situation and Warwick had brought 24 field pieces, guarded by a force of some 1,200 Almain hand-gunners, to do just that. These guns were carefully wheeled into position, pointed up the hill and guarded, with true Teutonic fussiness, by military gentlemen from Germany. Arrangements which were regarded with growing interest by those at the top.

Warwick retired to his tent for dinner and a well-earned rest after the exertions of the day. Arrangements for security were in place and all ought to have been well. The rebels would surely be over-awed by the opposition, for were not his lands-knechts the cream of Continental soldiery? Matters would be speedily concluded and all could go home.

Not a bit of it. Before the guns could be properly entrenched, the rebels descended the hill in force — as a contemporary account has it: *". . . All bowmen, swords and bills. . . ."* Arrows flew and, like their Italian counterparts in the West, the mercenary hand-gunners legged it swiftly to the rear. Ket's peasant soldiers carried 18 of the 24 guns victoriously back up Mount Surrey and the Earl was left with uneaten dinner and egg on his face.

Inevitably, since the rebels were surrounded, the subsequent battle a day or two later ended in Warwick's favour and Ket the Tanner met a sad fate, hanging in chains from Norwich Castle but, it was a very close-run thing. Sir John Smith, in his 1590 book 'Certain Discourses Military,' instances the battle when arguing in favour of retention of the war-bow. He records recognition of the power of archery, used by those with right and purpose on their side, from both Warwick (whose horse was shot from under him by arrows) and the captain of his German mercenaries alike[2].

But, what of the men themselves. This was no undisciplined band of bucolics wound up by rabble rousers. Many of them would have seen military service and all were perfectly familiar with their weapons and the drills associated with them. They and their leaders were well versed in the ways of war.

We have an account of these sturdy bowmen from one who saw them in action during Spanish wars against the Moorish invaders. Does it perhaps have a contemporary ring?

Padre Fray Antonio Agapida wrote of them . . .

".... They were a comely race of men, but too fair and fresh for warriors; not having the sunburnt hue of our old Castilan soldiery. They were huge feeders also, and deep carousers, and could not accommodate themselves to the sober diet of our

---

[2] ibid. The Duke (of Northumberland) brought in foure and twentie field peeces, to the cheefe charge whereof he appointed Coronell Courpenick an Alman and a great soldier with his regiment of Almains, which was twelve hundred, the most of them brave shot, and old soldiers.'

troops, but must fain eat and drink after the style of their own country. They were often noisy and unruly in their wassail, and their quarter of the camp was prone to be a scene of loud revel and sudden brawl. They were withal of great pride; yet it was not like our inflammable Spanish pride Their pride was silent and contemptuous. Though from a remote and barbarous Island they yet believed themselves the most perfect men on earth, and magnified their Chieftain, the Lord Scales, beyond the greatest of our Grandees.

"With all this they were marvellous good men in the field, dexterous archers and powerful with the battle-axe. In their great pride and self-will they always sought to press in the advance and take part of danger, trying to outvie our Spanish chivalry. They did not rush forward like the Moorish or the Spanish troops, but went into the fight deliberately, and persisted obstinately, being slow to find out when they were beaten.

"Withal they were much esteemed yet little liked by our soldiery who considered them staunch companions in the field, yet coveted but little fellowship with them in the Camp. . . ."

The archers who fought at Fenny Bridge and Mount Surrey were lineal descendants of these formidable fighters, xenophobic to a man and conscious of their martial superiority, if not always an advantage of arms; those who opposed them did well to respect their courage and tenacity.

And there we, who are of their line, will leave them.

The Battle of Fenny Bridges, 1549

THE BATTLE OF BLATCHINGTON HILL, 1545

LOOK FOR the battle of Blatchington Hill in any history book and you look in vain. Remote in time, its very site covered now by waves, this local skirmish is remembered only for the man whose charismatic leadership saved the East Sussex town of Seaford from French invasion.

Yet, it had an importance on the National scene that far outweighed its local nature; for by his vigorous defence at East Blatchington, on July 26th, 1545, Nicholas Pelham and his band of honest Sussex bowmen and billmen, persuaded French Admiral Claude d'Annebault that enough was enough and that further attacks on the English coast would be fruitless.

Defeat at this engagement terminated the French campaign of 1545 and d'Annebault, forthwith, set sail for France and home.

Henry VIII's French campaign of 1544, mounted with such determination and, in alliance with Charles V of Spain, had gained the port of Boulogne for England and this, with Calais, had left the King with strategic domination of the Channel.

All was not well with this uneasy alliance however. By 1545 France had concluded

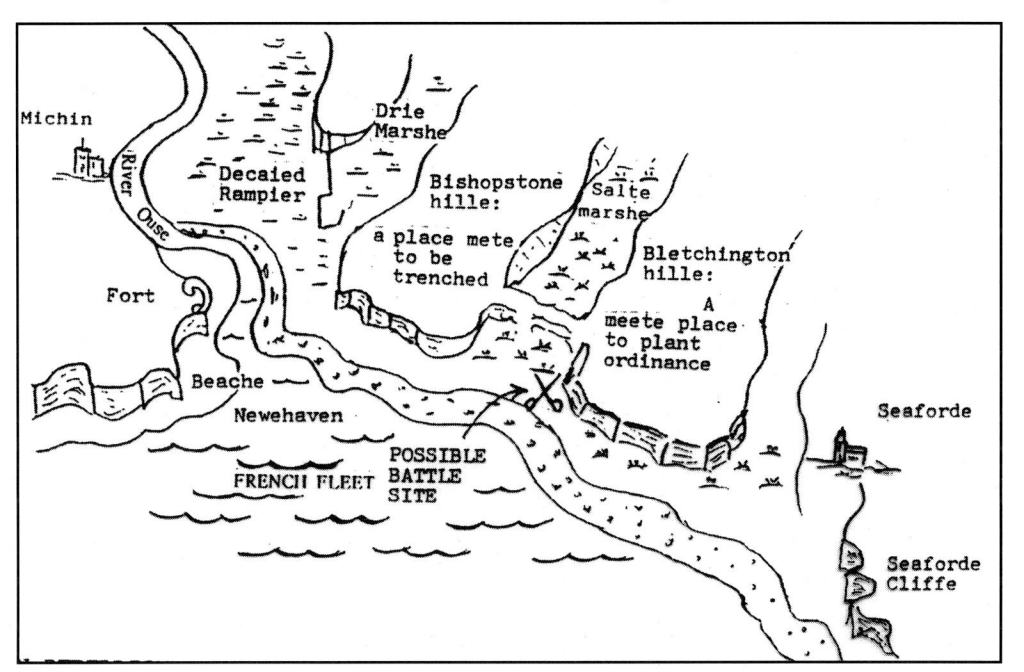

THE BATTLE OF BLATCHINGTON HILL, 1545

a separate peace with Spain and, England, now isolated, was left to feel the full fury of the French King, Francis I, whose avowed intention it now was to invade and exact retribution. All along the South coast, town and county militias were mustered at strategic points and bowmen, musketeers and billmen stood in readiness for the expected onslaught.

Beacons were made ready and, in Southampton water, protected by formidable shore batteries, Henry's small but efficient force of galleys and fighting sail, headed by the flagship 'Henri Grace a Dieu' ('Great Harry') with Viscount Lisle in command, awaited d 'Annebault's arrival.

Wisely perhaps, Henry did not invite full confrontation. Although the indecisive sea-battle that followed was marked by the loss of his vice-flagship, the recently refitted 'Mary Rose' (Vice-Admiral George Carew in command) it resulted in the withdrawal of a French force which, having landed earlier on the Isle of Wight, had been summarily dealt with by its defenders who wreaked havoc amongst it.

This failure to breach the defensive wall still smarting, the French fleet returned along the South coast en route for home, looking for easier pickings whilst on the way. Thus it was that the ships which anchored in the sweep of Seaford Bay on the evening of July 25th contained many who ached to get ashore for mayhem and plunder. Trouble was not long in coming; watchers on high ground overlooking the bay saw the first signs of French presence on the morning of the 26th. Great gouts of smoke rose from burning buildings as the troops swept ashore and the Portmen of Seaford, under their leader, Nicholas Pelham, joined with comrades from the immediate area to protect both town and property.

Although important in medieval times as the outlet for the River Ouse (or the 'midWynde' to give it an earlier name) and a 'limb' of the Cinque Port, Hastings, the town and port of Seaford had lapsed into near decay through silt and shingle movement by the early 16th Century. The mid-1530's had seen a new port created below the village of Meeching, where Newhaven harbour now stands and, by 1545, this had virtually replaced the 'Old Haven' at 'Bishopstone beach,' itself successor to the original at Seaford.

Whilst there was perhaps some trade by barge from Bishopstone and, although technically still a port, it is unlikely that Seaford prospered. With defences in scale, it was doubtless seen as an easy and suitable prize by d'Annebault's frustrated men.

What happened then was certainly not planned. The French landed in considerable force, watched from vantage points by the defenders. They burnt the first habitations they found, perhaps warehouses and fishermen's huts at Bishopstone harbour (where now is 'The Buckle') and then pressed inland heading for Seaford town.

Coming upon a light wooden bridge over a deep and fast flowing river they crossed, only to be met on the other side by a hail of arrows, shot to effect by a group of archers lying in wait within the confines of a small fort, concealed from view by the bridge.

Reeling from this sudden and unexpected attack and forced back against the river bank by the arrow-storm, their retreat across the river was cut off by billmen who destroyed the bridge.

Thus pinned down by bowmen, musketeers and billmen alike, their plight became apparent to their commanders on board. With cannon brought laboriously ashore and manoevred into position, d'Annebault eventually relieved his beleagured troops and a weary, dispirited and sadly depleted rabble struggled back across the river to their ships, leaving the port-men victorious. The would-be invaders then set sail for France, Admiral d'Annebault having decided that he would risk no more confrontations.

But, where was this engagement fought? One thing is certain, neither river, bridge, nor fort survive. They have long since succumbed to storm, shingle and tide. However, we can speculate.

In 1587, prior to the Armada threat, a survey of the coast referred to:

" *2 . . . Bletchington Hille, where an entrie was made by the ffrenche. . . .*"

The course of the River Ouse that once found outlet at Seaford, lay to the South of Hawth and Blatchington Hills, having meandered its way past Denton and beneath the lee of Bishopstone Hill. Probably much of this old watercourse existed in 1545, with an outlet in the area of what is now called the 'Buckle' — ostensibly so named from a local inn.

Although the south-western slope of Blatchington Hill has for several centuries been regularly defended by earthworks and forts, it is to the 'Buckle' that we look as a likely battle site. If the landing took place on the shingle shore between Seaford and Newhaven, at the place local folk know as Tidemills, then the bridge would have crossed the river at the Buckle. It would be entirely consistent with strategy for a small fort to both guard the old Haven and to offer some protection to the village of Bishopstone. This would give cover to the Seaford port-men and, important to subsequent events, would allow d'Annebault to see what was going on and eventually to recover his troops.

Some circumstantial evidence exists in favour of the Buckle as the site. In the 1587 map, both Hawth and Blatchington Hills have been combined, although in fact they are distinct. If, as is likely — even probable, the French landed to the South-West of the hill, then the Buckle is a prime candidate for the action.[3]

Notwithstanding the actual site, we know much of the man who led the defenders. Nicholas Pelham, later knighted, was 28 years old in 1545. Son of Sir William Pelham and Mary Carew of Beddington, he was a man of learning and letters, a patriotic statesman described by contemporaries as 'pure of spirit.' He died at the early age of 43 and lies beneath a monument in St Michael's Church at nearby Lewes. This bears the epitaph that lustily conveys the sentiments which his comrades-in-arms in the Blatchington battle no doubt felt for their young leader.

". . . *His valour's proof, his manlie vertue's prayse*
Cannot be marshall'd in this narrow room.
His brave exploits in great king Henry's days,
Among the worthye hath a worthier tombe.
What time the French sought to have sacked Sea-Foord,
This Pelham did RE-PEL-EM back aboord. . . ."

[3] The writer is an exiled Seafordian who, in the 1930's knew the Buckle well, lived nearby in East Blatchington and spent a carefree youth on the slopes of Hawth Hill.

As an aside, this son of a Carew had, in some small way, revenged the untimely death of his name-sake a day or two before. Certainly Seaford, Sussex and his country, have full reason to be proud of him.

About 3 p.m on 28th October, 1552, Henry Pert, Gentleman, went out to disport at Welbeck. He drew his bow so fully with an arrow in it that he lodged the arrow in his bow. Afterwards, Intending to make the arrow climb straight into the air, he shot the arrow from his bow with his fingers whilst leaning slightly over the bow, Because his face was directly over the arrow as it climbed upwards, it struck him over his left eyelid and into his head to the membrane of his brain. Thus, the said arrow, worth one farthing gave him a wound of which he immediately languished, and lay languishing until 12 p.m. on 29th October when he died at Welbeck by misadventure.

NOTE: A Farthing was 1/980th part of £1.00.

THOMAS WYATT'S REBELLION, 1554

THE BACKGROUND to the abortive rebellion led by Sir Thomas Wyatt, in 1554, is complex and symptomatic of the state of both Court and Country at that time. Indeed, had it not been largely a non-event, the final skirmish in this Chapter of skirmishes might be sub-titled 'The Battle of London.'

Edward VI, sickly only legitimate son of Henry VIII, had died prematurely, probably of tuberculosis and without leaving a universally accepted heir. Through what by most accounts was a debatable claim to succession, the Lady Jane Grey, daughter of the Duke of Suffolk and cousin to the late King, had been declared Queen. The termination of her all too-brief reign by execution was followed by proclamation of the Lady Mary who, as Queen Mary I, married Prince Philip of Spain, thus recovering England to the Catholic faith.

Queen Jane had been a Protestant and thus represented the Church's Reformation, carried out with such vigour by her grandfather. Her sponsor, the Duke of Northumberland, was thoroughly disliked by the country at large however and, sadly for the Lady Jane, whose reign as monarch was the shortest in this country's history, the opprobrium rubbed off by association.

Thomas Wyatt, born about 1521, was a soldier and a patriot with a background of military command. A devout Protestant himself, he abhorred the Spanish influence which now consumed the Court and, egged on by the Duke of Suffolk (Jane's grieving father) was persuaded to do something about it.

As commander of the Kentish militia, Wyatt had access to a substantial body of fighting men and in January of 1554, the Court and Privy Council were informed that he, with other like-minded military gentlemen, had stirred up insurrection. The Council, whose prime concern was the safety of the Queen, put London's own militia on stand-by and trained billmen, with archers and others of the Royal Guard, were despatched post-haste towards Kent and Wyatt, to scout and, if possible, quieten what was fast becoming a potentially explosive situation.

Meanwhile a nervous City was rapidly filling with armed men. A contemporary account:

> ". . . *the lorde Treasurer, being at the yeld* (Guild) *hall with the mayre and aldermen, declared that yt was goode to have a nombre of ijml* (20,000) *or ther aboutes in redynes for the safegarde of the cyte. . . ."*

Thus it was that by six o'clock on January 26th, 500 City of London archers and billmen under the command of the Duke of Norfolk and captained by Sir Henry Jerningham, were made ready and, on the 27th, this force moved off from Leadenhall towards Gravesend and the so-far triumphant Kentish men.

There, things were moving swiftly out of control. The strategically important Rochester bridge had fallen to the rebels on January 26th, a little in advance of Norfolk's scouting force. A number of minor skirmishes had already taken place, including one at Wrotham, where in 'Blacksoil Field,' Lord Burgavenny had encountered the rebel Sir Henry Isley and slain some of his men.

Although small in number, the Royal troops were well equipped and accompanied by some light ordnance. On their arrival at the bridge, a herald was promptly sent across to seek out Wyatt and declare that:

"... *all suche as wolde desyst ther purpose shuld have frank and free pardon*..."

There was some difficulty in delivering the message, since Wyatt was not particularly disposed to receive any declaration from the other side but it finally got through. To little avail though; for of the rebels, only Sir George Harper and his men had second thoughts and crossed the bridge.

However, matters then took a different and somewhat unexpected turn. One of the captains of the archer guard, a man named Bret, suddenly drew his sword and addressing his men and all the others, publicly threw in his lot with Wyatt.

In the ensuing melée, with part of the Guard on one side of the bridge and part on the other, confusion reigned supreme. His small force now largely dissolved, the Duke did the only thing possible in the circumstances, he retreated with what dignity he could muster, leaving behind much of his baggage train to the victorious Wyatt.

A contemporary source, whose loyalty is perhaps questionable, wrote:

"... *ye shoulde have sene some of the garde come home, ther cotes tourned* (torn) *all ruyned, without arowes or strynge on ther bow.* ..."

But now, with the rebels firmly in control of events and metaphorically breathing down their necks, it is difficult to say who were the more frightened, the Court or the City. Householders rushed thither and yon, the Mayor and Aldermen armed themselves for action and shops were barricaded against attack.

Typical of the atmosphere at the time was the action of one Ralph Rokesby, a serjeant-at-law who, fully equipped with his coat-armour, went to Whitehall Palace, and finding an unstrung bow in the Gatehouse, braced it, picked out a sheaf of arrows and remained there ready to defend his Queen (Mary I) until the last.

Meanwhile, a full muster of the London militia was now in hand. Drums beat, bugles sounded and all was bustle and noise. Cavalry were assembling in St. James Field (now St. James Park) whilst archers, billmen and pikemen gathered at their stations amongst the archery Marks in Finsbury Fields.

But Wyatt was on the move again. With a 2,000 strong army of augmented Kentish militia behind him, he was marching towards the City from Deptford, his vanguard in sight of and now within the range of the Tower artillery. Shots were fired but, unaccountably, all missed (one might idly speculate why?!)

With Tower Bridge gates shut and the Tower drawbridge raised, the Mayor and the Sheriff told shopkeepers to stand by their barricaded shops with weapons, ready to defend their property. Goods were taken off stalls, men ran to fetch armour and weapons, whilst women and their children took refuge indoors. All was chaos and disorder.

Wyatt was now in Southwark, where Lord William Howard's men were billetted. To a man they deserted to the rebel cause and joined him as he moved towards the City gate.

As might be expected, the Court at Whitehall was in turmoil. The Queen was calm however and visibly heartened by the news that loyal Sir Richard Southwell, having mustered 3,000 men, was at Blackheath awaiting her instruction.

Unable to reach the City past Tower Bridge, Wyatt changed his tactics. He marched his men towards the bridge at Kingston to cross the Thames, arriving there by midnight. Although destroyed, there was enough left for the rebels to cross by using boats secured to the remaining piers and, with little delay, they duly re-formed on the other side. However, now short of victuals for his men, Wyatt pressed on, to reach Brentford by the morning where he was spotted by the Queen's scouts.

Back in the City all was movement. In St. Paul's Churchyard the baggage train was preparing to leave. Twelve carts, loaded with bills, morice pikes, bows and arrows, spears, cannon balls, powder, shovels, mattocks, spades, baskets and other impedimenta without which no Tudor army could be considered complete, had been prepared and stood ready.

Wyatt was now at Knightsbridge and too close for comfort. At four in the afternoon word of his whereabouts reached the Court. Drums rolled and the Order given for the militia to assemble at the Charing Cross. Two battalions of pikemen and archers formed up close to the Cross, with cavalry commanded by William, Lord Howard (the Earl of Pembroke) close at hand in readiness.

Led by Wyatt and still fully confident in their cause, the rebels moved down what is now Constitution Hill, a small force heading for Westminster and the gates of Whitehall Palace, whilst the main force moved across St. James Park towards Charing Cross. Guns opened up on both sides, the Royal pieces getting the better of the exchange — on one occasion killing three of Wyatt's men with a single shot.[4]

Although Pembroke's cavalry had split the rebel army into two, it was itself dispersed and Wyatt pressed on. A rag-tag force of some 1,000 poorly armed defenders scampered into Whitehall Palace, closing the gates behind them as the Kentishmen and others pressed on between silent lines of fully armed householders, each prepared to defend their property if the need arose.

Disconcerted by a lack of welcome by the populace at large, the rebels poured along Temple Bar into Fleet Street and finally to the Ludgate of the City, only to find this barred and defended against them.

Here Wyatt stopped, uncertain now of his next action. He had expected London and the City to rise with him but, evidently, it was not to be. Whilst offering no resistance, the citizens lining his route had been quiet but unwelcoming. Finally, making up his

---

[4] These three, Edmond Pyrry, Anthony Adamson, and John Sympson are buried in St. Margaret's churchyard at Westminster.

mind, he turned and marched his men away, realising too late the trap into which he had fallen. For arrayed against him was a force of well-armed cavalry who immediately engaged his vanguard.

A fierce fight ensued, stopped only when Wyatt was advised that to continue would result not only in inevitable defeat but with considerable loss of life.

Thomas Wyatt, soldier and patriot, upholder of the Protestant faith and sworn enemy of Spain, died with dignity on the block at Tower Hill on Wednesday, April 11th, 1554. On Thursday, July 19th, Prince Philip of Spain landed at Hampton and, six days later, England had its first (and last) Spanish King.

POSTSCRIPT: On March 6th, some 300 schoolchildren had gathered in a meadow on the outskirts of London to play at the game of 'The Queen against Wyatt,' an early form of 'goodies and baddies.' Bows and arrows were used, and several on each side were wounded.

The boy whose misfortune it was to represent Philip of Spain was taken prisoner by the other side and summarily hanged, although, luckily for him, Authority stepped in before he was strangled. The Queen, who got to hear of this early example of pupil-power was, predictably, not amused and had the ring-leaders whipped, including presumably supporters of the unhappy infant Philip, to whom injury was added to insult.

Circa AD 2000, they would perhaps each have been given a counselling session and a change of school — but that is progress!!

Principal References consulted, and further reading:

GLOUCESTERSHIRE ARCHAEOLOGICAL SOCIETY RECORDS: VOLUME II. Gloucester Reference Library.

REVOLT IN THE WEST (THE WESTERN REBELLION OF 1549). John Sturt. 1987, Devon Books. ISBN 0 86114 776 6.

THE CHRONICLE OF QUEEN JANE. Ed.: John Gough Nichols. 1996. Facsimile Reprint Llanerch Publishers: Felinfach. ISBN 1 86143 014 0

SUSSEX RIVER. Edna & Mac McCarthy. Seaford. Privately published.

CERTAIN DISCOURSES MILITARY. Sir John Smythe. Ed.: J.R.Hale. 1964 Folger Shakespeare Library. Lib. Cong. Cat. No: 64-17765.

Part 8

Dawn and Dusk

The Battle of Lewes
The Black Prince and Battle of Najera
The Battle of the Spurs
The Battle of Tippermuir

Part 8

DAWN AND DUSK

THE FOUR engagements that make up this next Chapter differ from each other and, by doing so, illustrate the rise and fall of the bow in battle over a period of almost 400 years.

'Lewes' (1264). Where Simon de Montfort and his Barons showed Henry III who really ran the country.

'Najera'(1367). Outcome of the Black Prince's entrepreneurial adventure on behalf of King Pedro of Castile (nicknamed the Cruel for reasons only too apparent to his jaundiced subjects).

'Bomy' (1513). Known colloquially as the 'Battle of the Spurs' from the ignominious French retreat. The culmination of an adventure by the young Henry VIII, somewhat overshadowed by events at home, when his Queen, Katherine of Aragon, saw to the Scots at Flodden and,

finally, 'Tippermuir' (1644) where James Graham, Marquis of Montrose, accompanied by a large and intemperate MacDonald, dealt effectively with a Covenanter army on behalf of Charles Stuart (Charles I).

THE BATTLE OF LEWES, 1264

"...*And* in *the morwe of seynt Pancras, in the monthe of May, was the bataile of Lewes, between the kyng and the barons of the raume* (realm) in *whiche bataile manye men were sclayn on both parties: and in this bataile the kyng was taken and Sr. Edward his sone, and Richard erle of Cornewayle and manye othere were lad in diverses castelles. And in the same yere appered stella comata* (uncertain, but possibly shooting stars/meteor shower) *which endured xv dayes.*..."

THE CHRONICLE OF LONDON.

TO UNDERSTAND those circumstances leading to the confrontation between a baronial army commanded by Simon de Montfort and the Royal forces of King Henry III on the heights above Lewes, in East Sussex, we must first consider the political climate.

The initial stirrings of dissent between the King and the powerful barons who formed his administration, occurred in the unlikely setting of Sicily. A grandiose attempt to stave off bankruptcy had prompted the rulers of that Island to offer their kingship to the highest bidder. Henry, whose capacity for embracing doubtful causes was equalled only by his ability to lose them, was busily seeking the necessary wherewithal to secure this doubtful plum for his second son, Edmund 'Crouchback.'

Understandably, this exercise — together with a disastrous attempt to regain his French possessions, a totally unproductive exercise against Llywellyn ap Gruffyd (as wily a Welshman as ever stole a leg of beef) and a bruising clash with the Pope over the Sicilian venture — caused his barons to mutter 'enough is enough' and, led by Simon de Montfort, to make martial arrangements to curb the ill-founded royal enthusiasm.

Simon de Montfort was a close family member. He was married to Henry's sister, Eleanor of Provence and, until then, they had been great chums. Marriage, however, has a habit of alienating in-laws and, the wedding breakfast over, matters between the two went rapidly down hill. Whilst he was undoubtedly dedicated to the concept of English nationalism and a better way of life, Simon was born and bred a Frenchman; he had a quick temper and although he may well have understood the language, there is doubt whether he spoke English at all.

A constitutional crisis arising out of the inability of Henry to regard oaths as anything more than so much hot air, plunged the country into a state of virtual anarchy and, in 1263, battle lines were finally drawn. Simon proved a capable and effective leader; he gained the support of Llywellyn, who was in no doubt as to which side his bread was buttered and, with Henry's Queen being in France drumming up support for the royal cause, he marched to secure the Cinque Ports against invasion by any mercenary force from thence.

For a time mediation was in the air and a truce of sorts was arranged. Henry however, as volatile as ever, broke this twice and it became obvious to all that if anything was to be settled, it would have to be by military means.

So it was that Simon de Montfort gathered his forces and divided them into three parts. His sons, Henry and Simon, took one each whilst father took the third. Son Simon rapidly got himself into serious trouble; his army was defeated at Northampton and he was captured. Meanwhile, sibling Henry was prevented from joining forces with Llywellyn as planned and things were not shaping too well for the family firm.

The King meanwhile was in hot pursuit of Simon pére who, having abandoned the prospect of relieving Northampton and returning Simon fils to the fold, was contemplating the sack of Rochester. Wisdom overcoming valour however, he wisely withdrew and turned back to London and relative safety. Henry meanwhile, surviving forest ambushes by Montfort's Welsh archers, had straggled back across the Kentish Weald from his abortive attempt to catch Simon at Rochester and was now settled in some creature comfort within the Cluniac Priory of St. Pancras, to the South of Lewes,

THE BATTLE OF LEWES, 1264

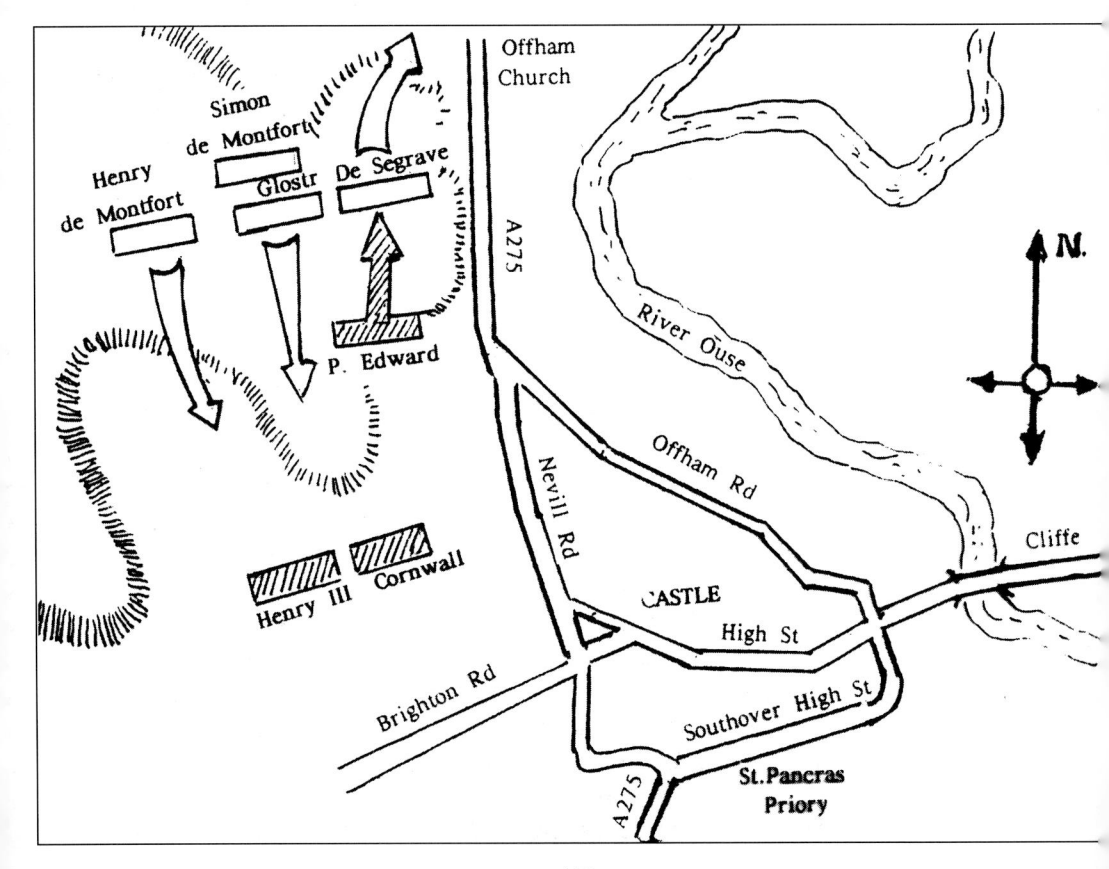

county town of East Sussex. Prince Edward, with the cavalry, being billetted in and around the Castle.

Meanwhile, de Montfort, with his small baronial army, had left London on May 6th, and was now encamped at Fletching, a village some eight miles to the North of Lewes. His intention: to bring the King to battle promptly and before royal reinforcements could arrive.

The morning of the 14th dawned bright and clear and saw the rebel forces en route to their chosen battle site: the plateau at the top of Offham Hill. Each side was well endowed with spies and de Montfort's deployment was watched with increasing interest by Prince Edward from the Castle turrets.

The baronial forces were drawn up in four divisions, or 'battles,' with de Montfort in charge of a reserve in the rear, an unusual but thoughtful tactical arrangement for the time. His troops were distinguished by white crosses sewn on the backs and fronts of their tunics. To his left he placed the Londoners: a raw, untried and probably largely untrained levy, strengthened by a contingent of mounted troops.

Before the King could deploy his forces, the alarm had been raised in the town. Prince Edward — who had a particular dislike of London and Londoners for personal family reasons quite unconnected with either politics or warfare — led his cavalry in a charge against them and chased them smartly off the field. A hot-headed and ill-conceived pursuit and one, moreover, that both kept him effectively out of the subsequent action and isolated the King.

The detail of the Battle of Lewes is unclear, with several accounts of what happened next. However, it is apparent that de Montfort not only held his ground when attacked by the King, but probably took advantage of the disappearance of Edward and his cavalry in a cloud of dust and small stones to advance down the hill.

Although Henry's Division fought bravely when attacked and, for a while held its own, the outcome was settled when de Montfort's reserve entered the fray. Retreating Royalist forces were cut down as they floundered in the mud of the River Ouse, or forded the smaller Cockshoot* brook that flows to the south of the Priory.

By the time Prince Edward had returned from chasing Londoners, the result was beyond doubt. Earl Richard of Cornwall (the king's brother) was holed up in a windmill, from which he was evicted with some ignominy and father was back at the Priory he had left that morning, seeking sanctuary.

Simon de Montfort had won and won convincingly. Henry was now a puppet king, with de Montfort and his barons in charge and Prince Edward was, for a time at least, under direct control. Matters changed here however when, at Hereford, a trusting Simon (who really should have known better) gave permission for the Prince to exercise outside the town on the understanding, freely given, that he would not wander off. Predictably, however, given the family's casual attitude to promises: On May 28th, Edward, mounted on a good horse and giving his guards the slip, galloped off into the sunset, making successfully for Roger Mortimer's castle at Wigmore and freedom.

---

* As a schoolboy in the 1940s. the author often walked beside this little brook with school friendsduring the dinner hour.

Montfort and he were to meet again at Evesham, on August 4th, 1265, where matters took a different turn. In a fiercely contested battle, during which many of his Welsh spearmen took an early bath, Simon was grotesquely butchered, his son Henry killed and his field army destroyed. After a decidedly hairy few minutes, in which he was obliged to wave his arms about a lot and shout in a loud voice: "I am Henry of Winchester your King, do not harm me." Henry III was returned to Kingship; his Prince lived to become Edward I ('Hammer of the Scots') and the barons retired to their castles, lowered their portcullises and resumed their feudal lives.

POSTSCRIPT. The general subject of this series of battles is the longbow at war. Whilst the 13th century certainly saw archery and archers deployed, their tactical use en masse was yet to come. The prelude to the battle at Lewes did involve the handbow however, since accounts exist of Welsh archers ambushing the royal army as it straggled through the Wealden forest. Ambush was fundamental to Welsh warfare, and their rough elm bows were ideally suited to close range destruction, as those charged to keep order in the Marches knew full well.

Whether Welsh bowmen were amongst the foot-soldiers massed on Offham Hill is not said; indeed infantry weaponry generally is scarcely mentioned in contemporary documents. There is little doubt that Llywelyn's spearmen were there with him and, perhaps mercenary crossbowmen were also present but, the marriage between English and Welsh bowyery that was to produce the devastating English yew war-bow was still in the making and, the massed flight of death-dealing English battle-shafts was a generation hence.

It has been said — and sometimes repeated by those who should know better — that the Welsh 'invented' the longbow. Firstly, of course, the description does not appear until two centuries later. The 'bendbow,' the 'handbow,' the 'English bow,' or the 'lugg': Yes! But the 'longbow'? No! Secondly, the hand bow was in regular use as a weapon for personal defence in the English shires, and had been since the Anglo-Saxon invasions.

Much has been made of a 'short bow' in contrast to a 'long bow,' since the military historian, Charles Oman, first coined the description in the 19th Century but, in truth, bows came then, as they do now, in all sizes and most Archer Antiquarians and historians of today believe that the description arose to distinguish the handbow, held longways, from the horizontally held crossbow.

It is true, of course, that the mid-13th Century was a watershed for military archery; not least of course for those who had perforce to train in the heavier weapon and to re-think draw-force lines, since drawing to the chest is not conducive to shooting in a heavy weapon. Although at this space in time it would stretch credibility to claim a connection, it is of passing interest that the earliest of the Robin Hood legends contains reference to a gift of 100 (stronger?) bows for the use of him and his men; one supposes in replacement of weaker ones in current use. We may infer that he drew a strong bow since, in other ballads, the strength of his weapon is noted, whilst at an archery tournament he is offered a bow and derides it as "right weak gear."

If he drew to the ear, his eye to arrow relationship would certainly have given him advantage over those of his opponents who, perhaps, still drew to the chest. A thought worth considering, since at some time in the 13th Century a change in style no doubt took place.

Indeed, if the Robin Hood of the 'little geste' were a role model for impressionable peasants and yeomen, one wonders whether, perhaps, Authority not only approved of the subliminal messages to move up in bow-weight contained therein, and directed at those who first heard them, but actively publicised them, and — who can say — perhaps even helped in their creation!

THE BATTLE OF NAJERA

THE CAMPAIGN which culminated in the battle of Najera, in Castile, on April 3rd, 1367, lasted a mere 45 days. During this brief time, the Black Prince, his commanders and his army, had marched some 130 miles, fought many skirmishes (not all of them successfully) and one major engagement.

Although this major battle was won and, won decisively, it left no satisfactory solution. Rather, as we will see, did it merely postpone the inevitable.

We think of the Black Prince today as the young, charismatic leader of his father's Vanguard at Crecy; a spirited fighter cast in his father's mould. True, he earned his spurs that August day in 1346, but he was destined, before an untimely death, to command armies brilliantly in his own right.

Although not exactly the stuff of legend, his exploits in Spain showed him to be an able soldier, if perhaps lacking something in the strictest of commercial senses.

The King of Castile — aptly named Pedro the Cruel — was, as might be surmised from his title, unpopular with his subjects. Capitalising upon this delicate situation, Enrique, his bastard half-brother, sought the crown for himself and called upon Charles V of France for material aid. Freely given, this took the form of an expeditionary force, under the control of able French commanders. Principal amongst these: Bertrand Du Guesclin, a formidable character whose personality was not dissimilar to that of the Prince and, Marshal d'Audrehem, an antagonist of dubious probity and one of whom the Black Prince had some personal knowledge.

One might justifiably use the term 'nominal' in the context of control, since with the French force were 'routiers,' or 'free Companies.' These were bands of ex-soldiers, many of them English. Owing allegiance to no-one but themselves, their free-booting activities had provided headaches for Authority since the conclusion of the Crecy campaign.

The period leading to the final battle was marked by skirmishing; hard-fought guerilla activity by small, out-riding groups consisting typically, on the English side, of a few men-at-arms, brothers in chivalry, with some 20 horsed lances and around 300 mounted archers.

Now here, now there, they harassed Enrique's troops to some effect as and when they could. Since equally, Enrique's men did the same, a continuing state of attrition developed which touched raw nerves on either side and this remained a feature of the Campaign.

Having reached the small town of Vittoria by late March and hearing from his out-riders that the Bastard's main force was there and in readiness, the Prince anticipated attack and mustered his men in battle order outside.

Preparations were premature however and, unwisely as it proved, the English army was stood down. During that night, Don Tello, Enrique's brother, moved with a sizeable force against the unsuspecting and, it must be said, unready English soldiery and a number were killed in their billets as they slept.

Fortunately, the vigilance of the Prince's brother, John of Gaunt, Duke of Lancaster, saved the situation from total disaster. Rapidly rallying men to his banner on a nearby hill-side and quickly joined by archers from the Prince's Division, his bowmen poured volley after volley into Don Tello's troops as, their task done, they quickly departed the scene.

Although Enrique still showed no sign of wishing a major engagement, understandably the Prince kept his men at battle-stations during the succeeding day — much to their disgust, since they were tired, unwashed, and hungry. Unsure now of their position after the near catastrophe of the night attack, wary captains bivouaced their troops overnight, with lookout posts in readiness for any repeat performance.

However, vile weather and numerous minor skirmishes with the French ensured that no-one got much sleep. Clearly this situation could not continue; protracted guerilla warfare was not on the English agenda and, realising that the terrain was unfavourable to them, the Prince and his commanders took the decision to pull back from Vittoria.

Thus it was that, having crossed the Rio Ebro on April 1st, English forces had reached the small fortress of Navarrete the following day. Once there, the Prince learned from his scouts that Enrique was encamped outside the substantial town of Najera and seemed, this time, to be seriously preparing for battle. Moreover, he had established a strong position involving the protecting banks of a nearby stream.

This was not to the liking of the English and, since the site had not been mutually agreed (still then the common preliminary to a battle) it was decided to alter matters. Accordingly, under cover of darkness, the Prince's battalions moved silently behind a small ridge, to appear on Enrique's flank.

Taken totally by surprise and having now lost the initiative, the entire Castilian army had hastily to regroup, their subsequent disposition noted carefully by the Prince and his leaders.

The opposing armies were broadly matched in strength, although the English were probably the better disciplined. The core of Enrique's forces consisted of some 15,000 men-at-arms, 6,000 or so crossbowmen and over 4,000 armed horse — light, highly-manoeverable cavalry

The Prince drew up his troops in the usual three Divisions, or Wards. The forward Division, or Vaward (that facing Enrique's Vanguard) was commanded by John of Gaunt and consisted of dismounted men-at-arms, supported by a large number of longbowmen. Behind the Vaward was the Prince's Division, also dismounted and, to the rear of that was a mounted Division, held as a reserve.

It is difficult to judge Enrique's tactical plan — if indeed he now had one — since all went wrong quite early on but, to place his two most able commanders, du Guesclin and d'Audrehem in the Vanguard, where they could not influence the activities of the rear Battalion, seems not to have been strategy of the highest order. Certainly, his light cavalry, lacking firm leadership by Don Tello, chose discretion rather than valour and ran when faced by the Prince's mounted Division. But, we move a mite too fast!

Having lost the advantage of position, Enrique was not anxious to open the batting and, for a while, there was stalemate. The Prince, however, not wishing to lose the initiative gained by re-positioning and, fully conscious of French guerrilla tactics by night, decided upon attack.

Accordingly, the Duke of Lancaster's men, lances shortened, moved forward to meet the opposition, accompanied by heavy covering fire from the archers. At first matters did not go his way; Enrique's vanguard was numerous, well-led and contained many battle-hardened routiers of good quality. Vigorously met, the English line reeled back in some disorder.

However, before the French could capitalise on this situation, the English Middleward (the second Division) was brought into play and slowly the initiative was regained. At this point there was mass desertion from Enrique's men, almost half of whom melted as snow into the surrounding vineyards and countryside. A retreat became a rout and by the afternoon the Prince had been assured of victory.

That evening matters were consolidated; the Prince spending the night in the com-

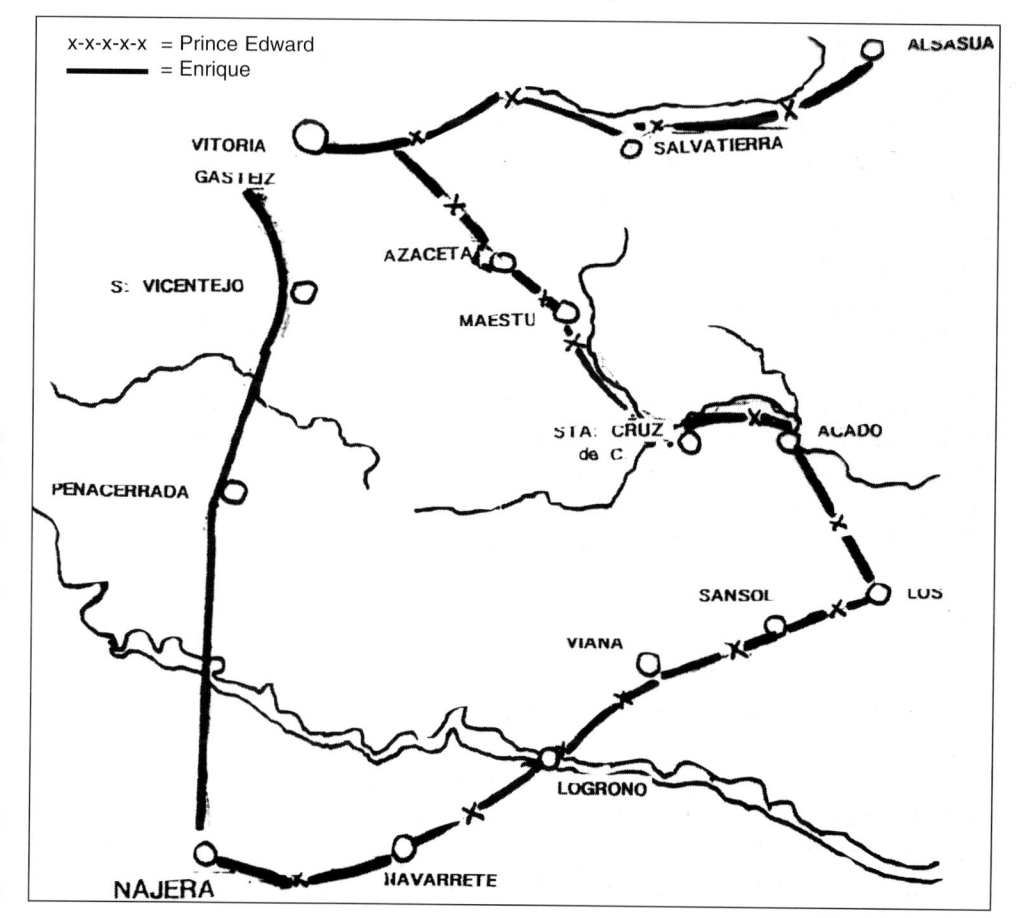

THE BATTLE OF NAJERA, 1367

fortable quarters formerly occupied by Enrique, whose whereabouts at that time were unknown. The aftermath brought good news for the Prince: both Du Guesclin and d'Audrehem had been taken alive and were awaiting his pleasure. Whilst the former was treated as chivalry required, entertained to a much-needed wash and a good dinner, the latter had some fast talking ahead of him.

The Prince forcefully reminded the discomfited d'Audrehem of an unpaid ransom following his capture at Poitiers, adding, with some emphasis, that an important part of that arrangement was the Marshal's oath not to bear arms against him in the future. Why, he demanded to know, should he not now be terminated out of hand.

It is a measure of the wily Marshal's honeyed tongue, coupled with either magnaminity or a lack of resolve on the Prince's part, that he escaped on what may seem now to be a dubious chivalric technicality. He gained his life by observing that since he was there on someone else's behalf, he was not directly fighting the Prince and the terms did not therefore really apply.

The Prince duly reported his victory to Joan, his wife, adding that he and his army were then to move to more comfortable surroundings in the city of Burgos if ". . . *so that we shall complete our journey successfully with God's help. . . .*"

An unfulfilled hope as it transpired, for as everyone knows, an essential part of any Service is the Invoice. The Prince duly presented his: a massive 2,720,000 golden florins.

This aspect of the undertaking seems not to have occurred to Pedro however, or if it had, then he had judiciously awaited a successful outcome before contemplating payment. In consequence the Prince was obliged to wait for six months, with an increasingly restless army, before any substantial payment was made at all. It was well into 1368 before he was finally recompensed and then not by the apparently impoverished Pedro.

Although Najera was a personal triumph for the Prince and his commanders and a consolidation of his considerable military skill in very difficult terrain, it was largely a political non-event, since Enrique invaded again. Predictably, the Prince declined any further involvement with the parsimonious Pedro, whose murder in 1369 clinched the Castilian power struggle in Enrique's favour.

The Castilian campaign, gallantly fought, achieved little and cost much. Indeed in one sense it may have cost more than mere money, since an illness contracted by the Prince during the campaign may have contributed to the long-standing tuberculosis from which, in 1376, he ultimately prematurely died.

THE BATTLE OF THE SPURS, 1513

SOME engagements during warfare come oven-ready as it were, for contemporary media attention. One has only to consider the battle of Agincourt — interpreted and presented ad nauseam since Henry V's triumphal return in 1415. Others, with equal potential, have unaccountably been missed.

The Affair at Bomy, hard by the fortified French town of Therouanne and known as the Battle of the Spurs, is one such, combining as it did in equal quantities, bravura and farce.

In 1513, Henry VIII, 23 years of age, head-strong and physically in his prime, determined to exercise his perceived right to honour and glory by mounting a major attack upon the most powerful monarch in Europe at the time, Louis XII of France. In this endeavour he was joined by Maximilian I, Holy Roman Emperor: at 54, an astute Statesman liberally fuelled by self-interest, but whose subsequent military advice, borne of much experience in Continental warfare, the young Henry both endorsed and usually took whenever it was offered — which was often.

As was practice at the time, Henry's army of some 35,000 troops consisted of a fore-ward, a middle-ward and a rear-ward, each of which was separately landed at Calais. Of these, the fore and rear-wards were quickly despatched to the intended Target. Although this may originally have been Boulogne, the capture of which would have been useful to Henry; through the influence of Maximilian (whose fingers were seldom far removed from the pie) the final destination proved to be the fortified town of Theouranne, at whose gates they arrived on June 22nd.

The Port of Calais had been English since its capture by Edward III in the mid 15th Century. A bustling town and port, a substantial proportion of whose population was English, its habits were largely those of an English town and its rules were made at Westminster. Its prosperity was founded largely upon the wool 'staple,' augmented by herring fishing and farming within 'the pale.'

Henry obviously felt at home there. Ambassadors, dignitaries and the common people alike were formally and informally entertained to a show of his personal prowess with the longbow when, we are told, he *". . . cleft the mark in the midst and surpassed them all, as he surpasses them in stature and personal grace . . .,"* a forerunner, perhaps, to his later display at the Field of the Cloth of Gold.

The middle-ward, with Henry firmly ensconced, remained at Calais for a month until July 21st when it too departed to join the others. Contemporary accounts demonstrate the pomp and panoply with which the young King surrounded himself. Of the 16,000-strong force over which he had command, more than 2,000 were non-combatants, there to serve him personally. His tents, totalling some 4,000 feet of canvas, filled two large wagons; whilst the piece de resistance, a two-roomed pre-fabricated wooden house with fireplace and chimneys, filled a further twelve.

More germane to the task in hand were the military supply carts. The middle-ward was provided with 90 of these, as were the other wards. Some 5,200 bows, in batches of 400, occupied 13 wagons whilst 86,000 bowstrings in 20 barrels (seemingly 4,300 bowstrings to each barrel) required an additional two carts. As an aside, over 16 strings to each bow does rather suggest a continuing lack of faith in the country's stringers, despite the formation of their Guild a century earlier to ensure quality

Finally, 10,000 sheaves of arrows needed a further 26 carts to carry them. A formidable assemblage of military hardware to supplement the archers personal equipment, for the bowman was still a significant military arm and his bow a decisive weapon in many engagements.

After a number of military adventures — many of which by pure luck turned in the Royal favour — the fore, middle and rear wards of Henry's army stood re-united out-

The Battle of the Spurs, 1513

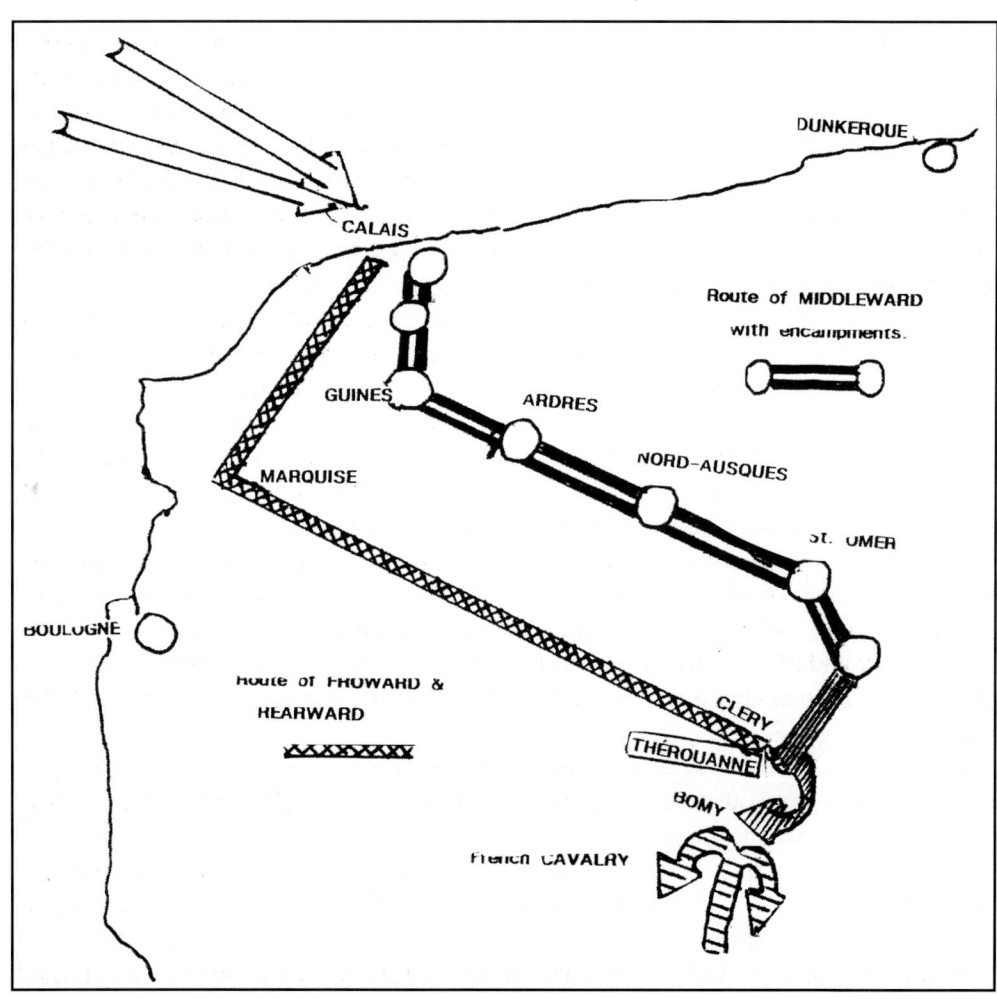

side Therouanne. A statutory request for its surrender having been summarily refused by the inhabitants, the task of reducing it now began in earnest.

By now, although the town had been under siege for over a month, supplies had been filtering through slowly in sufficient quantity for hardship to be at least partially averted. This clearly had to stop, otherwise matters could remain at stalemate indefinitely. Accordingly, after advice from Maximilian, Henry ordered the River Lys, upon which Theouranne stood and from whence most of the trickle of supplies had come, to be bridged. Despite an untimely diversion, through Henry's stubborn insistence (against military advice) that the Royal Tentage remain standing, surprise was achieved. A strong detachment from the middle-ward crossed and took up position to the South of the town.

A number of light guns, backed by cavalry, were quickly installed along the crest of a low ridge and a strong force of archers placed on their flank. None too soon as it happened. Intelligence had reported a powerful contingent of enemy troops advancing towards the town under the command of de Pienne and the personal instruction of the French King.

In addition to this potentially dangerous force, another smaller gathering was concerned with a rather different matter. For Louis, who must have been the despair of his tactical commanders, had decided on a novel, if unmilitary, means to provide succour to the loyal subjects of his besieged city. The plan was simple. A number of French cavalrymen were each invited to carry a side or two of bacon on their steeds. They were required to gallop to the town walls, drop the bacon beneath these and retire as speedily as appropriate. The grateful townsfolk would then collect the flitches after dark and all would be well. That at least was the theory.

Meanwhile, the French cavalry, under de Pienne, secure (they thought) from serious trouble, advanced with confidence towards Therouanne, only to be surprised at the village of Bomy by the cavalry of the English middle-ward. Moreover, on the near horizon and adding to their predicament, were the banners of the English and the German infantry under the respective commands of Henry and Maximilian. Reining in sharply, their discomfiture was complete when, to their dismay, they received a painful volley of arrows from archers who appeared on their flank.

Realising with horror that complete encirclement was a distinct possibility and that salvation lay only in instant flight, the entire French army turned on its heels and despite strenuous efforts by its officers to halt the rout, headed back to base and safety. Henry and Maximilian were thus treated to the curious sight of the backsides of the flower of French chivalry retreating at full pelt into the middle distance, shedding armour and weapons as they went.

The speed of this dis-engagement had one beneficial effect: casualties were light, numbers varying from 40 to 400, many of them falling to the flank-attack by Henry's archers.

Somewhere en route they were joined by the victualling project who, assessing the reality of the situation, had wisely chosen to discard the bacon in order to save their own.

Although it was Maximilian who had engineered it, Henry was inordinately proud of his battle and wrote to tell his Queen about it. She was dutifully lavish with her praise, writing:

> "... the victory hath been so great that I think none such hath been seen before. All England hath cause to thank God for it, and I especially, seeing that the king beginneth so well...."

Basking in supercharged if somewhat illusory glory, Henry was brought back to earth sharply a month later when, after the great English victory against the Scots at Flodden (for which he could take no credit whatsoever), Queen Katharine was disposed to write, a mite tactlessly perhaps:

> "... *This battle hath been to your Grace and all your realm the greatest honour that could be, and more than ye should* win *the Crown of France, thanken be God for it....*"

As a side-note to Flodden, it is a measure of England's martial superiority at the time to recognise that with 35,000 men under arms in France, an effective tactical fighting force of some 25,000 could still be raised by the Earl of Surrey to deal effectively with the Scots.

With all hope of survival gone, the leaders of the French garrison at Therouanne had little choice but to agree surrender terms. They struck a hard bargain though, being allowed to leave with weapons and in full armour. Both Henry and Maximilian stood to watch, as a 4,000-strong force of cavalry and infantry rode or marched with pride through their camp, en route to the main body of the French army.

But what of the town itself? Within a fortnight all but the cathedral and the houses of the clergy had been razed to the ground. As a town ,Therouanne ceased to exist and, with its destruction, the Battle of the Spurs passed into history and, some might hope, oblivion

From the New Forest Documents. (2nd December, 1247)
John, the son of Edonis de Lyndhurst and Simon le Theyn were taken by the Foresters with bows and arrows for harming the deer. Afterwards they were hanged for theft.

THE BATTLE OF TIPPERMUIR, 1644

TIPPERMUIR (or Tibbermore as it is known today), last of the set-piece battles employing the long-bow as a weapon of war, was little more than a skirmish and very much 'minor league,' compared with the major engagements of the Civil War.

Although numbers involved were comparatively small, as someone once said, it isn't size that matters, it's what you do with it and, if anyone knew what he was about and had the will to do it, that person was James Graham, 5th Earl and 1st Marquis of Montrose.

To set the scene: Scottish affairs were in some disarray. A land-feud between Campbells and MacDonalds had come to a head, with MacDonalds from Ireland spilling Campbell blood. Insofar as the situation was recognised and the invading force considered at all by the covenanting military folk in London and Edinburgh, it was dismissed as a raggle-taggle of naked 'Island hopping' Irish, led by a 'blood-thirsty monster.' This latter being one Alasdair MacColla Macdonald, a red-bearded fighting Gael of huge stature, dynamic personality and uncertain temperament; rather unfairly dismissed by some present military historians as "... *brave, but a bit thick*..."

That there was a fundamental flaw in the covenanters appraisal slowly impinged; for whilst MacColla undoubtedly had his own agenda, closely linked to recovery of the MacDonald territory usurped by Argyll Campbells, he was rather more than just a loose cannon in the Scottish ship of state.

He and his Irishmen were on the rampage and Campbell castles were falling like leaves in Autumn. Archibald Campbell, Earl of Argyll, covenanter extraordinary, with more than a little personal concern in the outcome, was charged with putting matters right. By July 22nd, a force of some 2,600 men had been gathered and the seeds of retribution sown.

That the seeds fell on stony ground was in large part due to MacColla's ability to merge with the scenery whenever confrontation seemed unlikely to produce advantage and, thus it was that his wanderings finally brought him to Atholl and the beginning of a fruitful, if unusual, liaison with Montrose.

The two were certainly an unlikely pair. Montrose was a thoughtful and charismatic leader of men, with the ability to seize initiative wherever the slightest opportunity offered. MacColla's reputation, on the other hand, was based upon brute strength and a dominant personality, able to deal constructively with recalcitrant Irish and thieving Campbell alike.

In contrast to the accepted covenanting view, MacColla's small army was, in fact, a well-trained and cohesive force, experienced in battle and, moreover, well led. Whilst the liaison of two such disparate leaders could scarcely be imagined, yet it proved virtually invincible.

Having met at Blair Atholl and, through sheer force of character, persuaded innately hostile Atholl Highlanders (whose attitude towards their brother Gaels was in danger of taking a negative turn) to accept the Irish as fellow freedom fighters, Montrose, with MacColla and his men, began the march on Perth.

It is a measure of his devious strategy that he moved by way of Glen Cochill and the Sma' Glen since, on his way, he met — and was perhaps rather less surprised than he might have been — Lord Kilpont, Sir John Drummond and Lord Maderty, with a newly-raised force of 500 Highlanders, en route to join the covenanters.

Persuasion paid off and one suspects, predictably. Lord Kilpont — a Graham and thus a kinsman to Montrose — threw in his lot with the Royalists. He was not to know that this would lead to his early death.

Thus, as dawn broke on the morning of Sunday, September 1st, Montrose and MacColla, with their ragged and unpaid army, broke camp and moved with determination towards Perth and destiny.

A mile or two from that city things were stirring by now. Aware from scouts that the Highlanders and the Irish were advancing rapidly and without opposition, the covenanter levies were hastily assembled to defend life, limb and property.

Montrose, fully in charge of events as ever, had calculated correctly that his rapid tactical advance would surprise and, in this he was right. With their leader Argyll away on business resolving his own problems, the levies were under the command of his protegé, William Ker, 3rd Earl of Lothian. However, he too was off-watch dealing with bureaucratic business in Edinburgh. Reponsibility for defence fell therefore to the understandably reluctant third reserve, David Wemyss, Lord Elcho, an aristocrat whose misfortune it was to be in the wrong place at the wrong time.

With between 5,000 and 6,000 men at his command, Elcho had a marked numerical advantage. Moreover, his armament was superior and although his troops were lukewarm in enthusiasm and quality, at least some were defending home and family and could be expected to show interest in the achievement of a successful outcome. As a measure of the opposing force, it was said that Montrose and MacColla had just one barrel of gunpowder left between them; something of an exaggeration perhaps but, symptomatic of the situation. Certainly, at one point, the right-flank Highlanders added stone-throwing with slings to their repertoire.

It would be wrong to say that Montrose relished the forthcoming fight. He was not to know the true calibre of Elcho's men; as a fledgling Royalist leader he was in a dangerously exposed position, faced by considerable odds. His credibility as a military tactician hung heavily in the balance.

Ragged it might be on the surface; however, his army was in good heart. MacColla's troops were veterans of the Irish wars and the Highlanders were men to whom battle was an essential part of manhood. Time though was not on his side; covenanting armies were powerful things, superior in manpower and armament and invariably well commanded; moreover, intelligence had told him that one such was on its way to Perth.

Weighing up the situation with his captains, Montrose decided his battle plan. Contemporary practice placed infantry in the centre, with cavalry flanking. Montrose, however, had no cavalry as such — beyond a few mounted troops. After consultation and with MacColla's agreement, he therefore placed the Irish in the centre, defending the right wing with Atholl and Badenoch Highlanders under his own command, whilst leaving the left to Lord Kilpont and his men.

It has been fashionable to describe Montrose's army as badly served with weapons, having few muskets and only bows and arrows. It is true that he was short of powder for his muskets but he was himself a practised archer and would have been well versed in the power of the bow. The lesser of his problems would have been the weapon, the greater would have been its strategic use, since it is doubtful whether his men had been trained to shoot en masse. Only in this tactical respect would he have had some doubt about the efficacy of the weapon.

Whilst the archers might well have dealt effectively enough with a frontal cavalry charge had the opportunity come, in the event things were to turn out rather differently. Montrose, MacColla and Kilpont, had advanced their troops in good order towards the opposing forces, steadied them and, when well within musket range and bow-shot, were ready to commence the action.

Lord Elcho's captains had deployed the (to us today, quaintly named) 'Forlorn Hope,' an experienced company, forward of their main battle line, with the object of drawing and cutting off pursuit from some of MacColla's centre. Unaccustomed as they were to the Gael's way of fighting, the tactic worked only too well. To their dismay, the entire centre of Montrose's army, having discharged one musket volley, detached itself as one man and roaring blood-curdling Gaelic battle-cries, arrived at full belt, brandishing sword, dirk and battle-axe, to the extreme terror of 'Forlorn Hope' and luckless levies alike. The Lowland defenders of Perth had experienced their first — and, for many, their last — 'Highland Charge.'

Whilst the Highland bowmen on the left flank had scarcely time to nock shaft to string before their opponents melted away in total panic, Montrose's Atholl Highlanders on the right flank had rather more to do for, opposed by Elcho's cavalry, which put up stern resistance, their bows were busy and arrows flew in profusion.

Within minutes, retreat became rout and, although actual battlefield casualties were comparatively small in number, Gaelic blood was up; after carefully removing clothing to prevent it being soiled, every fleeing soldier brought down was summarily despatched.

The triumphant Montrose called for the immediate surrender of Perth and, as he had now no forces with which to defend the city, this was promptly agreed by the Provost, Robert Arnot. Magnanimous in victory, Montrose was circumspect in his demands, reassuring the anxious Provost in passing, that although they were running riot in the suburbs, MacColla's Irish would not enter the city proper.

Alasdair MacColla actually did rather well personally out of the battle; apart from weapons, their clothing and other loot taken from dead covenanters, with which the quality and general appearance of his army was substantially improved, he left the premises with 50 Scots pounds from the city's coffers for his own use. One suspects the Gaelic equivalent of Danegeld here but, no doubt, the alternative appealed rather less to the city fathers.

James Graham, Marquess of Montrose, was to live to fight and win more battles against covenanter armies before his untimely death by execution; this, his first against organised and significant oppostion, was surely the catalyst for those victories yet to come.

POSTSCRIPT: In case it should be thought that the bow and arrow in Scotland were archaic things in the 1640s, circumstantial evidence is that this was not so. In Edinburgh, during the period 1630 to 1675 over 40 'bowers' (makers of bows) are recorded, and many more seemingly plied their trade across Scotland. True, they had other 'strings to their bows' in that some were 'club makers'and others made spears and lances, but it is as bowers that they were known, an indication of the importance of their calling.

As a relevant aside, although the Records of the Royal Company of Archers show that a Robert Munro was sent to England in 1676 to ". . . *be bred for making bows and arrows . . .*" and, an assumption is made by the writer of the History of the Company that the trade had, by then, fallen entirely into disuse, there were, however, at least two prospective bow- making instructors of merit in the City at the time. Robert's father, Hew Munro, to whom he had (earlier?) been apprenticed or, if Hew were past teaching, then Andrew Forrester — appointed 'his Majesty's master bower' in 1675 in succession to Alexander Hay, by whom he had been instructed and who was lately of that title,

It is curious that neither was selected to sharpen up the young Munro's skill; perhaps father was too frail, and Hay was too busy. Certainly, fletcher (sic) Egertoun in London did his job well, and young Robert was accounted a great success by the Company.

Principal References consulted, and further reading:

BATTLES IN BRITAIN 1066 - 1746. William Seymour: 1979. Book Club Associates.

LIFE AND CAMPAIGNS OF THE BLACK PRINCE. Richard Barber. 1979. The Folio Society.

HENRY VIII AND THE INVASION OF FRANCE. Charles Cruikshank.1990. Alan Sutton Publishing. ISBN 0 86299 768 2.

HIGHLAND WARRIOR — ALASDAIR MACCOLLA & THE CIVIL WARS. David Stevenson. 1994. Saltire Society. ISBN 0 85411 059 3.

RYMES OF ROBYN HOOD. R.B.Dobson & J.Taylor: 1997. Alan Sutton Publishing. ISBN 0 7509 1661 3.

SCOTTISH ARMS MAKERS. Charles Whitelaw: Arms & Armour Press. ISBN 0 85368 201 1

1558. The 6th August was burled at Poulie (St Pauls) churchyard an archer, the which was sIain at St. James fair In the field, shamefully for he was paunched with his own sword.

Part 9

Scotland the Brave

The Battle of Falkirk

The Battle of Bannockburn

The Battle of Nevilles Cross

The Battles of Otterburn and Homildon Hill

Battle of Shrewsbury

The Battle of Flodden

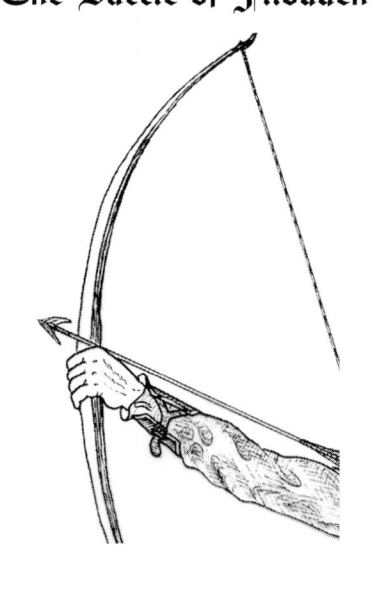

SCOTLAND THE BRAVE

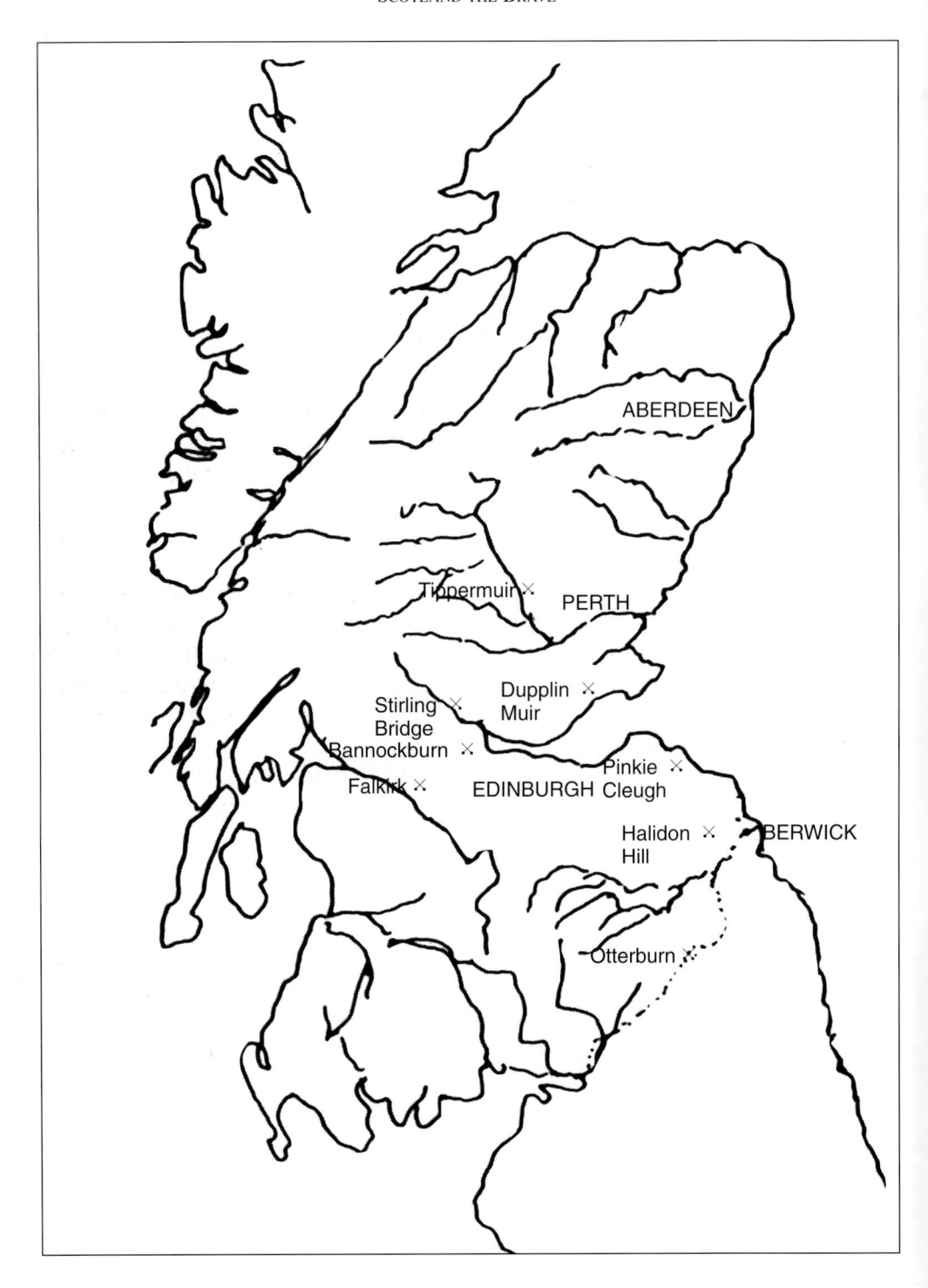

SCOTLAND

Showing the location of Major Battles

PART 9

SCOTLAND THE BRAVE

RELATIONS between the three Nations which share this Island have never been easy. Although we band together to meet our common foes and are formidable when we do, across the years more British blood has been spilt on our native soil than elsewhere.

Nowhere has this carnage and bloodshed been more truly seen than in the confrontations between England and Scotland — over land or political power.

The six battles which follow span a century. They begin with Falkirk in 1298, where Edward I avenged the disastrous English defeat by William Wallace at Stirling Bridge. They continue with Bannockburn in 1314, when Robert Bruce decimated the English archery and England learned a painful lesson in martial skill and, Neville's Cross in 1346, where Robert's son, King David Bruce, was defeated, to be held captive in the Tower of London.

Otterburn (1388) and Homildon Hill — fought in 1402, when Harry 'Hotspur' Percy battled with the Archibald "Tyneman"* Douglas, were followed in 1403 by Shrewsbury, where the two erstwhile enemies combined forces in conflict with King Henry IV, conclude the Chapter.

---

* The Loser.

TIIE BATTLE OF FALKIRK, 1298

AFTER THE battle of Stirling Bridge, where the English. under King Edward I's Treasurer, de Cressingham, had been out-manoevred and soundly thrashed by determined forces led by William Wallace, Edward himself turned his attention to the subjugation of the Scottish people. At the time of Stirling he had been otherwise occupied and the Scots, learning of his absence, had risen at Wallace's call.

On his return to England, the King picked up the reins of power once more and after travelling on pilgrimage to St. John of Beverley — under whose banner he had already tasted victory against the Scots — he mustered his army of 16,000 foot soldiers and archers and 2,000 men-at-arms at Roxburgh.

As the English army moved deeper into Scotland, Wallace retreated strategically beyond the Forth, plundering and laying waste as he went. Edward, meanwhile had reached Edinburgh and had camped to the West of the city whilst waiting upon the arrival of his ships with their stores.

Due to circumstances beyond the control of himself or seemingly anyone else, just one ship arrived however and that carried only wine. With what in hindsight appears a curious lack of judgment, he made this unexpected bounty readily available to his troops. The result was immediate and dramatic. Civil war erupted between English and Welsh foot soldiers and archers, resulting in a threatened desertion to Wallace and Scotland by the Welsh.

When told of the impending problem, Edward was dismissive. He is alleged to have replied:

> "what matter if enemies join enemies. Welsh and Scots alike are both our foes. Let them go where they like, for with God's blessing, in one day we shall get revenge on both nations. . ."

According to one account, the Scots, led by Wallace who believed Edward to be in retreat, arrived at Falkirk and made ready for attack. The King however ordered his men to proceed to Linlithgow some eight miles away, declaring that there was no need for Wallace to follow. He would return and meet him.

That night the army camped on the moor outside the town, the men-at-arms using their shields as pillows. An uncomfortable night, made more so in Edward's case, since during darkness his horse trampled him, fracturing two of his ribs.

Despite the pain, however, Edward mounted and on the morning of July 22nd, he gathered his troops and led them towards the Scottish position, hard by

Callendar Wood to the south of Falkirk and the battle.

Wallace had with him untrained forces of 10,000 foot soldiers, mainly pikemen but supported by a few hundred archers. These, with their 12-foot pikes, were formed in circles, or 'schiltrons,' anticipating formations adopted by the British army many centuries later. Edward, however, relied on the well-tested and more conventional three 'battles,' or 'wards' and had his men form Va(n)ward, Middleward and Rearward divisions.

The King did not wish to attack at once, he wanted firstly to rest his troops after their march and give them their provisions. The barons though, were restless and eager for the fray to begin and prevailed upon the Monarch to open the attack.

Reluctantly he agreed and mounted English men-at-arms led the charge against the Scottish ranks. They were unable to force their way through the hedge of pikes however and, although the Scottish cavalry and the archers turned and fled the field, the tightly-packed schiltrons withstood charge after charge of the English knights.

Despairing of breaking this impenetrable barrier, Edward, after several hours, turned to his bowmen — as yet still an almost untried arm of his fighting force and ordered them to shoot into the massed ranks. Soon arrows were pouring like hail towards the exposed bodies of the luckless pikemen and, before long, the effect of these concentrated volleys could be seen as the circles gave ground and finally broke.

Both mounted and dismounted men-at-arms were now able to get in amongst the Scots and, unwieldy pikes being of little use as close quarter weaponry, put them to lance and sword.

Casualties were large on the Scottish side, with some 5,000 foot soldiers and 100 knights slain; whilst on the English side 200 men-at-arms fell. William Wallace, victor of Stirling Bridge, had been defeated by superior generalship and took ship for France, from whence he eventually returned to conduct guerilla warfare from the woods and hills, finally to be ousted and brought to London for execution.

Falkirk was unusual, perhaps even unique, in the disparate number of men from England and Wales that were involved. Despite his contemptuous dismissal of them, had the threat by the unruly Welsh to change sides materialised, Edward would have been seriously embarrassed, since numerically the composition of his army was diverse. Ten thousand-five hundred foot soldiers, archers and spearmen had been 'requisitioned' from Wales, against 1,000 bowmen each from Chester and Lancashire.

As in all battles in which cavalry is involved, it is the horse that suffers. We know from the subsequent inventory that at Falkirk 111 horses, or around 5% of those taking part, were killed during the charges. To carry the point a little further before leaving it for other matters, the mean value at cost of the knightly war-horse in 1298 was £10.2s, most being actually valued at under £10. One hundred shillings was the lowest acceptable valuation for the inventory however and, although perhaps unfair, the suspicion is that many of the mounts forced into battle by their resplendent riders were little more than unwilling country hacks

BANNOCKBURN, 1314

THIS is a tale of two men — one a King of England, weak son of a war-like father; the other a Scottish patriot, a brave, charismatic leader of men, inspired by injustice and with single-minded fervour to rid his land of an heriditary oppressor.

The English King: Edward II. The Scot: patriot and acclaimed King: Robert the Bruce.

The battle, which took place on the marshy flats of the Bannock Burn on June 23rd and 24th, has been described as the most lamentable defeat ever suffered by an English army and the only pitched engagement in recorded medieval history in which well-led and well-armed infantry totally overwhelmed the cream of contemporary mounted chivalry.

As always in these early battles, there are significant discrepancies between the various accounts, both in the matter of numbers of troops involved and in the disposition and sequence of events on the battlefield itself. Numerically the English may have mustered some 20,000 men, many horsed but of whom an unspecified, perhaps a small number, were foot-slogging archers.

Bruce may have commanded about half that number, largely infantry, including some archers but with a leavening of 500 picked horsemen. A motley collection of 3,000 enthusiastic 'sma' folk,' untrained and undisciplined, completed the picture.

Although number-wise Edward had the advantage, it was Bruce who had selected the battle site. He had prepared well and, moreover, had the advantage of fighting both on, and for, his own land.

He was positioned strongly on dry rising ground, adjacent to New Park and a mile or so beyond the River Forth. Close by was the Bannockburn ditch, which gave its name to the subsequent battle. His encampment lay between New Park and Kings Park. Some three miles behind him was Stirling Castle, besieged by Edward Bruce and the reason for the English presence.

A truce had been arranged between the commander of the castle and Edward Bruce, brother to Robert, the gist of which was that if an English army had not come to its aid and was within three leagues (nine miles) by Mid-Summer Day, then Stirling Castle would capitulate.

Faced with the real possibility of losing a tactically important stronghold to increasingly bellicose Scots, Edward was reluctantly obliged to persuade his Barons to support a relieving force. Because the 11th hour was rapidly approaching, this army — well-armed and equipped despite its speedy formation — had force-marched beyond the Scottish border, to encamp well within the statutory distance of the Castle required by the truce.

The Battle of Bannockburn was essentially a two-day affair. Although dealing with

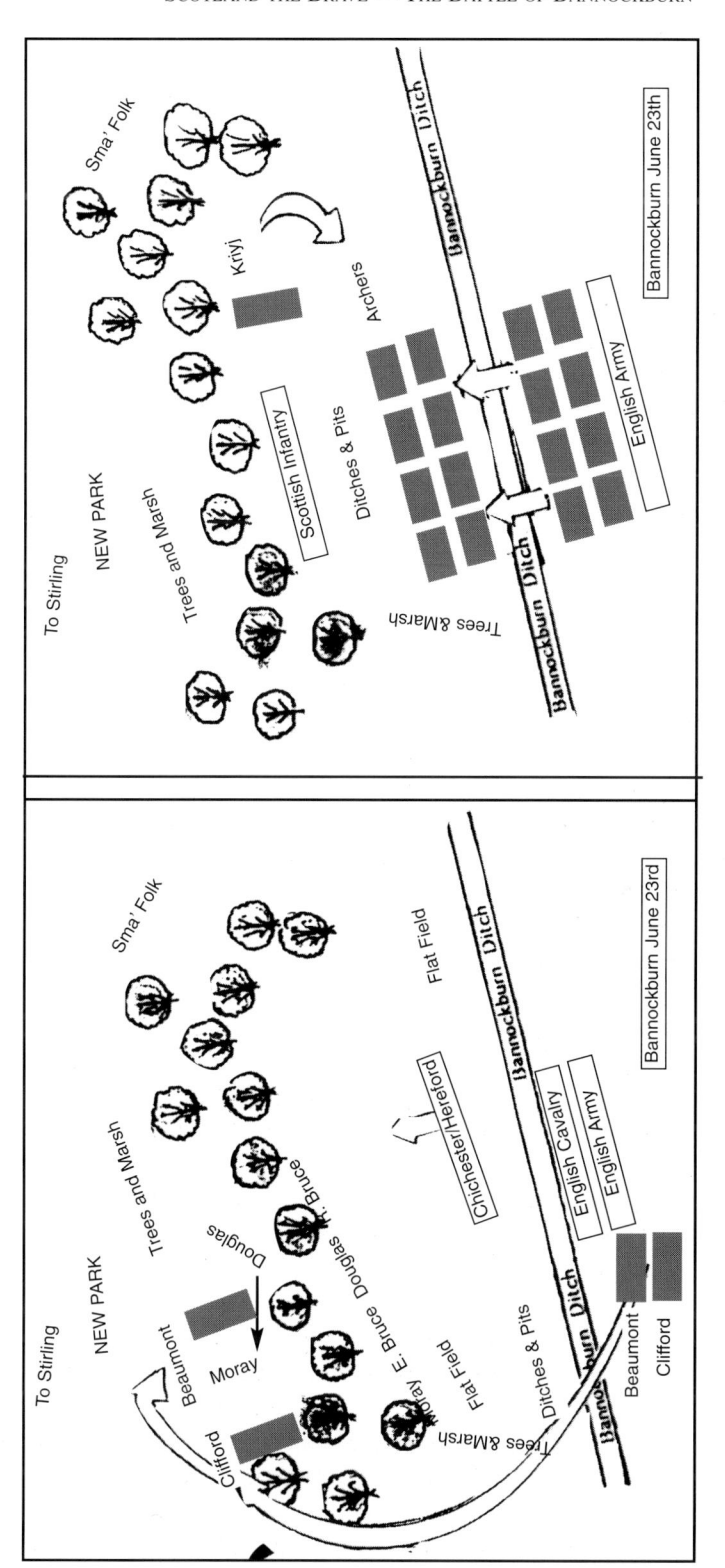

THE TWO-DAY BATTLE OF BANNOCKBURN, 23rd & 24th June, 1314

Robert Bruce was uppermost in Edward's mind, the relief of Stirling Castle was the prime reason for his presence. With this in mind therefore, he despatched Lord Robert Clifford and Henry Beaumont with a strong cavalry force of some 800 men-at-arms to break the surrounding ring.

It seems to have been in the King's mind that this force could slip unnoticed past Bruce's men without inviting confrontation. Like other theoretical exercises during those two days, practice however, proved otherwise. Thomas Randolph, Earl of Moray, with 500 infantry, stood in his way, spears outward and in defensive formation.

Whilst perhaps not forced to fight — for they were mounted and could have returned from whence they came — Clifford and Beaumont chose to do so. Leading charge after charge they were unable to penetrate the Scots wall of spears. Horses were killed and men-at-arms thrown to the ground — but to no avail.

Reduced finally to throwing spears, lances, darts, maces and even swords and knives at the dogged Scottish infantry, they could not break through. Meanwhile, James "the Black" Douglas received Bruce's agreement to join the fray and advanced to assist the hard-pressed Earl of Moray and his men. This manoeuvre was watched by Edward who, not for the first time in the battle, misinterpreted the movement as flight.

With victory seemingly in sight, the English vanguard crossed the Bannock ditch, only to find the bulk of the Scottish first and second Divisions not only largely intact, but in well-disciplined battle formation, with Bruce in personal command.

The next piece of action has passed into Scottish legend. With Robert Bruce seemingly there for the taking, one Sir Henry de Bohun — a fire-eating English man-at-arms — put spurs to horse, couched his lance and in full panoply of war charged directly at him.

The Scottish King was seated on a nimble palfrey however, having not yet mounted his battle-stallion and, accepting the challenge, turned smartly as the over-enthusiastic de Bohun thundered past, swinging his great battle-axe down on Henry's head with such force that it broke the haft.

Exit Henry: 'cleaved,' so it is said, 'to the brisket.' Questioned later about the wisdom of this encounter by anxious commanders, Bruce only remarked laconically that he had broken an 'aye guid axe.' (As an aside, precipitate action seems to have been endemic to the de Bohun's. Henry's namesake, Sir Humphrey, had perished at Boroughbridge a few years later in much the same way.)

Preliminaries dispensed with, the battle began. Some English forces led by the Earl of Gloucester had by now crossed the burn and were engaged by Bruce's battalion. Matters did not go their way however; Gloucester was unhorsed, barely escaping capture and, in some disarray, the English troops fought their way back across the water.

This confrontation and its result was watched with keen interest by the Scots and, in some considerable dismay, by the English. With Bruce now properly prepared, the Scottish Divisions moved against their foe and a hard-fought struggle ensued. The English cavalry, having limited space to manoeuvre, made a fighting retreat across the Bannock ditch to lick their wounds and, joined by the remnants of Clifford and Beaumont's unsuccessful Castle relieving force, to prepare for the morrow.

Twilight was a miserable time amidst this gloomy English camp. There had been some limited success against Bruce during the day it was true, but nothing that could be counted a victory. The enemy was still in position and Stirling Castle was as yet unrelieved. The troops had seen the defeat of the vanguard and knew of Clifford and Beaumont's problems with Moray and Douglas. Feelings of foreboding were spreading throughout the ranks and there was much shuffling of feet.

As twilight turned into dusk, English commanders tried, with limited success, to inject fresh spirit into flagging troops. However, with nightfall all settled down into an uneasy sleep amongst the soggy terrain of the Bannock burn — an 'evil deep, wet march' as a contemporary described it with feeling.

Morning broke and enthusiasm evaporated further with the news that during the night. Alexander Seton, a Scot in the service of King Edward, had defected to the opposition with his retinue.

It was at about this point that the King called a hasty Council of War. The English were at some disadvantage; Bruce had carefully selected the battle site and had prepared pits and trenches and laid iron calthrops to break up any mounted charge. Moreover his men were well-led, well-armed, had enjoyed more than just modest success on the preceding day and were in good heart. Clearly the initiative lay with him.

Various strategems were discussed; one — which given the Scottish propensity for personal pillage might just have worked — was to fall back behind the tents in the expectation that the Scots would break ranks to loot. This was dismissed out of hand by the King, who categorically refused to appear in retreat. Noticing that the Scots were now kneeling (in prayer) he seemingly mistook this activity for pleas for mercy and against the advice of two of his commanders, Sir InghamUmphraville and Gilbert de Clare, Earl of Gloucester, clinched matters by mounting his horse in preparation for a frontal onslaught.

The vanguard, including archers, moved forward across the burn and once in position, there was some sporadic shooting on both sides. To little effect by the Scottish bowmen, due perhaps to the lightness of their weapons; rather more so by the English archers on the right flank although, before they could get fully into their stride, they were attacked and chased off the field by Bruce's small force of picked cavalry, led by Robert Keith, Earl Mareschal of Scotland.

Meanwhile the English cavalry charges had begun and were to continue for a very long time. The shock of each impact was absorbed by the Scots however, fighting being particularly fierce around Gilbert, the young Earl of Gloucester. Having been forced to fall back the previous day, he had need to restore his martial credibility and went into the thick of things with this uppermost in his mind.

Although he fought like a demon, he was singled out for particular attention and, after having been stabbed with spears, was finally knocked off his horse. Once down, his body bleeding from numerous spear thrusts and his head battered by clubs, he died under the hooves of his horse.

This was the turning point for many of Edward's men. Certainly the front line broke and, crashing through the second and third Divisions, were followed by the disciplined

MOUNTED ARCHERS FROM WALES AND THE ENGLISH SHIRES

ranks of Scottish schiltrons. From behind the hill, the camp followers and the poorly armed levy (the sma' folk) joined in the fray. This proved the last straw, the English army dissolved into a rout, with men struggling to recross the tidal Bannockburn ditch and so to the River Forth

Seeing that all was now lost Edward himself left the field closely followed by Bruce's men and after considerable difficulty, finally made his way to safety.

English martial pride was not only seriously dented, it was decimated. One of the largest, most professionally led, best equipped and effective fighting forces in contemporary Europe, had been brought to its knees by an army of well-led infantry.

The CHRONICLE OF LONDON dismissed the affair with tight-lipped asperity:

"... *This yere of oure lord a M'cccxiiij the kyng Edward with a ryall oost (royal host) went into Scotloud: and upon Midsomer day faught with the Scottes at Strywelyn (Stirling) and, there he was discomfited and fledde, and moche of his peple sclayn . . . "*

England licked her wounds. Lessons were there to be learned. Clearly battle tactics required an overhaul. Whether another more martially inclined commander would have taken Edward's tactical decisions is naturally questionable. As has been remarked elsewhere, hindsight is a wonderful thing. The withdrawal of Douglas's force to support the Earl of Moray against Beaumont and Clifford was seriously misread. The English vanguard, under Gloucester and Hereford, was badly mauled in consequence; whilst the spectacular demise of Sir Henry de Bohun did nothing whatever for English morale.

The employment of cavalry against determined opposition from well-armed and disciplined spearmen proved disastrous; whilst the potential destructive power of archery against the schiltrons was not seemingly utilised as it might, or should have been. Had Edward known of the Scottish cavalry and its location (and one would have expected his scouts to have reported this) then matters on his right flank might have been better arranged and his archery used to more effect.

Bannockburn was followed by much Scottish raiding in the Border area and Bruce had things more or less his own way for the next two decades. However, when English and Scottish forces next met, at Halidon Hill, things would be ordered differently.

Henceforth, English men-at-arms would fight dismounted, shoulder to shoulder. Protecting their flanks would be serried companies of archers (themselves shielded by pit and sharpened stake), disciplined and ready to deal coldly and effectively with both approaching cavalry and infantry. Mounted bowmen from Wales and the English shires would ride proudly alongside England's chivalry, each confident in the other's role. Arising from the stench of death and defeat at Bannockburn were the military tactics that a generation later were to win victory at Crecy.

In 1460, 'OSMOND BARS' — a superior quality of Baltic Iron was used for arrow heads, fish hooks, and the like.

NEVILLES CROSS, 1346

THERE is little obvious connection between the homeric battle that took place at Crecy ridge on August 26th, 1346, and that at Neville's Cross in County Durham on October 17th. A link there was and it was close.

Philip VI of France, his army destroyed and his martial abilities shattered by English chivalry and English and Welsh bowmen at Crecy, had appealed to his Scottish ally, King David Bruce, to give diversionary help by taking an army into unprotected England in the hope — vain as it happened — that this would persuade Edward III to hasten home and thus give Philip chance to regroup his forces.

David was well aware that most experienced English commanders were with Edward in France and, that in theory, there might be no effective force to bar his way. Thus, in October, with an army of some 20,000 men, he crossed the border and, having sacked the Abbey at Lanercost, he marched on towards Durham, laying waste as he went.

Clearly matters had to be taken in hand and speedily at that. Thus it was that whilst the Scots occupied themselves with plunder and loot, the Archbishop of York, with the Northern Earls, Ralph, Earl Neville of RabyNeville and Henry, Earl Percy of Northumberland, called out the Border levies to muster at Bishop Auckland, some 20 miles south of Durham.

This hastily gathered force of around 15,000 men formed into battles and began its advance towards David and his Scots. The meeting came rather sooner than expected; a Scottish raiding party, 500 strong, out for loot and mayhem and led by Sir William Douglas of Liddesdale, met the English vanguard head-on and were summarily routed. King David's first intimation of English readiness for defence was the appearance of Douglas's panic-stricken remnants.

It was clearly necessary to prepare for confrontation and so King David formed his army into three Divisions. Robert, High Steward of Scotland, led the first Division to the King's left, whilst command of the second, the right wing, fell to the Earl of Moray and William Douglas. The King took charge of the centre of the line.

The English meanwhile had mustered around Neville's Cross, one of several ancient crosses which surrounded Durham. The position was favourable to them: a ridge some 200 feet in height gently sloping towards the Scottish positions but, steep enough to slow an advance. The infantry was formed up in three Divisions, cavalry to the rear and archers to the fore. Lord Henry Percy commanded the right wing, Sir Thomas Rokeby the left whilst the aptly named Ralph Neville took overall command from the centre.

Although Lord Graham sought permission to open the attack with a charge by his cavalry, the King refused his request and gave orders for a general infantry attack. The

Scots moved forward but, an intervening ravine caused a bunching together of the right and centre Divisions. The resulting mass of men was a perfect target for English archery and Scottish casualties swiftly mounted.

Seeing this, Lord Graham mustered his cavalry and charged the leading bowmen, scattering and dispersing them. However, at close range his horse was shot from under him and he had to make his way back to his own lines on foot.

Seeing the result of Graham's action, Robert, the High Steward, led his spearmen in an attack on the disorganised archers, forcing them back into Lord Percy's Division. The situation was saved by a cavalry charge led by Edward Balliol, which rolled the Scottish Divisions back upon themselves; whilst the archers, now reformed, were once more shooting into the mass of spearmen.

Attacked in the centre by Earl Neville and on the flank by Balliol's cavalry, the Scots began to give way and, although close-quarter hacking continued for some time, the end was inevitable. Despite David rallying his troops again and again and the remaining Scottish men-at-arms forming a steel ring around their King, the Royal banner eventually fell and defeat became a rout.

King David was taken prisoner by Sir John Copeland. Legend says that he struck Sir John in the face with a mailed fist, seeking to be killed rather than captured but taken he was and conveyed in triumph to London's Tower.

Although the army which defeated King David at Neville's Cross was a scratch force and untried, it contained within its ranks those essential ingredients for future English success: the valiant men-at-arms, dismounted and stubbornly defending every inch of ground whilst, supporting them, the formidable war-bow and the murderous English battle-shaft. At Durham, in October, as at Crecy in August, the combination proved invincible.

From the History of Salisbury.   In 1408. A body of men attached to the Earl of Lancaster quarrelled with Salisbury men on Fiskerton Bridge, killing three with arrows and swords. The City inhabitants were summoned by bells to deliberate concerning this and a cessation of hostiities appears to have been brought about by a Minstrel hailing from Wales. Hence the following entry in the town's Exchequer books:-
"To a certain Minstrel from Wales for purchasing peace and for making him a hood, because he had lost his hood in defence of the city in the insult offered on the bridge at Fiskerton by the men of the Earl of Lancaster . . ."

OTTERBURN, 1388 AND HOMILDON HILL, 1402

ALTHOUGH truces between England and Scotland were a regular feature of the Middle Ages, they were transient affairs and broken at the will and whim of those Border Lords who held the Northern reins of power. Thus it was that Earl Percy of Northumberland, his son Henry 'Hotspur' and the Scottish house of Douglas, were in more or less constant conflict.

The battle of Otterburn is commemorated in an anonymous poem which leaves us in no doubt about the instigator.

> "... It fell about the Lammas Tide, when the muir-men win their hay
> That the doughty Earl of Douglas went into England to catch a prey ..."

James, 2nd Earl of Douglas, had led a raiding force into County Durham, plundering as he went and had reached the gates of Newcastle where, in a skirmish, he had captured 'Hotspur's' lance pennon. This he bore away in triumph, to the chagrin of 'Hotspur,' who swore to recapture it before Douglas reached the border. Hearing this, Douglas remarked that the pennon was hanging in front of his tent and that if Henry wanted it back, then he knew where to come to get it.

Although with much difficulty 'Hotspur' was prevented from launching an immediate mission of recovery — his Barons fearing that the challenge was bait for a Scottish ambush — a day later he and his army set off in pursuit of Douglas and the missing flag.

Thus it was that on August 19th, the English forces found Douglas and his marauding army encamped for the night at Otterburn. 'Hotspur,' true to his name, paused only to send Sir Thomas Umfraville with 3,000 men to outflank the Scots and launched an immediate attack.

Douglas, who held a strong defensive position, divided his men into two divisions. One he despatched to engage 'Hotspur,' whilst the other he led personally against Hotspur's right flank.

It was now dark and with almost no visibility, Hotspur's archers were at considerable disadvantage. Whilst they and the men-at-arms struggled with the advancing Scottish Division, the flanking attack, led by Douglas, crashed into their right, pushing their line back towards the River Rede. During this melee, Douglas was killed and Hotspur captured.

> "... This deed was done at Otterburn, about the breaking of the day,
> Earl Douglas was buried at the braken bush, and the Percy led captive away ..."

Sir Thomas Umfraville, given the job of outflanking the Scots, found their camp which he attacked and ransacked and, having done so, departed for home Had he carried on

CAVALRY APPROACHING TO ATTACK A GROUP OF ENGLISH ARCHERS

to attack Douglas from the rear, things might have ended differently for Earl Percy but, having successfully concluded his own mission, with the independence of spirit that has ever identified the Northerner, he decided that no more was required of him.

Although the Scots were masters of the field, they did not press their advantage. Whilst the English had been badly beaten in the night-time engagement, it was now daylight and, given leadership, the archers were capable of reforming. Earl Douglas had been killed but 'Hotspur' was a captive. Otterburn was a Scottish victory but a hollow one.

Warfare, whether ambush, skirmish, or set-piece battle, was a way of life for Borderers and raids continued intermittently as chance allowed. Never one to let opportunity slip, Archibald Douglas took advantage of English concern with Owain Glyndwr's Welsh ambitions and entered England with an army which he marched as far as Newcastle, before retreating heavily laden with loot.

'Hotspur,' ransomed and back in the bosom of his family once more, raised the Northumbrian militia and, in a smart outflanking move, made for the River Till to cut off Douglas's retreat. Learning of the English presence from his scouts, Douglas quickly looked for a suitable place to defend. He chose Homildon Hill, a rise of several hundred feet with a flattened top and then set about organising his forces into defensive schiltrons.

It rapidly became apparent to 'Hotspur' that the position was proof against advance and accordingly, he turned to his archers for the solution. A scouting party of several hundred longbowmen was dispatched and these engaged the schiltrons at long range causing some casualties. Moving closer, as the distance between archer and spearman shortened, so casualties increased until, galled into action by the incessant hail of arrows and with their own archers ineffective, the spearmen were left with no choice but to move downhill.

Retiring slowly and with discipline before the mass of oncoming spearmen but, still keeping their distance, the archers continued their volleys until, with the entire Scottish army on the move towards them and now at the foot of the hill, they moved aside to allow Hotspur's men-at-arms to attack. Despite attempts to reform their defensive schiltrons, the Scots had by now lost not only men but, of more importance, many of their commanders. Seven prominent nobles were killed and over 80 barons and knights taken for ransom. Douglas himself lost an eye and was wounded four times by hissing English war-arrows. With confusion turning to rout, the battle was lost.

If the common English bowman had a Battle Standard, then Homildon Hill would be written large upon it.

From the Diary of Henry Machyn, Citizen of London, 1557: " The 27th May at afternoon was a woman great with child slain. going in Finsbury field with her husband, with an arrow shot in the neck. The which she was a puterers (pewterers) wife."

THE BATTLE OF SHREWSBURY, 1403

ALTHOUGH other internal conflicts had in the past matched and in the future were to match Englishman against Englishman, the engagement that took place at Shrewsbury on July 21st was in one sense, unique, for it brought together in common cause the most unlikely of companions in arms.

Archibald Douglas, that thorn in Northern English affairs, had been taken by the Percy's at Homildon Hill a year before and was held an honoured captive by them in hopeful exchange for a significant ransom. King Henry IV, with an eye to the Exchequer, claimed Douglas as a Royal prize and the putative ransom for the State and had made his demand clear. Even clearer however was his captor's determination not to hand Douglas over.

Henry Percy, Earl of Northumberland, had presented the King with his account for various services rendered — including inter alia, an unpaid for campaign in North Wales and the arrangements that preceded Homildon Hill; a total that amounted to a very respectable £60,000.

Disputing the figures however, the King (or perhaps his Treasurer) made a final offer of just £40,000. Conscious of the short-fall (in today's parlance the offer would have been termed 'derisory') and with his possession of Earl Douglas a trump card, Percy claimed the ransom for himself.

THE BATTLE OF SHREWSBURY, April 21st, 1403

Although the Earl of Northumberland had aided Henry Bolingbroke to regain his Dukedom of Lancaster, his subsequent usurpation of the throne (as Henry IV) from King Richard II had disturbed the sensitive North-country political scene and had not, moreover, been part of Percy's personal agenda.

Relations, already cooling rapidly, were not therefore aided by Henry's parsimony and a Royal directive for Henry 'Hotspur' to present himself in Wales to help deal with Owain Glyndwr was met with a categoric refusal to budge.

Positive in all they did and with the army victorious at Homildon still mustered, Earl Percy called on the family firm to help. With Thomas Percy, Earl of Worcester and their erstwhile enemy, the one-eyed Douglas and his border warriors in tow, he set out for a showdown with the King.

Reaching Chester they were joined by Cheshire archers and Welsh 'friendlies,' with a promise of help from the King's arch-enemy, Owain Glyndwr, whom he was to meet at Shrewsbury.

Meanwhile, the Prince of Wales — later Henry V — who was raiding in North Wales, heard from his scouts of the Percy's march from Chester and turned his forces in that direction. Alerting Henry IV, his father, who was en route with a sizeable army to deal with a Scottish problem, the two joined forces and awaited Percy's expected arrival.

On July 21st the two armies faced each other. On one side 'Hotspur,' with Douglas but not his promised ally, the wily Glyndwr — who may have had a suspicion of the ultimate outcome. On the other, the King with his commander, the young Prince of Wales, untried in major conflict. Each force was broadly matched in numbers; each had a substantial and effective archery contingent.

'Hotspur' had positioned his army on a low hill some two miles North of Shrewsbury, at the base of which was a large field planted with a ripening crop of peas. On the further side of this field and facing 'Hotspur,' the Royal army was massed. Standing just outside normal bow-shot, some 300 yards apart, they awaited confrontation.

Both armies adopted similar positioning. A centre Division comprising men-at-arms, fronted by a substantial force of longbowmen, with additional archers on each flank.

In keeping with protocol, when two English sides met in potential conflict, a peaceful settlement was attempted. The King sent forward the Abbot of Shrewsbury to negotiate suitable terms with 'Hotspur,' taking the opportunity in the meantime to create knights from amongst his followers.

With daylight diminishing and no settlement agreed, King Henry broke off negotiations, suspecting (probably correctly) that 'Hotspur' was delaying matters deliberately in the hope of receiving Welsh reinforcements from Glyndwr.

Hostilities now began in earnest. Previously just out of bowshot, the archer vanguard of the Royal army moved forward into the pea field, treading with difficulty though the tangled mass of plants. Once within range, the Cheshire archers of Hotspur's forces opened up and loosed an arrow-storm amongst them. As usual casualties were heavy but the advance continued until within range themselves, the Royal bowmen started to inflict casualties upon Hotspur's ranks.

Of the rival longbowmen, those from Cheshire were the more deadly — these were the archers whose pay was greatest when serving the King — and, under their marksmanship the King's leading Division began to wilt and then gave way. Several thousand of his men turned tail and ran, followed by Hotspur's archers, who gave chase and, as they caught up, joined in hand-to-hand fighting with them.

By now the Royal men-at-arms were involved in the battle but had also given way under the pressure of the rebel charge. King Henry sent in his reserve Division to try to stem the flight of his troops; it was at this point that 'Hotspur,' with Douglas, led an assault into the King's Division in an attempt to reach and kill him. Several men, Royal look-alikes dressed in the King's livery, were slain in the belief that one was Henry IV himself. With the struggle at that point poised in Hotspur's favour, the King had been hurried away to a place of safety.

His son, the Prince of Wales (later Henry V), barely 16 years of age and with responsibility for the left of the line, now began to move slowly up the hill, his superior disciplined force outflanking those archers and men-at-arms of the rebel forces who had remained in position whilst their fellows were pursuing the King's men. Slowly the Prince's division swung around behind these troops, who now found themselves shot at from two sides. The remaining rebel archers and men-at-arms, realising that no quarter would be given, now fought furiously for their lives and, at this point, the young Prince of Wales received an arrow wound in the face. However, displaying the courage that stood him so well as King at Agincourt, he refused to leave the field and slowly the Royal army began to gain the upper hand.

It was now that fortunes changed. During the heat of battle, 'Hotspur' raised his visor to wipe his brow and was struck immediately in the head by an arrow, a fatal wound which dropped him on the spot. As word of his death spread, Hotspur's men gave way and fled the field, with the King's soldiers in hot pursuit.

A major defiance of Henry's sovereign authority had been successfully countered. He had been spared to face both Scottish belligerence and the growing challenge of resurgent Welsh nationalism.

Although Hotspur's death had proved the catalyst for King Henry's victory, the outcome of the battle was a close-run thing. Contemporary account suggests that the Royal forces actually sustained far more casualties than did Hotspur's rebels. As was ever the case in medieval wars, perhaps more died from sepsis following the suppuration of arrow wounds, than were despatched outright on the battlefield. Interestingly, it is said that one of the King's knights, Sir Robert Gousill, was murdered and robbed by a trusted servant as he lay wounded on the field. Seen in the act by a wounded Esquire who later recovered, the servant was brought to justice and hanged.

Hotspur's body was recovered from where he fell and buried. However, with rumour spreading that 'Hotspur' had survived, the King ordered his exhumation and, to emphasise the point, had the remains quartered and each portion sent to the country's major cities to be exhibited. Later Hotspur's widow was allowed to gather the pieces together and inter them at York.

Hotspur's uncle, the Earl of Worcester, taken captive with Douglas, was hanged, drawn and quartered and his head displayed on a spike over London bridge, whilst Earl

Douglas, a major reason for Hotspur's rebellious activity, was back once more in captivity.

The CHRONICLE OF LONDON, departing from its usual cryptic dismissal of National events, devoted a number of lines to the battle and its outcome. This account, although set down some 50 years after the event, evidently draws upon contemporary comment and makes interesting reading, if only because it is specific about the fate of the unfortunate Harry Percy and his brother Thomas.

It is apparent that the latter was accused, perhaps with some justification, of being less than dedicated to the prevention of the conflict and, seemingly because of this, paid the ultimate price for the consequences of procrastination.

> *". . . This same yere (1403), on Maudelyn even, betwen Englysshemen and Engllysshemen was the sory batail of Schrovesbury, that is to seye betwen kyng Herry and Sr. Herry Percy sone of the erIe of Northumbeland; the whiche Sr. Henry Percy was there sclayn and there beryed and, on his syde the erIe Douglas of Scotland lost his on eye and Sr. Thomas Percy brother to the said Sr. Herry was there taken and kept too dayes after on lyve and, for he was embassator before the batall betwen the kyng and Sr. Herry Percy, manye a good man loste there hys lyf, wherfore they seyde Sr. Thomas was drawen, hanged and beheded, and his hede ['with a quarter of Sr. Herry Percie's hedde'. . ., vide another Manuscript] sett upon London brigge; also in the said bataille the prynce was schot in the heed wyth an arowe and, the erIe of Stafford sclayn undyr the kynges banere, and Sir William Graunsell, with manye othere knyghtes and squyers (gentilles, and good yomen) and forasmoche as som peple seyde that Sr. Herry Percy was alyve, he was taken up ayen out of his grave, and bounden upright between too mille stones, that alle men myghte se that he was ded. . . ."*

The short term political effect of Shrewsbury was to consolidate Henry IV's Royal position. However, during the 10 years before death settled his future, he had to successfully confront Owain Glyndwr, Owain's ally and son-in-law, Edmund Mortimer and the ubiquitous clan Douglas. History tells us that, largely through his son, he did; Glyndwr faded from the scene, his dream shattered.

It is worth contemplating for a moment the might-have-been had 'Hotspur' won and not been slain at Shrewsbury. If the English political power base had then moved to include Glyndwr, the country might with time have looked very different. A document: the 1406 'Tripartite Indenture,' reveals Glyndwr's aims.

The realms of England and Wales would be partitioned into three. Edmund Mortimer would take — presumably as King — the Thames Valley and the area to the South. The North, including much of the Midlands, would fall to the Earls of Northumberland, whilst Glyndwr, in furtherance of his aim for a strong and dominant Celtic West, would extend the boundaries of the Principality, recovering land within the Western English shires: from the Severn to Worcester and thence to Bridgnorth in Shropshire; north then to Kinver and on to the source of the River Trent; from there to the source of the Mersey, following that river to the sea.

It is strange to think that the sure aim of that unknown longbowman, whose bodkin-pointed battle-shaft sank deep into Hotspur's brain, may have secured the continued right of many of his fellow countrymen to be known as English. But, such is chance.

NOTES:
The substance of the preceding six battles follows Articles written by A.E.H. (Ted) Bradford which appeared within early copies of 'The Glade' archery magazine.
The writer was recently asked to instruct two young archaeologists in archery on the Shrewsbury battlefield site, and taught them the rudimentary skills of shooting in a long-bow on the very ground occupied by the Royalist bowmen, losing an arrow in so doing. It is a passing thought that this traditionally made wooden, 21st-Century shaft, shot in peace, will have joined the many thousands that must have fallen there on that fateful day half a millennium earlier!

The Forester. From an early Treatise on bow-hunting.
He must know how to shoot well in a bow. To train his scenting hound to follow a trail of blood. To stand properly by his tree. To remember the placements of the archers with him. To observe the wind, by which he should know the direction the beasts will take, and thus where he should place his archers.

To cut arrow shafts. To be handy with a crossbow. To make a bow-string if necessary, to cut up and skin a Hart. To direct his scenting hound well. To sound his horn in all the ways a Hunter needs.

THE BATTLE OF FLODDEN

THE BATTLE OF FLODDEN, which took place in Northumberland on September 9th, 1513 arose from circumstances which were complicated and had their origins in the quick-sands of Medieval European politics and intrigue.

James IV of Scotland, enthroned in 1488 whilst in his teens (following the unfortunate demise of his father, murdered after falling off his horse) had won the affection of his countrymen and had raised Scotland to a position of some eminence in Europe. In 1502 he had married Margaret Tudor, daughter of King Henry VII of England, thus forging a fragile and, it must be said, largely theoretical friendship between the two countries. Ten years later however, in 1512, he made a political decision which was to end this friendship and heap misfortune upon Scotland.

Many years previously the Scots and the French, who had both suffered at the hands of the English, had agreed a pact of mutual support in the event that England attacked either. In 1512, James had renewed this 'Auld Alliance' and, in so doing, sadly signed his own death warrant and that of much of his nobility.

In June, 1513, his brother-in-law, now Henry VIII of England, a young man anxious to demonstrate his martial clout, in company with Maximilian, the Holy Roman Emperor elect, invaded France to support the Holy League. In July, James asked Henry to call off his campaign. Henry refused and, James, as a man of honour, would not abandon his ally. The die was cast and war was inevitable.

THE ARMY OF KING JAMES

At the end of July, James began assembling an army on the outskirts of Edinburgh. It contained the flower of Scottish chivalry: 15 Earls, 20 Barons, many Bishops and hundreds of Knights, each with their own retinue. The exact number mustered is unknown but it is believed to be between 50,000 and 100,000, including the "sma' folk": local levies of doubtful advantage whose presence was motivated largely by self-interest. A French contingent under the Comte d'Aussi was also there to teach Scots the use of the 18-foot-long Continental pike. Artillery, a comparatively new arm was also present. James, like his brother-in-law Henry, was proud of his large cannons which left Edinburgh pulled by some 400 oxen.

On August 22nd this huge, slow-moving army, crossed the River Tweed at Coldstream and captured the English border strongholds of Norham, Wark, Etal and Ford.

The latter was occupied by the personable Lady Heron, whose husband had earlier been taken hostage by the Scots. What may or may not have been a scurrilous tale, has it that she allowed herself to be seduced by the lascivious James, in an attempt to regain her husband and, inter alia, delay the Scottish advance. Whether true or not, history records that James, once more fully booted and spurred, took his leave of her after enjoying her charms for a couple of days and, scarcely the act of an honourable man in receipt of female favours, burned down her castle around her ears

Henry VIII, fully aware of the Alliance, had astutely anticipated the Scottish move and, on his departure, had appointed Thomas Howard, Earl of Surrey, as Lieutenant General of the North, to guard both the Country and his young Queen.

"My Lord, I trust not the Scots, therefore I pray you, be not negligent" were his parting words. Accordingly, when news of the Scottish preparations reached Surrey, he sent out a call-to-arms throughout the north and, on August 1st, set up a recruiting Headquarters at Pontefract in Yorkshire.

Richard Assheton, of Middleton in Lancashire (whose likeness appears in Middleton Church), was in charge of the Military School at Middleton Hall, where the sons of Lancashire gentry received their military and equestrian training and where archers honed their skills. They were amongst the first to answer the call, making their way directly to Homby Castle, near Lancaster, the ancestral home of Sir Edward Stanley, Commander of the Lancashire and Cheshire contingent.

Middleton Hall was renowned as a school for archery. Even at this late period in its use, great emphasis was still placed upon constant practice of the English warbow and its battle-shaft. In the hands of a competent archer it was still a most devastating weapon in contemporary warfare and was again to prove its worth at Flodden

Constant archery practice took place at Middleton and there are place names in the vicinity of the Town which tell of this. Although now long gone, the spot is still pointed out between the 'Olde Boar's Head' Inn and Middleton Church, where butts were placed for practice, whilst in Archer Park the 'Middleton Archer' Public House now stands. There were Butts placed at nearby Stannycliffe Hall, home of the Knights Templars, in whose Crusades Middleton archers also took part.

A curious but unsubstantiated legend persists in the Middleton area, that the archers sent to greet the Scots were left-handed men and, this is perpetuated by the statue of a left-handed archer placed outside the local inn. The tale gains some slight credence from the fact that King Henry took the cream of his archer force to France, leaving the northern archers, with those unsuited to his needs, behind. It may be argued perhaps, that sinistrals were omitted in favour of right-handed (dextrous) men, but the perception rests to be proved.

PREPARATIONS FOR BATTLE

On September 3rd, Surrey arrived at Alnwick, in Northumberland, leading an army of some 26,000 men, strong in archers and billmen. Although he possessed more cannon than the Scots, they were of smaller calibre and their range was limited. A cavalry unit of 1,500 men, led by Lord Dacre, also arrived that day, as did Surrey's eldest son, the Lord Admiral Thomas Howard, who brought with him 1,000 armed sailors. Surrey's force thus consisted of a cross-section of northern society, with local

Lords, gentry, yeomen and peasants forming the backbone of his hastily summoned army.

Just how far Surrey went to recruit his force is borne out by a curious piece of poetry recorded in Newbury in Berkshire. If this is to believed, bowmen from this southern town were called upon to travel north to fight, with distinction, at Flodden.

The English had serious problems. Due to the extended communications and, perhaps, indifferent planning, food was short even at that early date. During the next few days supplies failed entirely and men were obliged to keep up their strength just by drinking water. Although morale remained high and Surrey had the loyalty of his men, many had not eaten solid food for four days when the battle commenced.

On September 4th, the English Commander sent a messenger to the Scottish King, offering to do battle on September 9th, on Millfield Plain, saying that he would:

"gyve the sayde Kynge batayle by Frydaye next at the furthestte"

On the following day Surrey marshalled his army in battle formation.

The English were to fight in two divisions, a vanguard under Admiral Thomas Howard and, a rearguard under Surrey himself. Each Division consisted of a large central body flanked by smaller wings. The right wing of the vanguard was given to Edmund Howard, the Admiral's younger brother, who had under him about 3,000 men, including a contingent of Stanley's archers from Macclesfield in Cheshire, led by Christopher Savage (subsequently killed, to a man, in the first Scottish assault). His left wing was under the veteran knight, Sir Marmaduke Constable. The main body of the rearguard was centred on the banners of the Earl of Surrey, on whose right was the Yorkshire company of Sir George Darcey.

Bringing up the rear was Stanley's contingent of Lancashire and Cheshire archers and billmen. Although many from his force had been taken to swell other units, Sir Edward Stanley retained all his Lancashire archers, amongst whom were the Middleton men.

On September 7th, Surrey was alarmed to see that James had occupied Flodden edge, a virtually unassailable position. Although he reminded James of his agreement to fight on level ground, the Scot refused to abandon his chosen spot. Surrey was too experienced a soldier to attempt a frontal attack and, after discussion with his field Commanders, they decided to march north-east, first crossing the River Till then, after several miles, turning due west and re-crossing the river to take up a position to the north of James and his army. This had the triple effect of cutting off supplies, preventing James from retreating into Scotland and, hopefully, tempting him off Flodden Edge. The following day the English marched out of Scottish view, to camp that night in Barmoor Wood.

The plan worked. James was worried by the English move. Suspicious of Surrey's intentions he ordered his army to move and take up position on Branxton Edge, another defensible position about one-and-a-half miles further north. Here he finally positioned his men. On the extreme left he placed the Earl of Home and his pike columns. To their right were the men of the Earls of Crawford, Errol and Montrose. In the centre were the King's Columns, with the Earls of Cassilis and Glencairn, whilst held in reserve were the formidable Highlanders of the Earls of Lennox and Argyll.

THE BATTLE.

At dawn on September 9th, the English, leaving their horses and what supplies were left and carrying only their weapons, moved out of Barmoor Wood. Thomas Howard, the Lord Admiral taking the vanguard, manoevred the cannons across the Till at Twizel Bridge. Surrey following with the main body, crossing by the ford at Castle Heaton, about a mile downstream.

It was shortly after mid-day when a breathless scout galloped into the Scottish camp and reported to James that the English, with trumpets sounding and banners flying, were bearing down on him from the north. In total disbelief, James mounted his horse and rode to see for himself. Having confirmed the sight he rapidly re-arranged his troops and stood ready and waiting.

FLODDEN'S FATAL FIELD
THE BATTLE OF FLODDEN, September, 1513

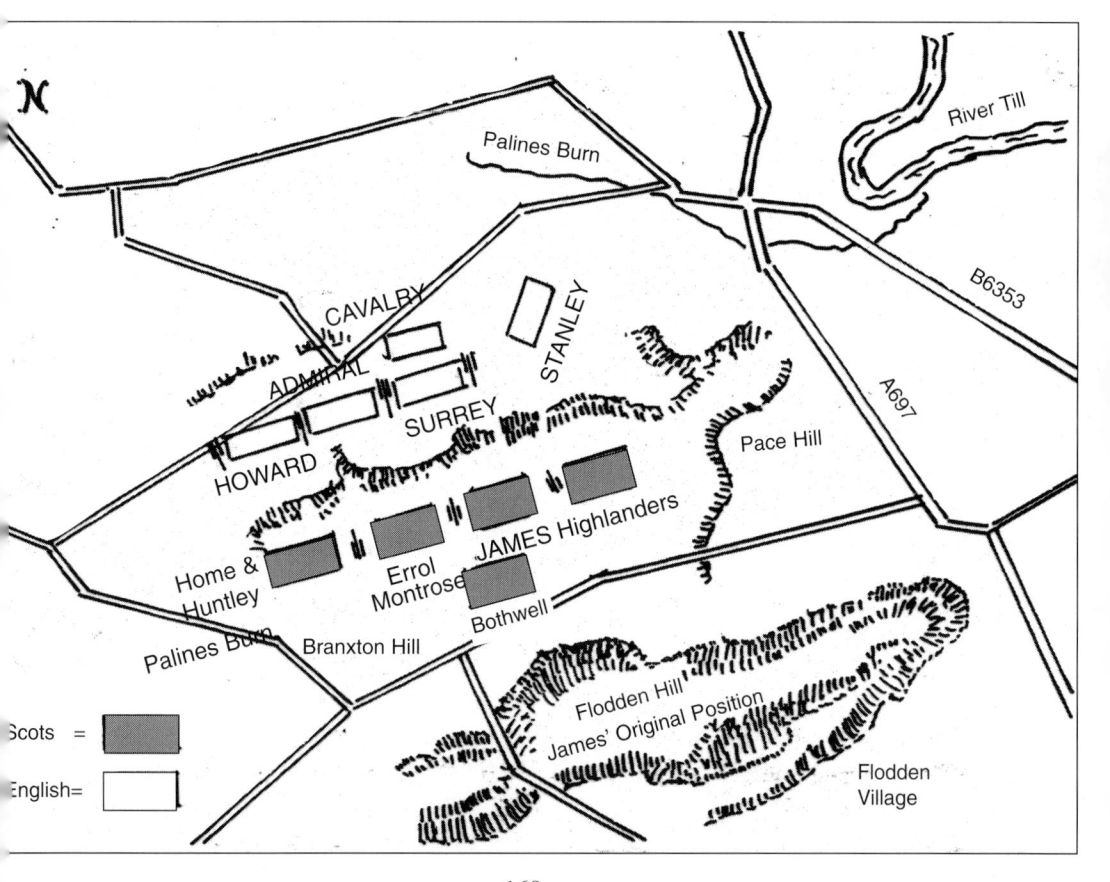

Meanwhile, the weather had broken, rain reducing visibility as the English marched southwards. When the advance scouts topped the Pallinsburn rise they were dismayed to see the entire Scottish army lined up in battle order less than 800 yards away.

After some re-marshalling the English formed up on Pallinsburn. The two armies were now face to face, separated by a small valley, the Scots on the higher ground. A deep silence fell. The time was a quarter past four.

A deafening roar from the Scottish cannons broke the silence, the missiles passing over the English as the barrels could not be depressed sufficiently. The English cannons responded, making large gaps in Home's Borderers on the skyline, who, with the Earl of Huntley's Highlanders, were the first to descend the hill.

The English right flank took the full impact, being driven back 200 yards. Men were trampled underfoot as the Scots, with their huge pikes slashed, maimed and mutilated. They continued to pour down the hill until the English, including the lightly-armed Lancashire archers, now outnumbered ten to one, turned and ran. Edmund Howard was unhorsed three times before managing to fight his way to the relative safety of his brother's Division. The situation was not finally restored until Surrey had ordered Dacre's cavalry into action, killing many Scottish noblemen and routing their pikemen. When the English right collapsed and Edmund Howard's men were seen to flee, King James dismounted and, seizing a pike, led his household to the front rank. Horrified, his Commanders begged him not to put himself in danger, but to no avail. His hasty action meant that the Scottish army was now effectively leaderless, with no-one in overall command but the English had little time to recover the situation before both central Scottish Divisions advanced.

The result was now finely balanced. However, nature now played her part; for between the two armies was a deep bog and a gulley, unseen from the Scottish position. These two natural obstacles slowed the Scottish advance. As the enemy emerged from the gulley the English archers loosed off an arrow storm, throwing the tightly packed columns into disorder. The initial momentum ceased and with the Scots now forced to fight at a standstill, the English billhooks chopped their long pike shafts into useless pieces.

The outnumbered English took no prisoners, being determined to *"be rid of all that came to hand,"* and the disordered columns of Errol, Crawford and Montrose were savagely repulsed with heavy losses, including all three Earls who were slain with their men.

King James' column, some 15,000 strong, now crashed into Surrey's Divison of 7,000 Yorkshiremen but they held their own, taking terrible toll of the Scottish nobles in the front rank. Lords Maxwell and Herries were amongst the first to fall. Help soon came from the Admiral's sailors and together, they set upon the Scots with renewed ferocity as bodies piled up in the hollow near the English position.

The fighting in the centre of the battlefield went on interrupted for at least two hours, when it gradually became clear that the Scots were losing the fight. Gathering together his household once again and all others that he could muster, James led them in a last furious charge towards Surrey's personal banners. Although his desperate onslaught broke through the English front ranks, his men fell in increasing numbers, until finally his Standard-bearer was cut down by his side. Single-handed the King fought his way to within 20 feet of Surrey before being beaten down and slain.

The battle had now reached a critical point, for the 5,000 Highlanders held in reserve under Lennox and Argyle were preparing to charge from Branxton Edge to join the fray. This intended move had been anticipated by Sir Edward Stanley however, who took the bold decision to climb the hill and attack the enemy from the rear. Silently leading his men up the almost vertical eastern slope, they arrived unnoticed by the Scots. Once positioned, deadly battle-shafts were swiftly notched and, at a signal from Stanley, the Lancashire bowmen, amongst them the Middleton archers, loosed off volley upon volley of arrows, taking terrible toll of the Highlanders.

Stanley then formed up his billmen and, as the Scots fled, they pursued them, hacking and slashing in all directions. The Earls of Argyle, Lennox and Caithness were killed, doing all they could to rally their troops.

Through his intrepid leadership, Stanley and his men had routed the Highlanders and thus virtually assured English victory; for if these men had not been defeated, their reinforcement of James' Household division would have turned the tide of battle.

Richard Assheton, mounted and armoured, was in the thick of the fighting around the King, taking prisoner Sir John Forman, Knight and Sergeant-porter to the Scottish King and Alexander Barrett, the High Sheriff of Aberdeen. On his return from the battle Richard Assheton dedicated his banner and armour to St. Leonard and placed them in the family Chapel.

Assheton was knighted for valour, and received privileges for his Manor.

And, what of the Scots? Their losses were appalling; 10,000 dead is now generally believed, against English losses of around 3,000 men, many of whom fell on the right flank. It is said that every family or town of note lost someone at Flodden. Typical was Selkirk. Three weeks before the battle, 70 men had marched out bravely to the cheers of the townspeople. Four days after the battle, one distressed youth, the sole survivor, staggered into the town square with the terrible news. Truly, Friday, September 9th, 1513, commemorated by the Scottish pipe lament 'The Flowers of the Forest' is regarded as the saddest day in Scottish history.

The Parish Church of St. Leonard, Middleton, on the outskirts of Manchester, records the valour of its archers in a stained glass window dating from the battle. The Flodden Memorial window, originally of three-light design, was installed in the north wall in 1515 as a thanksgiving for the victory and the safe return of the Middleton contingent; it shows the archers and their leader kneeling in prayer before the battle. The archers have shoulder-length hair and are wearing blue court-mantles. Each man carries a bow-stave with his name above it. Richard Assheton and his wife are wearing scarlet cloaks. Sadly, the window was neglected during the following centuries and allowed to fall into disrepair; although now reconstituted, much of the original glass was broken and missing. A link with our heroic past, it has a special meaning for longbowmen. It may be viewed by arrangement.

References consulted, and suggested further reading:

BATTLEFIELDS OF BRITAIN. David Smurthwaite. Guild Publishing. 1984.

MY WOUND IS DEEP. (A History of the Later Anglo-Scots Wars 1380-1560.) Raymond Campbell Paterson. John Donald Publishers Ltd. 1997. ISBN 0 85976 465 6.

THE REVOLT OF OWAIN GLYN DWR. R.R. Davies O.U.P. 1997. ISBN 0-19-285336-8.

OWEN GLENDOWER (OWAIN GLYNDWR). Sir J.E. Lloyd. 1931. Llanerch Publishers Reprint 1992. ISBN 0 947992 89 8.

CHRONICLE OF LONDON. Llanerch Publishers photo-reduced reprint, 1995 ISBN 1 86143 000

From the City of London Court of Aldermen.

1572. Sir Thomas Offley and Sir John White are appointed to go to my Lord Keeper for the delivery of the Certificates for archery and to inform his Lordship that it is very inconvenient and perilous to suffer apprentices within this City to go a-shooting according to Statute and therefore in their Certificate they have certified that they have taken Order for such as use shooting as conveniently can or may, and to understand how his Lordship hath liking of that word 'convenient,' and make report to this Court (of Aldermen).

Part 10

Against All Odds

The Battle of Crecy
The Battle of Poitiers
The Battle of Agincourt

ARMED WITH HIS CLOSE-QUARTER WEAPONS AN ARCHER SHOOTS TO GOOD EFFECT WHILE THE ENEMY IS STILL AT A DISTANCE

PART 10

AGAINST ALL ODDS

THE CAMPAIGN which culminated in confrontation at Crecy began in a thoroughly desultory way. In response to serious provocation by Philip VI of France — whose fleet had raided both Jersey and the English South coast — a small expedition, funded by Edward III and led by Sir Walter Maunay (Manny) landed on the Flemish island of Cadzand in November, 1337 and, by dint of well-organised archery, defeated a substantial French force.

This was followed in 1339 by Edward's determined attempt to bring Philip to battle. In accordance with contemporary chivalric custom, a formal challenge had been sent to the French King and had been accepted. Although Edward's well-paid but luke-warm allies were reluctant to stand up and be counted, there was sufficient resolve for Edward to be reasonably confident of victory — a view which seemingly Philip shared, since although the armies confronted each other in martial array at a pre-selected spot close to the village of Buironfosse, no battle took place.

The astrologer of King Robert of Sicily, ally to Philip, had consulted the stars and advanced the suggestive view that matters would not go the French King's way, a comment which carried some weight with his vacillating German allies and, after a pro-longed pause, the army mounted its horses and retired to Avesnes, 10 miles nearer home.

Vainly did Edward attempt to persuade Philip and his star-struck comrades that a challenge made — and moreover accepted — was a serious matter. His offer to fight at Avesnes met with no more success than at Buironfosse; although — or perhaps because — the disposition of Edward's troops was known to Philip and his erstwhile allies through the capture of an English scout; the German princes with their retinues were heading homeward. Having no-one with whom his army could do battle, the frustrated young Edward was obliged to do likewise.

The opening round 'of the 'Hundred Years' War' therefore ended almost in farce.

Following Edward's abortive attempt to engage Philip in combat during 1339, matters improved to some degree in 1340. The great sea-battle at Sluys had terminated, after much bloody hand-to-hand fighting, in victory for the King; he had endeavoured to consolidate this success on land, by laying siege to and taking the heavily fortified and strongly defended town of Tournai. Stubborn resistance, coupled with unenthusiastic allies, proved too great an obstacle however and the outcome was a barely satisfactory truce. The first set-piece battle of the 'Hundred Years' War' was not to take place until September 30th, 1342, when the Earl of Northampton contested Morlaix with Charles de Blois. (See Part 5.)

The early phases of the French campaign were dominated by the almost entrepreneurial adventures of many charismatic men, whose exploits are overdue for wider recognition. Outstanding amongst them: Robert d'Artois, a French knight owing allegiance to King Edward, who captured the city of Vannes by breath-taking subterfuge; Sir Walter Manny, of Auberoche fame and Sir Thomas Dagworth, whose tiny force of English longbowmen decimated a much larger French army at St Pol de Léon. It was men such as these who formed the bedrock of King Edward's successful campaigning.

THE BATTLE OF CRECY

AN EARLIER Chapter described Edward's increasingly desperate march to avoid entrapment by French King Philip VI and — with the help of Gobin Agache — a successful crossing of the River Somme at the ford of Blanchetaque.

Now safely across that major obstacle, Edward felt relief. Moreover, his army was united in its praise for him as leader for, as one man, they trusted him implicitly. Their faith in him was absolute. He would not let them be defeated. For Edward, a miracle had happened. As he settled his army for a well-earned rest that night in the forest of Crecy, north of the Somme, he must have felt that in the eyes of the Almighty his cause was just. So French Philip wanted a fight did he? Well, by the God of Battles and Saint George of England, he and his 'goddams' would see he had one.

The French army, disheartened by failure to catch Edward and pin him with his back to the river, bivouacked in the vicinity. The next day, August 25th, it doubled back and made for Abbeville, where it stayed the night.

With confrontation now inevitable, Edward led his men to the edge of Crecy Forest (some nine miles away) where he spent the day seeking a site suitable for battle. He halted on the banks of the little River Maye, close to a small village called Crecy-en-Ponthieu. There, on a small ridge and in consultation with his commanders, he prepared to take up a defensive position.*

Although Edward had selected his position on Crecy ridge and was prepared for a set-piece battle, he had no assurance that King Philip would wish to join him. Confronted in the recent past by ranks of English men-at-arms and archers in battle order, resolve had vanished as snow in summer and there was no guarantee that this would not happen again. Moreover, there had been chance enough for battle en route, had the French wished it.

The Vallee aux Clercs below Crecy ridge was some 2,000 yards in length and lay between the villages of Crecy-en-Ponthieu and Wadicourt. The rise of land varied between 100 feet and level ground.

At the highest point of the ridge, some 700 yards from Crecy village, stood the

---

* There is inevitable variation between authorities concerning numbers in the English army prior to the engagement and, learned discussion will continue. However, the King's confessor, Richard Wynkeley, was present and recorded an account in which he estimated numbers at 17,000. Lt.-Col. Alfred Burne in his 'Crecy War' approaches the matter from a different aspect, that of initial shipborne transportation. He takes the figure of 700 vessels (the lowest recorded) and excluding sailors, horses and war equipment, suggests an average of between 20 and 25 combatants to each, or a total of between 14,000 and 17,000 men.

Allowing for garrisoning and losses en route, Colonel Burne submits that a force of some 12,000 or 13,000 troops faced the French on that fateful August day.

AGAINST ALL ODDS — THE BATTLE OF CRECY

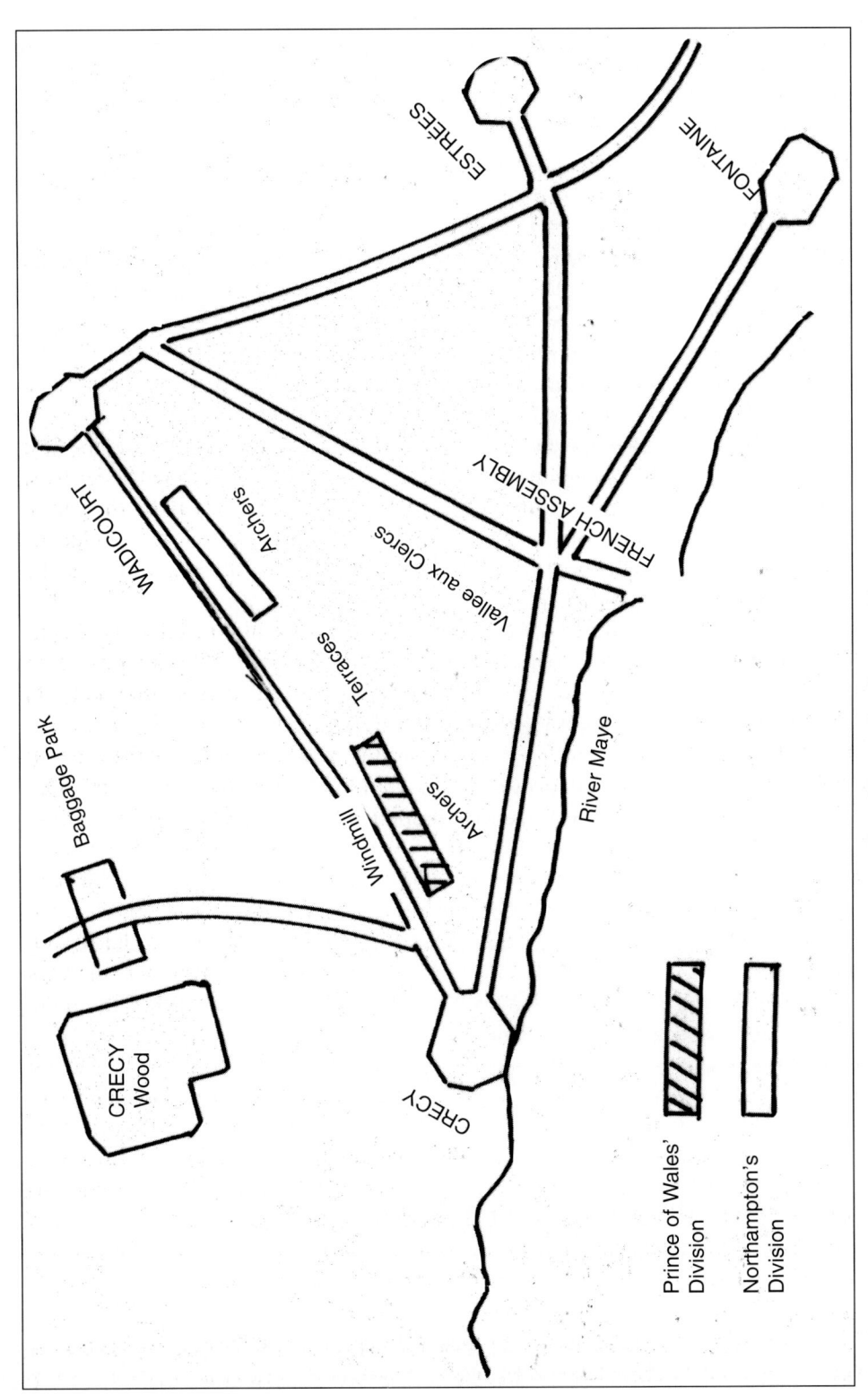

THE BATTLE OF CRECY, 1346

windmill that King Edward was to use as a vantage point during the battle. To its rear, a few hundred yards away, lay the Bois-de-Crecy, a small wood linked with the village.

The overall position was strong but had a potentially weak point on the left flank, where the ground was level with no river obstruction.

Edward gave leadership of the right flank to his young son — to be known later as the 'Black Prince' — with the Earls of Warwick and Oxford for guidance. His well-being was in the charge of the King's trusted friend, Godfrey de Harcourt. The weaker left was placed in the keeping of the experienced Earl of Northampton, whose brilliant defence at Morlaix had earned him Royal praise. The third division, that of the King, was held in reserve a little behind the others in the centre of the line.

The baggage train lay in a circle on the edge of Crecy wood, within its 'walls' the horses, for Edward's men-at-arms fought dismounted. The arrow wagons were uncovered and boys made ready to re-stock the front-line troops.

There has been much academic argument and military scholarship concerning the positioning of archers and it is of no purpose for this brief account to enter the lists. Suffice it to say that archers placed in wings on the flank of armies will, by the nature of their volleys, force attacking cavalry or infantry to bunch as they approach a line of men-at-arms. By bunching they become disorganised and disoriented; whilst in the case of cavalry, horses fall and bring others down around them.

As had been shown at Falkirk, Halidon Hill and Dupplin Muir, the effect is of confusion and to the significant advantage of waiting troops. It is thus reasonable to assume that Edward and his Field Commanders placed their archers substantially on the flanks. It seems likely also that pot-holes were dug to slow cavalry advance.

With positions finalised and no sign of Philip or his army, Edward gave the order to break for food, with instructions that at the sound of trumpets positions were to be resumed. Men relaxed, the August sun was strong and the day was warm if, a little sultry, with storm clouds building. Rain threatened and a short shower came to dampen the grass. Whether archers unstrung their bows — as is legend — or indeed whether at this point their bows were actually strung, is conjectural. As an archer, the writer is ambivalent about the matter but feels it unlikely that bows would be left strung with no reason. Why, or indeed whether, strings were kept under caps is another matter of some mystery to practising longbow archers. But, we will leave the stories as they are.

It was now four o'clock. Vespers had been said and the sun was slowly sinking before the French army made its tardy appearance. Firstly the household troops and, with them, Genoese mercenaries — some 6,000 crossbowmen under their leader Ottone Dorian. Following them were the Allies, notably blind King John of Bohemia, John of Hainault (brother-in-law of Edward) and other foreign dignitaries, each with their personal contingent. A total of many thousands.

Lastly, and providing by far the largest contingent, came the local 'levee en masse,' armed with whatever came to hand but virtually unorganised and tactically uncontrollable.

Although vastly out-numbered, the English watched with increasing confidence as disordered manoeverings dissolved into virtual chaos. Although French Commanders had recommended and Philip had agreed, that there be a period of consolidation before battle was offered, this was not to the liking of the French men-at-arms. They pushed ahead and with them the 6,000 mercenary Genoese crossbowmen who formed the forward line. These brave unlucky men were without their protective shields and, being eventually established in some sort of order just 150 yards from the English line, they prepared to do their duty.

But 150 yards is point-blank range for an English war-bow and, before they could load their weapons, volley upon volley of iron-tipped battle-shafts drove into them, whilst the roar and whistle of iron and stone cannonball from Edward's gunners startled the horses of the assembling cavalry.

The effect was panic. In their struggle to get away from this deadly fire, the retreating crossbowmen impeded the French advance and were cut down by the men-at-arms. They retaliated and a miniature battle developed amidst the French front line as the Genoese defended themselves.

Having ridden down and cleared this self-inflicted obstacle, the Count d'Alençon, with a corps of the elite knights of France, rode at the English right flank and engaged the Prince of Wales' Division in hand-to-hand fighting. With the rest of the French line in semblance of order (although the arrow-storm continued its dreadful toll) men got through and, charge after charge now assaulted both flanks. Fighting was exceptionally fierce on the right flank and Godfrey d'Harcourt, concerned for the safety of the young Prince, ran to Northampton's Division to ask for aid, simultaneously despatching a messenger to Edward to ask for the reserve Division to be brought into play.

Although it is seemingly on record that he despatched 20 men-at-arms to help out and that these, with Northampton's counter-attack, turned matters in the Prince's favour. Famously, the King refused fuller support, allegedly replying: *"Let the boy win his spurs."*

Edward had every reason to be proud of his young son, since according to his own testimony, no fewer than 1,500 French men-at-arms lay dead or dying in front of his Division.

As night fell, it became clear that Edward had the victory against enormous numerical odds. However, matters were not yet over; for the following day saw a powerful force of French levies from Rouen and Beauvais heading swiftly towards the battlefield. Encountering English troops under Northampton and Warwick — whom initially they took to be friendly — they were engaged and slaughtered by the archers, before the remnants were chased off by mounted men-at-arms.

Whilst the record of the battle is largely from English sources, there are odd references from French accounts which add a little more to the story. Preliminary to the opening of the battle, four experienced French knights approached the English lines without being seen *"less than an arrow's flight away"* and reported their disposition to Philip who, having seen the chaos of his own army, directed that battle should not be joined until next day. This order either did not reach the ranks, or if it did, was not obeyed and the charge of his over-enthusiastic knights provided a momentum that it proved impossible to stop.

Although each account confirms a storm, there is some doubt as to when it occurred. The English have it well before the battle proper; the French, just as the engagement began, making the rising ground slippery and muddy.

The threat to the Prince, so evident as the battle progressed and which almost achieved its objective, resulted from an abortive French charge led by Jacques d'Estracelles. One knight who did make it through the English lines and, beyond, was Thierry de Sancelles, mounted upon a splendid black horse given him that morning and bearing the Standard of his master, Jean de Hainault. As Froissart remarks: *"Not considering himself talented enough to return"* he set off quite alone, leaving the noise of battle well behind, eventually to reach Cambrai with banner intact.

King Philip, searching vainly for a scapegoat, picked rather obviously upon Godemars du Fay, erstwhile defender of the Blanchtaque ford and directed that he be hanged. Godemars, who had sensibly kept out of the way, was allegedly disposed to respond that whilst undoubtedly he had lost the ford, Philip had lost France Whether this logic swayed the King or not, matters quietened down and Godemar's life was spared.

A final and most curious comment from French sources concerns the Order of the Garter, founded by Edward shortly after the battle. It is said that *"this was created to reward those of his officers who had served him best at Crecy,"* going on to add that 'Garter' was the Welsh word used on the day of the battle for rallying. Whilst it is reasonable to assume that the Welshmen present had a rallying cry drawn from their own language (beyond noting that 'garter' is not a Welsh word — although 'gartref' [home] is) there seems no credence for this most interesting suggestion.

In the matter of the Order itself however, although commonly believed to have originated from an incident at Court involving a lady's embarassment, an authoritative source has it commemorating an incident in battle (perhaps Crecy) when Edward had given his own garter as a rallying emblem. But there we will leave this stuff of legend.

THE BATTLE OF POITIERS, 1356

THE CAMPAIGN which culminated in the battle outside the town of Poitiers, was in essence complex and, to some extent, dis-ordered in its conclusion. As originally conceived there were to be three separate operations, loosely associated (synchronised would be too precise a description) but independent of each other.

That with which we are concerned was led by Edward (the Black Prince), and began on July 6th, 1356, when elements of his Anglo-Gascon army set out from Bordeaux for assembly at Bergerac, on what was described by Edward as a chevauchée. The word is difficult of definition but, to the Prince, it's meaning was clear. He would carry fire and sword into the heart of enemy country, meet and defeat his armies in battle and, if all went well, link up with either the King or Henry, Duke of Lancaster, leaders of the other two operations.

Edward's 6,000-man army was strong in archery. Six hundred bowmen, 500 from Cheshire led by Sir Richard Stafford, provided an experienced core, although arrows for these elite troops had proved something of an initial problem. Because the King had requisitioned all the country's available stocks for his own uses, in order to obtain the necessary number the Prince had been obliged to offer the fletchers of Cheshire, who were required to work overtime, *"such sums as will encourage them in their work."*

The army duly assembled on August 4th, and the chevauchée was under way.

Marching some 10 miles a day and, systematically devastating the countryside, the Prince reached the fortress of Romorantin on the 29th of the month. Here the main castle was taken after a brisk engagement whilst, to persuade the remaining garrison to leave, the Keep was set on fire.

With Romorantin successfully subdued, the army moved on, reaching Amboise by September 7th. Here the prince stopped, hoping perhaps to meet the King on the Northern bank of the River Loire. This proved impracticable however, since bridges were well defended and the river was in flood.

In something of a quandary as to his next move, the Prince held a Council with his commanders. The city of Tours, on the river bank, was a prize well worth considering containing as it did, the Duke of Normandy, Comte de Poitier but, its defences were strong. Edward had no siege train and success was therefore questionable. There was no sign of either the King or Henry of Lancaster and there were indications that the French army was in the offing. Moreover he had collected a great deal of treasure en route and had no great wish to lose it.

His mind finally made up, the Prince now moved South and, by September 11th was at Montbazan. In the meantime, messengers from cousin Henry had arrived to report that he was held up on the wrong side of the Loire and could get no further.

Edward was now effectively on his own and again with choice of action. There was

AGAINST ALL ODDS — THE BATTLE OF POITIERS

ON THE MARCH

THE ENGLISH ARMY GETS READY FOR A CHEVAUCHEE

a chance to move speedily back towards Bordeaux, ahead of French King John II, or he could stay and fight. Although the decision may have been forced upon him by subsequent circumstances, there is some evidence that he consciously chose the latter and, by September 18th the die had been cast. The French were in martial array across the road ahead and engagement was inevitable.

In accord with custom of the time, intercession for peace had been made by French cardinals and a brief truce had been reluctantly agreed by Edward, during which the enemy had consolidated some stragglers and tidied up their Divisions. Here there is a divergence of account. Whilst English sources are clear that the army was martialled in defensive position and that battle was both anticipated and sought; if the French are to be believed (although this would seem out of character), the Prince offered terms amounting to virtual surrender to be allowed to leave.

The concessions were seemingly rejected by the French as not going far enough however. A suggestion that the affair be settled by a contest between 100 of the best knights on each side having been dismissed as chivalric whimsy, formalities were concluded.

At some point, Edward is said to have gathered his archers together and to have encouraged them with a martial oration.

The gist of this (or rather a translation from the French, for it was set down by Geoffrey le Baker) follows:

> *"Your manhood hath been alwaies known to me, in great dangers, which sheweth that you are not degenerate from true sonnes of English men, but to be descended from the blood of them which heretofore were under my father's dukedom and his predecessors, kings of England, unto whom no labour was paineful, no place invincible, no ground unpassable, no hill (were it never so high) inaccessible, no towere unscaleable, no army impenetrable, no armed souldier or whole host of men was formidable.*
>
> *"Your lively couragiousness tamed the Frenchmen, the Ciprians, the Syracusians, the Calabrians, and the Palestines, and brought under the stiff-necked Scots and unruly Irishmen, yea, and the Welchmen also, which could endure all labor.*
>
> *"Occasion, time, and dangers maketh of ffearful men very strong and stoute, and doth many times of dull witted men make wittie: honour also, and love of the countrey, and the desire of the riche spoyle of the Frenchmen doth stirre you up to follow your father's steps.*
>
> *"Wherefore follow your antients* (banners) *and wholly be intentive to follow the commandement of your captaines, as well in minde as in bodye, that if victorie come with life, we may still continue in firme friendship together, having always one will and one minde.*
>
> *"But if envious Fortune* (which God forbid) *should let us at this present, to runne the race of all flesh and that we ende bothe life and labour together, be you sure that your names shall not want for eternall life and heavenly joy, and we also with these gentlemen, our companions,* (the men-at-arms) *will drink of the same cuppe as you*

shall doe, unto whom it shall be an eternal Glory and name to have wonne the nobilltie of France: but to be overcome (as God forbid) is not to be ascribed unto the danger of time but to the courage of men."

Having delivered this stimulating oration, the immediate area was scanned for suitable cover; this was found in the form of a long and thick hedge, extending from the ridge on which they stood to the marshy ground below.

Although the French claimed the English to be in retreat and that battle was joined on French terms, again there is divergence of opinion. English booty wagons with their guard of archers were on their way it is true and, if one may excuse pedantry, tactical withdrawal may well have been on the Prince's mind. Certainly Warwick, with the vanguard, was away from what was to be the main battlefield at the lower end of the hedge and here was attacked by Marshal Audrehem, one of the French King's two field Marshals.

This proved a seriously unwise move. A frontal charge was picked off by Warwick's flank archers, stationed on marshy ground and immune from attack but the charge petered out in disarray. Simultaneously, the English rearguard was attacked by Marshal Clermont. This move fared even worse than that of Audrehem since Salisbury's archers, positioned by gaps in the hedge, brought down French horsemen at point-blank range. Clermont himself was killed and the ragged remnants of his force retired in confusion.

With his opposition neutralised, Warwick now joined the Prince and together their combined force stood ready to take the brunt of the main French charge. Two thousand men-at-arms, led by the Dauphin, thundered towards the English lines, only to be broken up by the hedge, its associated ditch and other natural and man-made obstacles. Unable to breach the English line, the French retired in small groups towards the remaining Division, with numbers much depleted and without either their leader (for the Dauphin had been spirited away for safety) or his standard bearer, who had been rendered hors de combat.

At this point then, matters were broadly in balance. Although fighting defensively and, at this point, probably still outnumbered, Edward was in control of matters. The archers of the rearguard had performed well, holding their hedge positions against considerable odds, whilst those in the vanguard had proved vital in the break up of Marshal Audrehem's cavalry advance.

But now the French were assembling under King John and a further attack was imminent. There had been a lull in the fighting however, allowing the English to rest and re-group. Horses had been brought up and were made ready for battle and archers had retrieved and otherwise replenished their arrow stocks.

It was then that the Prince and his commanders decided upon a bold, even a foolhardy move, had it failed. Faced with advancing French men-at-arms, they would not continue standing in defence but would take the initiative by cavalry charge: a tactical decision almost unique in contemporary English warfare. Combined with this, a force of 60 knights and 100 archers, led by the Captal de Buch, would make their way to the rear of the French — when in position raising the Standard of St. George.

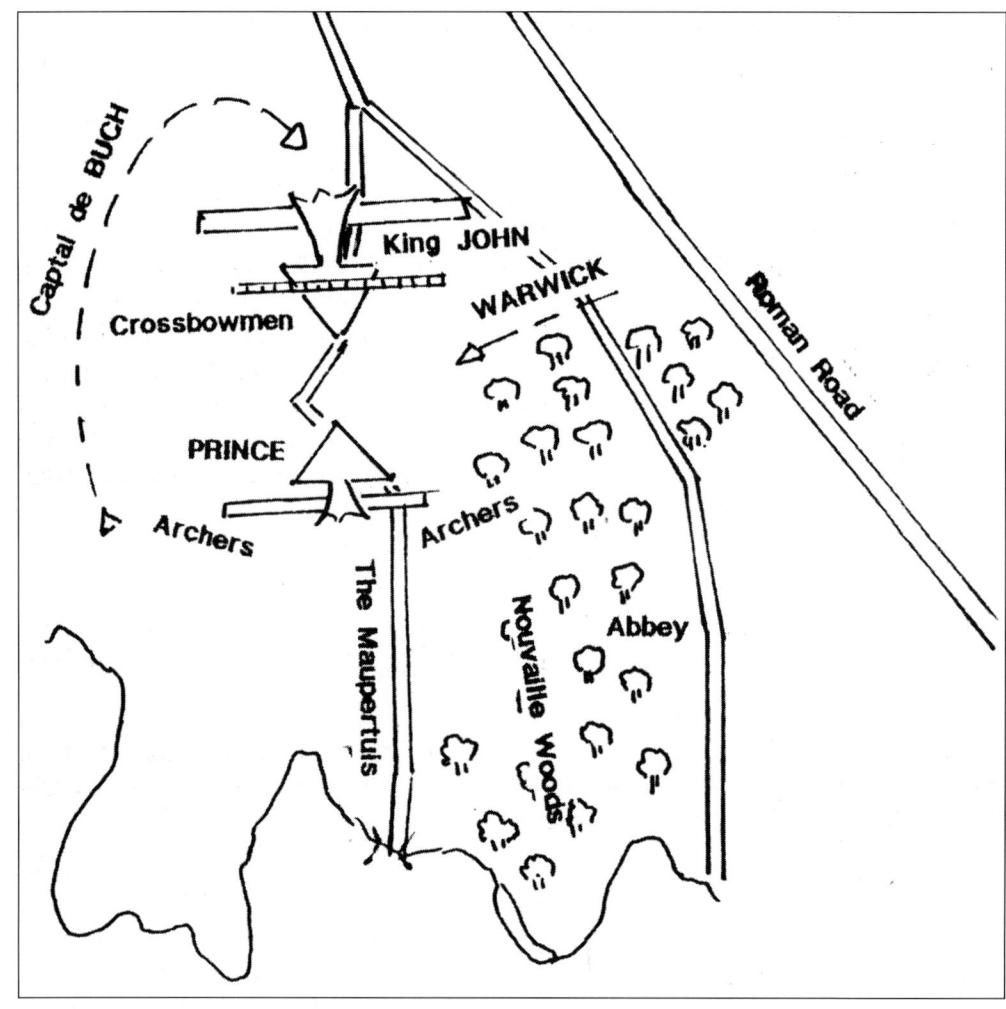

MAP OF THE BATTLE OF POITIERS, 1356
(Final Phase)

With the encircling move complete and the banner duly unfurled, English trumpets sounded and the cavalry charge was on. Led by Sir James Audley, who was unhorsed and seriously wounded in the subsequent melée, it engaged the French line of battle and after a fierce fight, in which the archers played their usual part, drove the French downhill towards the river. Here, in a water meadow during the late afternoon, matters were concluded. King John's brave bodyguard made their last stand; Geoffrey de Charny, bearer of the Oriflamme was killed and the Oriflamme — symbol of French aggression — was taken. King John was captured along with many of his nobles and the Battle of Poitiers was over.

In what was a thoroughly civilised feature of the time, whilst lesser mortals mopped up the opposition, it was proper for the victor to entertain the vanquished to a hearty meal and, Prince Edward did not depart from tradition. The dust having settled he, with

King John and other captured nobles, sat down to a sumptuous repast, provided largely from the French King's cuisine. However, between courses, news was brought that Sir James Audley had been discovered in a less than marketable state and the Prince excused himself to personally tend his fallen colleague. Happily Audley did in fact recover, to serve him and his King for many more years.

The Battle of Poitiers was not one that had been sought by Prince Edward. He was quite seriously outnumbered — accounts vary as they always do, but a conservative figure suggests a total of some 6,000 fighting men, including 2,000 archers. The French army, or armies (since its Divisions fought independently of each other) has been estimated at 20,000 including — inter alia by one account — a significant leavening of crossbowmen. Edward would have preferred to have slipped quietly away with his booty. He was no coward however and had implicit faith in the fighting qualities of his troops, both men-at-arms and archers. He knew that if he failed, it would not be through lack of valour. If he had to fight, then by God and Saint George he would show what Englishmen with backs to the wall could do and, this he did.

The CHRONICLE OF LONDON, succint as ever recorded that.:

"In this yere, that is to say the yere of oure Lord mccclvi, the xix daye of Septembre, kyng Jolin of Fraunce was taken at the bataill of peyters be the doughty prynce Edward the firste sone of kyng Edward, also Sire Philip his sone was taken with hym; and the Dolphin (Dauphin) *fledde"*

With the capture of King John, matters quietened for a while. Relations between England and France were formalised in 1360 by the Treaty of Bretigny. This was duly summarised by the London Chronicler:

"In this yere the pees (peace) was made between the kyng Edward, and kyng John of Fraunce, the xv of May... whiche othe (oath) was plight undir this forme: Charles [Regent of France in king John's enforced absence] dede lete solempnely a masse to be songen (solemnly ordered a Mass to be sung) and when Agnus Dei was thries (three times) seyd, Charles leyd his right hand upon the patene (the dish containing the Eucharist) wherupon lay Goddes body, and his lefte hond pressying don upon the masse bok, seyenge. "We swern (swear) upon the holy precious Goddes body, and upon the Evaunglies (Evangelists), fermely to holden anente (between) us pees and concord betwen the too kynges of Fraunce and Engelond, and in no manere to do the contrerie."

Treaties have a habit of sliding into obscurity however earnest the parties to them might initially be and, whilst all was well for a time, inevitably relations between the two countries deteriorated. Edward III died in 1377 and was replaced by Richard II until his deposition in 1399 by Henry IV. Henry was succeeded in 1413 by Henry V and the stage was once more set for confrontation.

King Henry V was conscious of his rightful title to Normandy, a claim vigorously disputed by French royalty and, his 1415 campaign, culminating at the field of Agincourt, was in furtherance of that aim.

THE BATTLE OF AGINCOURT, 1415

IT WOULD be difficult when presenting a popular account of this momentous engagement to write anything new, for the Battle has been analysed and re-enacted in various media forms almost ad nauseam. Indeed there can scarcely be an English archer, knowledgeable in the history of the country who, at the drop of a hat, cannot summarise what happened on that fateful St. Crispin's Day.

It follows that if this narrative is not to fall flatter than an unhorsed knight, then the approach must be different.

Since a number of cohesive accounts come to us from French sources and, these are not necessarily as familiar as those from Britain, we will begin by looking at certain well publicised events as they are said by French chroniclers to have happened.

The first is brief, of uncertain accuracy, but revealing in certain respects:

"... *the king of England landed in France with 4,000 men-at-arms and over 4,000 infantry armed with hauberks, great jacks, and axes, and 30,000 archers with axes, swords, and daggers. After capturing Harfleur, he decided to march overland to Calais. As he approached Rouen, an order had been given to prepare for battle against him, but nothing came of this because the Duke of Burgundy remained at Amiens and would not join.*

"*But, on Sunday 19th October a* (French) *herald informed king Henry that his king would meet him in battle on Saturday 26th. King Henry was joyful at the news and gave the herald 200 ecu's and a new robe. The French and the English were now very close to each other, and on Thursday 24th October, at the request of the English, fighting on the 25th was discussed because they had been short of victuals now for three days. The request was made that they should either be given battle or victuals and be allowed to pass unheeded.*

"*Now, this was the French strength. In their first Battle were 5,000 knights and esquires, and in the second there were 3,000, not counting the gros valets, the archers and the crossbowmen.*

"*When the English learned of this they chose a fine position between two areas of woodland. In front of these, but a little way off was another wood where they placed a large ambush of archers, and in one of the woodland areas on their flauk they put a large ambush of their mounted men-at-arms.*

"*On the 25th October our men advanced towards the English but on their way found the ground very soft. And when they sought to find 400 horsemen who had been ordered to breach the English battle-line they could only find 40.*

"*When attack time came, our archers and crossbowmen fired* (sic) *neither arrow nor bolt. Our men had their sun in their eyes so in order to better withstand and to*

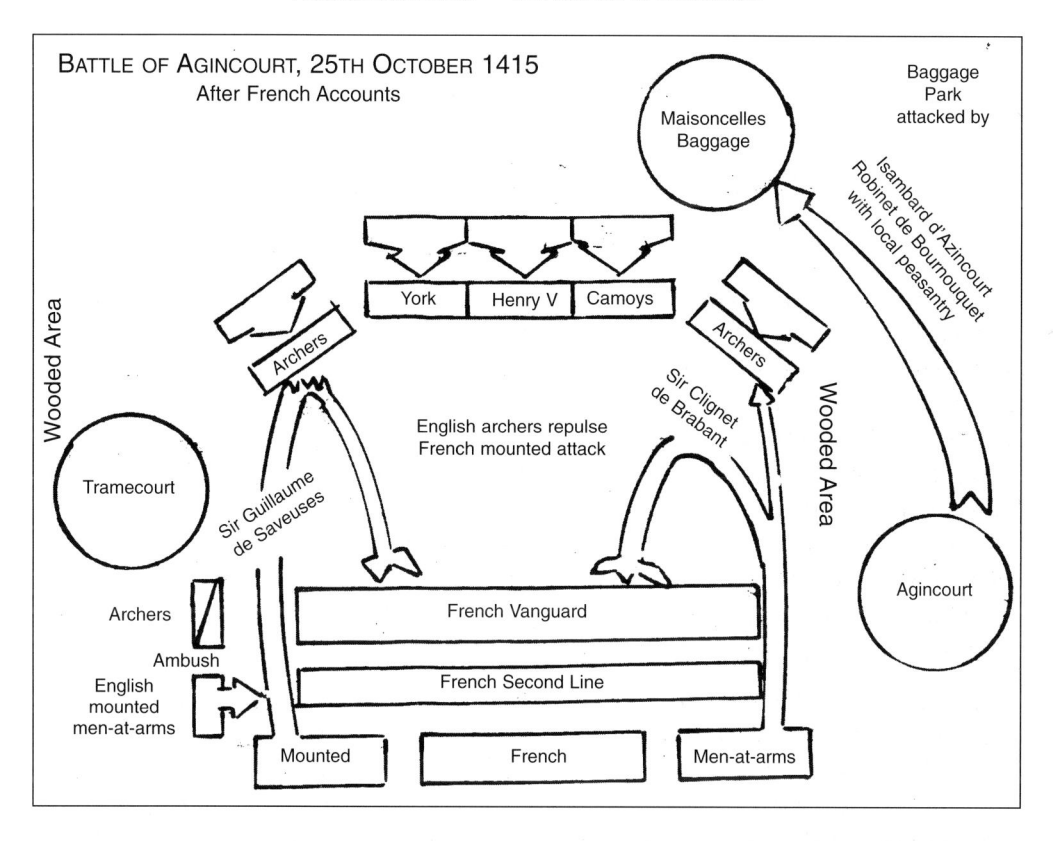

Battle of Agincourt, 25th October 1415
After French Accounts

- Maisoncelles Baggage
- Baggage Park attacked by Isambard d'Azincourt, Robinet de Bournouquet with local peasantry
- York, Henry V, Camoys
- Archers
- Sir Clignet de Brabant
- Wooded Area
- Tramecourt
- Sir Guillaume de Saveuses
- English archers repulse French mounted attack
- Wooded Area
- Agincourt
- Archers, Ambush, English mounted men-at-arms
- French Vanguard
- French Second Line
- Mounted French Men-at-arms

reply to the English fire they lowered their heads. When the English saw them in this position they advanced upon them so that our men knew nothing until they were hit with axes. And the archers who were behind the ambush party assaulted them with arrow fire (sic) *from behind.*

"Furthermore, the mounted men whom the English had put into the wood sallied out and came from the rear on to the second Battle who were close behind the first, - just two lance lengths away. the English horsemen made so great a cry that they scared all our men, - so much so that the second Battle took flight. And all that were in the first Battle were taken and killed."

This French account is to a large extent supported by others, although with significant variation in numbers. Thus, an overall figure of 38,000 said to have landed (of whom 30,000 are named as archers) becomes 22,000, of whom a maximum of 18,000 carry the bow.

Mention is also made of the small contingent of armed troops who, setting out from Calais to link with Henry's force, were confronted by *"men of Picardy"* and obliged to return.

Although mustering an overwhelming superiority of numbers, the danger of giving battle to an English army, particularly one containing a large number of archers, was debated at some length in Council before a decision was made to engage Henry V. Opposing views were advanced: 'doves' present thought that Henry should be allowed to pass unhindered because the outcome of battle was uncertain; whilst 'hawks' felt that they were powerful enough to defeat the English, advancing the reason that their armour was in bad condition and that the archers were poorly dressed.

Both options being considered, the 'hawks' gained consensus and it was agreed that there should be a cavalry charge to disrupt the archers.

As the defender, Henry had the advantage of choosing the site of course and, he chose wisely. The ground, so this French account continues, had been softened by rain and, when battle began, the heavily armoured men-at-arms could scarcely move their legs they sank so deeply into the mud.

The charge of the Lords on horseback came to nothing, since the archers aimed at the horses, which could not be controlled and turned in retreat, taking their riders with them. It is interesting that the dismounted French men-at-arms are reported as largely unhurt by the arrow volleys, since they were well protected, although they were out of breath on arrival at the English line.

The Duke of Alençon is singled out for particular praise, *"doing wonders that day."* In fact he worked his way sufficiently close to King Henry to hit him on the head with a battle-axe, before himself being despatched by an overly enthusiastic bodyguard whilst trying to surrender. Finally, there is adequate recognition of the part played by the archers who *"knocked down the French completely."*

Turning now to a summary of events recorded by three Frenchmen, two of whom were actually present. Enguerran Monstrelet, whose Chronicle dates from 1447 and with him, Jean Waurin and Jean le Fevre, present at the battle: Waurin with the French and le Fevre with the English army.

Vide this account, King Henry garrisoned Harfleur with 500 men-at-arms and between 1,000 and 1,500 archers. According to Monstrelet, the bulk of the army was then sent back to England, although according to le Fevre and Waurin, only the sick were returned. Henry then struck out for Calais with around 2,000 men-at-arms and between 13,000 and 14,000 archers and other men; a total of some 16,000. These figures are markedly different to a responsible English account which has just 900 men-at-arms and 5,000 archers.

Of the various adventures en route to Calais, a distraction at the town of Eu attracted particular notice. A head-strong local notable, one Lancelot Pierre, engaged an English man-at-arms in single combat. He was struck with a lance and paunched but, as he lay dying, he thrust a knife into his opponent and killed him on the spot.

The report of proceedings at Blanchetaque is revealing and offers an important variation from the usually accepted version, which suggests that because Marshal Bouciccaut was on the other side commanding a substantial French field army, Henry chose to move on rather than invite potential disaster.

By this account, whilst scouting in the area of the ford, a gentleman servant of Charles d'Albret, Constable of France, was captured and brought in for questioning. It was he who revealed Marshal Bouciccaut's apparent presence and, being believed, caused the change in Henry's plan. In fact, say both Waurin and le Fevre, the ford was virtually unguarded and Henry could have passed safely. Had this happened, then

Henry would have reached Calais without obstruction and there might have been no battle.

If the account is accurate, then the reason for this prevarication is unclear. If d'Albret was a 'hawk' however, the change in Henry's plan virtually assured confrontation and, this may have been the motive. A third account has it that whilst only lightly guarded, the ford had been staked and was in consequence impassable; whilst a painting in the Bibliotheque Nationale shows mounted English archers being repelled by French forces there. It is all very odd.

Blanchetaque or no, the Somme had to be crossed and arrangements were made for this at St. Quentin. The troops dismounted and, by dribs and drabs, passed across an existing but broken bridge. Once over, the army reformed into a cohesive whole and made ready to move off. However, Heralds sent by the Dukes of Orleans and Bourbon now approached Henry and offered him combat if he would appoint a place and a day. The King chose not to respond, other than to remark that he and his army would meet force with force wherever and whenever there was need. In fact a day was apparently agreed and, with confrontation arranged for Saturday, October 26th, preparations were put in hand.

Accounts vary at this point but the King is said to have advanced matters to Friday 25th because his men were short of food and this was seemingly accepted as a reasonable thing to do. The well-known incident involving the King and his lodgings is confirmed; Henry was wearing his coat-armour when he inadvertently rode past billets prepared for him. Asked to return, he replied stiffly that since he was in warlike array he would not retreat and stayed where he was. Accordingly, with (one suspects) some veiled mutterings from his personal staff and, probably from the vanguard also, those already ensconced upped-stakes and moved on and Henry settled in for the night.

Troops now made ready for the fight to come. Men-at-arms prepared their aigulets and archers renewed their bowstrings[1]. The night of the 24th did not pass without incident however — if the French accounts are to be believed! Provocation was provided by the Duke of Orleans who sent the Count of Richemont, with 2,000 men-at-arms and archers, to raid the English camp. The latter were ready however and English and French archers were briefly busy. The rest of the night passed without event.

Morning dawned and Henry, in full armour and mounted on a small grey horse, inspected his men drawn up in order of battle amidst a field of young corn. (Young corn? October?) He detailed, so it is said, just one man-at-arms, with 10 lances and 20 archers, to guard the baggage and arranged his fighting men in one Division of between 900 and 1,000 men-at-arms, flanked by archers. Waurin here particularly mentions Henry's warning to his archers that if caught they would lose the three fingers of their right hand. Other accounts suggest two — in accord with the contemporary two-fingered draw and release — but the point is academic.

---

[1] A wise precaution emanating pehaps from Erpingham, but one wonders whether this was a commonplace instruction at the time. Bowstrings were notoriously prone to breakage during the Agincourt campaign; the formation of the Ancient Society of Longbow stringmakers on August 2, 1416 arose directly from this circumstance.

Against All Odds — The Battle of Agincourt

Preparing for the Arrow Storm at Agincourt, 1415

Monstrelet expressly mentions 200 archers sent to a meadow near Tramecourt, close to the rear lines of the French. Whether this force actually existed seems questionable but the French certainly thought it did.

With everyone now ready, the stage was set for action. But not without the customary dialogue between each side. The French offered Henry safe passage if he would give up title to the Crown and return Harfleur. He might then keep Guienne and his Picardy territories. Henry replied briskly that he could be interested only if, in addition to Guienne, he had five other named cities, the King's daughter Catherine and jewels to the value of 500,000 francs.

Predictably these terms were not accepted and the day's business began. On the English side the veteran Sir Thomas Erpingham addressed the archers, exhorting them to fight with vigour against the French. He then threw his baton into the air and shouted *"nestroque."*[2] This signalled a general move forward and, when in their final positions, Henry and his men awaited the arrival of the French.

The pre-arranged plan to break up the flank archers was now put into practice. However, of the 800 selected for the purpose, when the time came just 120 were ready and willing to accompany Sir Clignet de Brabant on the Tramecourt flank and they were quckly routed. Matters were little better on the Agincourt side as, led by the brave Sir Guillaume de Saveuses, 300 lances rode against the flank bowmen. Galloping ahead, Sir Guillaume engaged the forward archers single-handed but, losing his horse against the stakes, was shot and killed almost at once. Rather than face the arrow storm then landing amongst them, his companions reined in smartly and turned for the French lines, crashing into the advancing dismounted men-at-arms with disastrous consequences as they did.

With the cavalry in chaos, the French forward battle line broken and the rear Divisions seriously disrupted, the archers emerged from behind their stakes and, throwing down their bows, drew swords, mallets, axes and falchions, laying into the enemy with vigour and determination, concentrating on killing or taking prisoners where ransom might be got.

However, although events were going Henry's way, matters were far from over yet. Two things happened in quick succession. The small baggage party had been attacked and overwhelmed by a strong force of peasantry led by two local men-at-arms[3], and — of greater potential consequence — a large number of French, with Bretons, Gascons,

---

[2] Although no-one really knows what this meant, it has been taken by many to mean 'now strike' in Midland dialect, or alternatively, and less likely 'knee stretch.' There is a third possibility however to which, having carefully considered it, the writer subscribes. '(Me)nee stroke.' 'Menee' alt.: 'Menie' (assembly). 'Menee' was an important hunting call or 'stroke' and would be well known to all present, not least Edward, Duke of York, contemporary author of the hunting book 'The Master of Game.' The cry would have been followed naturally by trumpet calls, as indeed it seems from the account to have been . The debate is ongoing.

[3] It is on record that Robinet de Bournoville and Isembard d'Azincourt, who led the attack on the baggage park, were subsequently apprehended and imprisoned for a substantial time by the Duke of Burgundy. In vain did they plead that they had presented King Henry's jewel encrusted sword to the Crown.

Against All Odds — The Battle of Agincourt

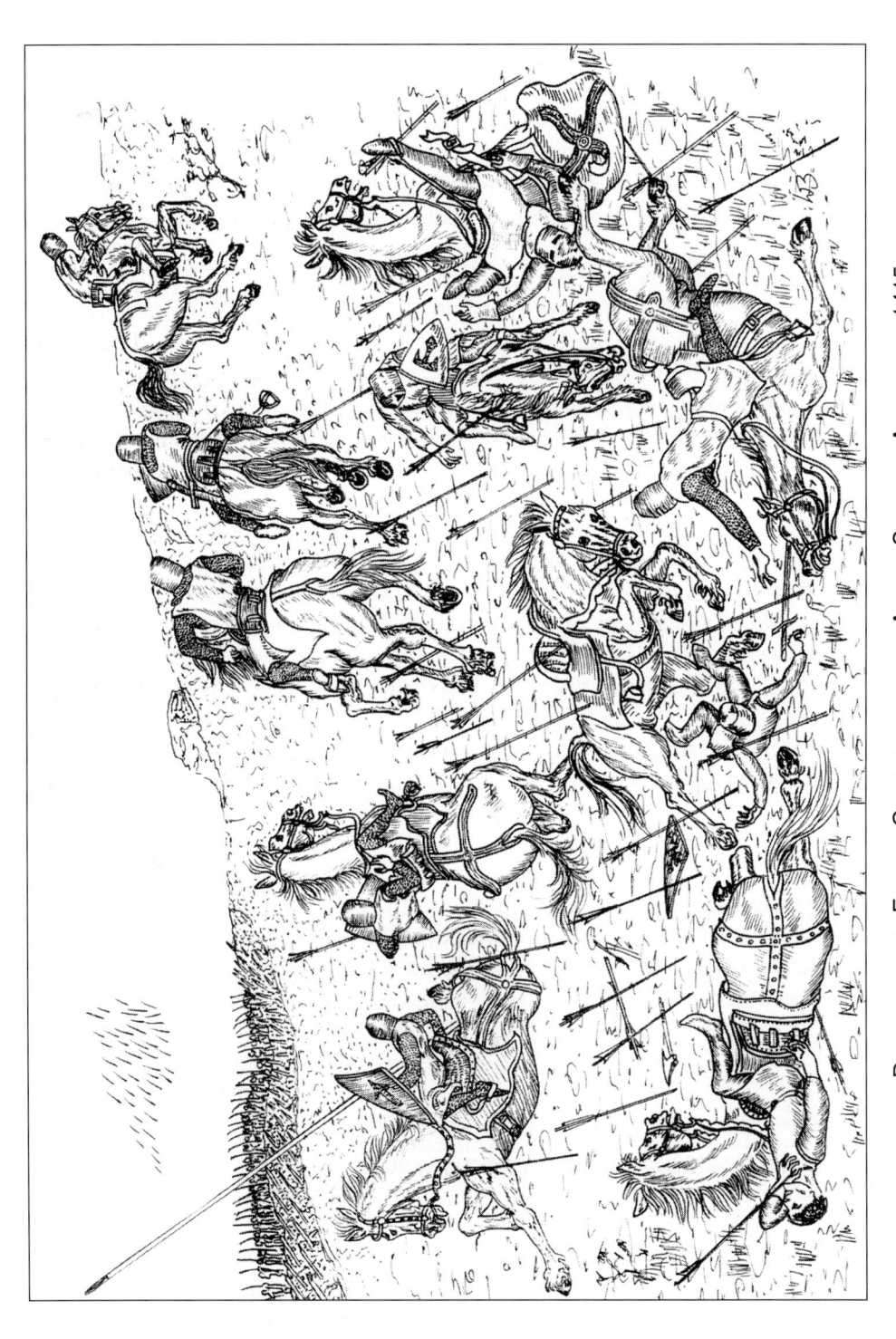

Damage to the French Cavalry after the Arrow Storm at Agincourt, 1415

Poitevins and others previously put to flight, had regrouped and were posing an obvious threat.

To Henry fell a vital decision. He did not waver. Behind him a large number of able-bodied prisoners, potential aggressors. In front, a substantial force seemingly ready to engage his weakened Division. He did not demur. He issued the order to kill all prisoners.

Naturally, this went down badly amongst those who were expecting rich rewards from ransom money and Henry had to detail a man-at-arms, with 200 archers (perhaps the Welsh) to do it for him.

This achieved, he faced the regrouped French, only to see them melt away.

Casualty counts for battles are notoriously inaccurate and French sources are probably no more correct than others. For the English losses of all ranks they offer two figures, one of 600, the other of 1,600. Their own total was incalculable.

Agincourt over, Henry's weary army resumed its interrupted way to Calais. Once there however, the expected rest and relaxation proved elusive. Admission to the town was refused, food was short and what there was, was expensive. Soldiers hoping for fat profits from loot and ransom of those prisoners saved from slaughter, had to be content with much less than the 'market value.' Waurin describes the soldiery as being *"very discontented"* and one senses a marked under-statement here.

King Henry, who had stopped at Guinnes en route to Calais, heard of the problem however and, with characteristic speed, arranged for shipping to take his victorious but thoroughly exhausted army back home.

Henry's march to Calais was an undertaking fraught with risk. He was brought to battle by French choice not his own. Whether his archers, arguably the power base of his army were ever adequately rewarded for their role is questionable. That chivalry was beaten from the field by the vigour and aggression of their actions may have been as unpalatable a fact to the English courtly class as to the French and, they had full reason to know.

Contemporary chroniclers could hardly dismiss the fact and tales man and broadsheet balladeer alike, praised their feat but many centuries were to pass before Authority ceded to bowmen Jack, Will and Jenkin the credit they were due.

Principal references consulted, and further reading.

THE CRECY WAR, A MILITARY HISTORY OF THE HUNDRED YEARS WAR FROM 1337 TO 1360. Alfred H. Burne, 1990. Greenhill Books. ISBN 1-85367-081-2.

EDWARD, PRINCE OF WALES AND ACQUITAINE. Richard Barber, 1978. Penguin Books Ltd. ISBN 0-7139 0861 0.

LIFE AND CAMPAIGNS OF THE BLACK PRINCE. Ed.: Richard Barber, 1979. Folio Society.

THE AGINCOURT WAR. Alfred H. Burne, 1956. Eyre and Spottiswood.

THE BATTLE OF AGINCOURT, SOURCES AND INTERPRETATIONS. Gen. Ed.: Dr. Anne Curry, 2000. Boydell Press. ISBN 0 85115 802 1.

THE CHRONICLE OF LONDON, photoreduced reprint. 1995. Llanerch Publishers. Felinfach. ISBN 1 86143 000 0.

Part 11

A Crown of Roses

The Civil War of York and Lancaster
The Battle of St. Albans
The Battle of Tewkesbury
The Battle of Towton

Part 11

A CROWN OF ROSES

*L*ASTING FOR some 30 years, the brutal 15th Century power struggle between the great Houses of York and Lancaster, termed by the Victorian historian and novelist Sir Walter Scott "The Wars of the Roses" (a romantic title, suggestive of quite unwarranted horticultural innocence) was punctuated by bloody battle between both factions, unremitting in their mutual hostility.

To describe the tangle of inter-connected happenings which collectively formed this internecine struggle as complex, understates the word. Men, some dominant, some domineered, strode across this 15th Century stage — their well-laid plans for power usurped and twisted by the fickle hand of fate.

It may help if some of the Principals are identified and their parts in the unfolding story briefly described. So we will start:

Lancastrian Henry VI, son of Henry V, succeeded him to the throne in 1422, to be deposed in 1461 in favour of Yorkist Edward, Earl of March, who reigned until 1483 as Edward IV. He was briefly replaced upon his death by his young son Edward V, who reigned for two months. The throne was then usurped by Richard III, Duke of Gloucester, son of Richard, Duke of York (killed at the battle of Wakefield). Richard III was killed at Bosworth in 1485 and replaced by Henry VII, Duke of Richmond, who established the Tudor dynasty. Other characters, some shadowy, some well-defined will move across the stage from time to time.

Now, add to the equation Margaret of Anjou, wife to Henry VI; a powerhouse of a woman whose single-minded determination to secure succession maintained the momentum of the struggle and directly fuelled the second Battle of St. Albans.

Now to this Chapter, in which four battles are described. The first, at St. Albans — and that which began the struggle for supremacy — took place in 1455. The others occurred within months, during 1461.

The town of St. Albans, dominated by its Abbey and really no more than a large village at that time, had the dubious distinction of playing host to two confrontations; each wasteful of life; each, in their own way, significant in their outcome.

CONTENTION IN THE STREET: The first Battle of St. Albans was fought in 1455. The principal antagonists: King Henry VI with Edmund, Duke of Somerset and Richard, Duke of York.

Edmund was a devious man with his own distinct agenda who, having displaced others with better claim, was now principal 'adviser' to Lancastrian Henry VI. Yorkist Richard, removed from favour and fully conscious of his lost political standing, was (with namesakes Richard, Earl of Salisbury, and Richard, Earl of Warwick) understandably concerned at the turn certain events were taking.

Fearing the influence which the three Richards might have with a potentially unstable Sovereign, whose recurring mental affliction was severely impairing his ability to govern, Somerset made a point of keeping close company with the King. With some apparent success, he constantly endeavoured to turn the King against the trio, despite the fact that he was mistrusted by the commoners, whose preference was for Richard, Duke of York.

The scene was potentially explosive and encounter inevitable.

CONFRONTATION: The three Richards had gathered an army (not large as armies go, but substantial enough to cause Somerset and the King alarm) and were assembling outside St. Albans, in Hertfordshire. Efforts to recruit a force in the area having signally failed, a patchy and somewhat smaller Royal army was hastily gathered together, consisting largely of the retinues of those Lords then present with the King in London, supported by men-at-arms and archers of the royal bodyguard.

So it was that on May 21st, King Henry VI, in company with Edmund Beaufort, Duke of Somerset, the Duke of Buckingham, the Earls of Pembroke, Northumberland, Devon, Stafford, Dorset and Wiltshire and, the Lords Clifford and Dudley, with other gentry and yeomen numbering perhaps 2,000 in all, rode towards St. Albans, resting at Watford overnight.

The King, having arrived and taken up position within the town, barricades were quickly prepared and preliminaries begun. Protocol, hallowed by tradition, decreed that confrontations between Englishmen should be preceded by endeavour at mediation and this duly took place. Heralds plied between the rival forces in vain attempt to stem the inevitable. All hope of peaceful solution ended however with the King's categoric refusal — heartily endorsed no doubt by Somerset — to hand him over for trial as a traitor and to accept York once more as principal adviser.

With the scene now set and York champing at the bit, matters eventually got under way.

THE FIRST BATTLE OF ST. ALBANS, 1455

There are several accounts of the ensuing fight. That contained within English Historical Documents 1327-1485 owes its accuracy to the Paston Letters, and serves well, since it is explicit of some detail lacking in more general accounts.

THE DUKE OF YORK, with Salisbury and Warwick, their knights, squires, bill-men and archers to the number of perhaps 3,000, prepared for battle at a place known locally as the 'Key field,' on the Eastern outskirts of the town. Meanwhile, Henry VI, well aware of the presence and almost certainly the strength of the opposition, raised his Banner at Butts Lane, off St. Peter Street, a place which went by the earlier name of Sandford. His instructions were that the immediate area be strengthened with barriers and, with this stronghold quickly arranged, he and Somerset sat back to await developments.

They were not long in coming. In anticipation of the King's and Somerset's arrival, York had spent three impatient hours in the field, his troops arrayed in martial order. With no sign of battle readiness on the Royal part however, he had no option but to seek out his enemy and attack. Thoroughly exasperated by now, an irritated York sent a messenger to the King demanding that he should "*. . . deliver such as we will accuse . . .*" Understandably, the reply was uncompromising and sharp. York was threatened with the penalty of treason if he did not pack up his tents and depart at once.

Faced with this impasse, someone had to do something and. with some reluctance, York took the initiative. After a brief Council of War, he and his commanders decided to storm the Royal barricades. Thus, between 11 and 12 o'clock, they broke into the town and through the barriers in several places, moving up Chequer Street towards the Market Place. Progress was painfully slow however; Lord Clifford and his archers defended every inch against York's men and stalemate looked increasingly more certain as time passed.

The King, with Somerset, had raised his Banner adjacent to what are today the Law Courts. Warwick however, either with intimate personal knowledge of the town, or good local intelligence, gathered his men together and, with a ferocious attack broke into St Peter Street, entering through a garden side between the Key and the Chequers Inns in Hollowell (Holywell) Street.

Once inside the barriers, trumpets were blown and, shouting: 'A Warwick!' 'A Warwick!' archers and men-at-arms set upon Somerset, Northumberland and Lord

Clifford with gusto, killing them and some 50 of their retainers. (A plaque recording Somerset's death is placed on a building on the corner of St. Peter's Street and Victoria Street.)

In this sortie, Durham, Buckingham, Stafford, Dorset and other Lancastrian nobles and gentry, were wounded by arrows; even King Henry taking a flesh wound in the shoulder.

The battle, such as it was, was now over. York, Salisbury and Warwick (whose archers had swung the pendulum of chance) now approached the King and, falling upon their knees, begged his forgiveness, asking him to accept them as his "liege men" and adding that — arrow wound apart — they had meant him no permanent harm. Faced with what was quite obviously a 'fait accompli,' the King had little choice but to agree terms and, with that assurance, York, Warwick and the others commanded "in the King's name" that the fighting should stop, which — in deference to York, although nominally to the King — it now did.

The following day, the King, with his new-found friends, rode to London where they stayed at the Bishop of London's Palace.

(An alternative description of the proceedings, vide the Dijon Archives de la Cote d'Or, is regarded as a more exact and less biased account, adding some detail to the story. Where the foregoing had York awaiting the King's response before starting the action, the Dijon account suggests an earlier pre-empting of the expected reply.) This is its gist:

Warwick, whose archers seem to have been in the thick of it, had placed guards on the approach lanes and streets and entering, quickly sealed off the market place. The real fighting began at about 10 o'clock but, because the area was restricted, only a few men could fight. Notwithstanding that, four of the King's personal bodyguard were killed by arrows as he watched, the King himself being struck and receiving a flesh wound in the shoulder.

After three hours of fierce fighting, it became apparent that the outnumbered King's men were getting the worst of the engagement and they turned to flee. At this point the Duke of Somerset, with his archers, retreated into the shelter of a nearby house in a desperate effort to save himself. He was spotted by York's men however and the house was promptly surrounded. His men resisted bravely, shooting from the windows and doorways, until eventually pole-axes broke down the door. But Somerset was not beaten yet; with some of his men he fought his way out, killing four of York's men himself before being struck down with a pole-axe and then wounded in so many places that he died.

Still the battle was not over at this point and the Yorkist faction had certainly not had everything its own way. Whilst Somerset was being dealt with terminally, York and Warwick's own men were under serious pressure from the King's men-at-arms (supported by elite archers from his personal bodyguard) and three of York's principal commanders, Lords Northumberland and Clifford, with Sir Robert Warrington, were slain.

The battle had now lasted for some four and a half hours but, with Somerset dead, further hostilities were unnecessary and it all ceased at around 2.30 in the afternoon, after the King had received and accepted protestations of loyalty from York and his fellow Lords.

Although the street-fighting was over, there was unfinished business to attend to and having received reports that Buckingham and the Earl of Wiltshire (the King's Treasurer) had accompanied the King and taken refuge in the Abbey, Yorkist soldiers stormed in to find and kill them both. Buckingham was found with ease and dealt with summarily; he had been severely wounded by three arrows and was in no condition to flee. Matters were different however for the wily Wiltshire who, having ransacked the Vestry, slipped off wearing monk's clothing and could be found nowhere in the vicinity. The Compiler of this account notes solemnly:

"... *until today, May 27th, no one knows whither he has gone!*"

It was in the Abbey, according to this Account, that the King received York and pardoned him, departing afterwards for London:

"... *to be received with great joy and solemn procession* ..."

The 'CHRONICLE OF LONDON,' characteristically terse, records the battle and its outcome but, after reporting the demise of "*the Duke of Somerset, therle of Northumberland, the lord Clifford*" adds, rather curiously "... *and a knight called Sr. Barthilmeu Nantwesil and xxv squyers, with other people* ..." Why this gentleman, whose name is vaguely Cornish, was singled out for recognition is unclear (a Gentleman Spear and member of the King's bodyguard perhaps?) — it matters little; for whatever reason the name Nantwesil is forever recorded for posterity.

The first Battle of St. Albans, ferocious encounter though it was and small compared with those to come, is considered by historians to have been of little consequence politically. Of those slain, Henry Percy, second Earl of Northumberland, was perhaps of most significant potential interest on the wider political scene. Power on the Scottish border Marches was very finely balanced and the removal of a major English player from the scene inevitably shifted initiative Scotland's way. Learning of the Earl's unlamented demise, an aggressive King James II, his eyes fixed firmly on Berwick, launched an immediate attack and, but for the stout resistance of the garrison, the clash at St. Albans might well have had wider and more serious consequences than it did.

True, the chess board pieces changed and were to change again; knights had fallen and castles too. True also, that matters did not always go the Yorkist way but, though time's wall was still unmarked, the hand of fate had sought, found and grasped the pen.

AFTERMATH: On the Duke of York's militarily implemented return to favour, he was, because of the King's "*infirmity,*" visited upon him by "... *the Most High Saviour, and hindering him from undertaking* ... *numerous matters of business* ..." given power to summon and dismiss Parliament and was ordained by the King as Protector and Defender of England and the Church and, its principal Councillor.

THE SECOND BATTLE OF ST. ALBANS, 1461

IF THE FIRST BATTLE of St. Albans in Hertfordshire could be dismissed as a mere skirmish by those who pontificate on such matters, then this certainly could not be said of the second which took place in February, 1461. This was a full-scale slog of a thing and one which, if possession of up-to-the-minute military hardware were the criteria, went very much the wrong way.

Richard Plantagenet, Duke of York, successful at the first St. Albans affair six years earlier and, erstwhile 'counsellor' of the King, had been ousted from that position of power in 1456 by the intervention of Queen Margaret. In December, 1460, his forces defeated in battle outside his Sandal Castle home at Wakefield and, unable to defend himself, he had been hacked to death in 'Cock and Bottle Lane,' Sandal, by Lancastrian soldiers. Two months later in London, his former companion, Yorkist Richard Neville, Earl of Warwick was 'protecting' King Henry VI, a troubled monarch whose tenuous hold on reality was diminishing by the day.

To compound his problems, Warwick had recently learned that a huge Lancastrian army, flushed with its successful elimination of the Duke of York at Wakefield and led by Henry's Queen with the Prince of Wales in tow, was slowly and ponderously making its way south, leaving havoc and mayhem in its path. Largely an ill-disciplined rabble of Welshmen, assorted Northerners, mercenary Scots and French, it had nevertheless a leavening core of battle-hardened men-at-arms and bowmen who bore (besides the livery of their Lords) the ostrich feather plume of the Prince of Wales. Despite the inequality of its composition however, it was a very considerable threat and Warwick was in little doubt of the intention of its leaders: to take London, dispense with the mentally challenged Henry and enthrone son Edward (backed by mother Margaret) in his place.

London traders were predictably concerned. The thought of this riff-raff making free with hearth and home induced almost terminal panic and they rushed thither and yon, burying their treasures and battening down in readiness for fate.

Although unfortunate in his choice of companions, Warwick was a prudent and cautious man. Carefully and with judgement, he gathered a large army, mustering(with his own retainers and those of the Earls of Arundel and Suffolk) some 25,000 men. He was joined by a contingent of hand-gunners provided by the Duke of Burgundy. Also present and later to play a key role in subsequent events, was a substantial contingent of archers: men of Kent, under their leader, one Captain Lovelace, a survivor of Wakefield.

The Lancastrian army, much of it scarcely under control, matched Warwick's Yorkist force in strength, if nothing else. However, Warwick's bowmen and foot-sloggers had the benefit of the most up-to-date military equipment around at the time

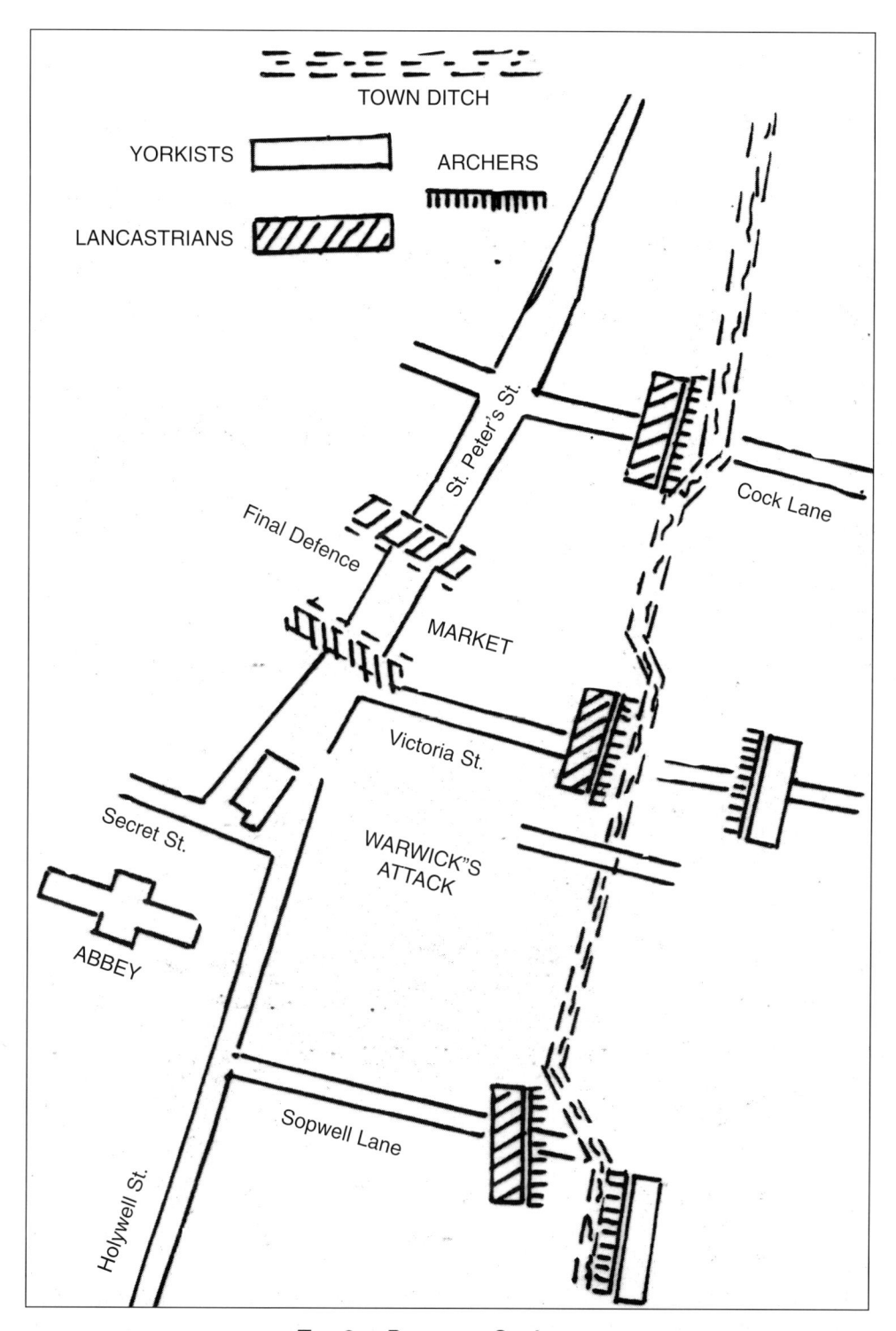

A Crown of Roses — The 2nd Battle of St. Albans

The 2nd Battle of St. Albans

although, it must be said, many medieval soldiers disdained it, preferring their traditional gear of leaden mallets, bows, swords, axes, spears and lances. Available for the more discriminating though, were pavises (large protective shields generally associated with crossbows and possibly intended for them if they were present) fitted with a folding leg and a flap, which could be raised up to permit a shot. These devices were studded with 3d (sic) nails, sharp end up, intended to act as a deterrent to horses when, having performed their primary function, the archers or the arbalesters laid them flat on the ground.

Nets, also studded with nails, were prepared to be hung between bushes and hedges to hinder horsemen and others in their attack. Caltraps (3 spikes joined, one of which always remained upright), together with a device very similar to the 'sting' used by present-day police against car-thieves, were there in numbers whilst the Burgundian hand-gunners, with contemporary Continental flair, had been provided with arrows an ell in length armed with a *"great mighty head of iron"* and fletched with six feathers, *"three in the midst, and three at the other end."*

Burgundian troops were well organised and drilled. Beside hand-gunners, with their crude and (when they didn't self-destruct) effective weapons, archers were also employed. The bows used by these men and, possibly, also by English archers in Burgundian employ, were of a distinctive type and different from English longbows in one particular: that of profile. Their limbs were deliberately recurved whereas, apart from any curvature resulting from the vagaries of grain, the English bow limbs are believed to have been largely straight.

(As an aside: to gain advantage from this recurved profile, modern experiment shows that 'Burgundian' style bows are at their most effective when used with long arrows. It would be instructive to know whether there was significant difference in arrow length between contemporary English and Burgundian shafts.)

To return to Warwick and his preparations. Although he moved North, he really had no clear idea of where the Queen and her army were. Whilst chance may have played a part (although there may have been darker implications), he decided on St. Albans and, once arrived there, with no evidence of the whereabouts of the Lancastrians and seemingly time to spare, he set about establishing his position at the convenient sites of Barnards Heath and Nomansland Common. He disposed his force on an extended front, to the north of the Heath, his left flank closest to the town, leaving a strong contingent of archers at the Watch Tower in the town centre.

With time apparently on his side, if ever a commander could be said to have covered every exigency then — at least in his own opinion if not that of his biographers — Warwick was that man.

Unfortunately for him however, matters were about to take a turn for the worse. Warwick still had little idea of where his enemy was. His 'prickers' (scouts) had failed to find it and, having regard to what he knew of the activities of the mercenaries, whose right to pillage was accepted virtually as a condition of service and whose depredations were still in process, he was probably right to think his enemy was still a distance away.

The first bad news came on the evening of February 26th. The Yorkist out-post at Dunstable had beeen over-run and its defenders all killed or captured. A contemporary account of this skirmish records:

> "... *the king's meinie* (soldiers) *lacked good guidance, for some were but new men of war, for the chiefest Captain was butcher* (by trade) *and there were the king's meinje overthrown only by the Northern men* (themselves little better than armed rabble). *And soon after, for sorrow it is said, the butcher hanged himself."*

Understandably concerned at the loss of his outpost but believing this to be just a marauding band of looters, Warwick took no action to put his men on stand-by and this was his undoing. The enemy had indeed arrived in force and, by a co-incidence of Yorkist unreadiness and Lancastrian subterfuge, had gained access to the town square. Taken by surprise and outnumbered, the Yorkist archers braced their bows, notched shafts and, shoulder to shoulder, not only held off the advancing Lancastrians but forced them back.

Although for the time being the status quo had been re-established, matters were quickly to turn against the gallant town force. Conscious of the way in which the first St. Albans affair had been won, by infiltration through back alleys and gardens, the Queen's commanders probed Warwick's defences to find a weakness. This they readily found in Catherine Street and, with a simultaneous attack from the George Street side, caught the archers in a pincer movement. Although arrow stocks were low and finally exhausted, once again these men fought bravely with bow, maul, sword and fighting knife, until inevitably they were eventually overpowered.

The Queen and her troops now had the town to themselves and, having consolidated their position, her commanders began their advance against the Lancastrians. Warwick was thus in something of a quandary. His reading of the position had been that the Lancastrian force would move towards him from the East to join him in a set-piece battle. He had not anticipated the fall of the town and the possibility of a Lancastrian advance from that direction. Matters had changed — and not for the better.

He had now not only to swing his battle line around to face the threat but, first to contact his commanders on the extended front through a maze of country lanes — a lengthy and difficult business. That eventually done, those very preparations made to welcome the enemy had then to be removed to allow the movement of troops. Meanwhile, Warwick's left wing, under Lord Montague, was about to take the full brunt of the Queen's forces. It is to their credit that they stood their ground, at least for a time. However, because of the lie of the land and the disposition of the centre and right wings, these were unable to reach them and matters swiftly became desperate.

The final straw came when Captain Lovelace and his men of Kent changed sides and defected to the Queen. Morale hit rock bottom. The Yorkist line broke and, although to his credit Warwick rallied his men, the inequality of numbers forced the inevitable. He gathered his remaining troops around him and, at Nomansland Common fought on resolutely until dusk brought an opportunity for ordered withdrawal. With 4,000 men under discipline, Warwick departed the scene and headed Westward to join the Earl of March, victor at Mortimers Cross.

King Henry VI, who had accompanied Warwick to lend Royal authority to the affair, was left sitting peacefully under a tree, singing to himself and laughing — if accounts are to be believed. With him Warwick left two trusted knights, Lords Kyriell and Bonville. The King had assured them of their safety when finally he was collected by his wife. The promise of immunity did not wash with the Queen however, who, seeing them merely as two potential further thorns in the Yorkist side, had them summarily despatched.

Although the key to victory at this second battle of St. Albans mirrored the first, through the initial taking of the town, Warwick was dealt a double blow by the defection of Lovelace and the men of Kent. It is speculative that the result might have been more in doubt had this not occurred, since the Yorkist centre and right wing were already on the move and, had Montague and the left wing held on a while, reinforcements, preceded by an attack from Warwick's cavalry might have made a difference to the outcome.

Lovelace is an enigmatic individual. Indeed there are those historians who deny his existence, seeing him advanced as flesh and blood merely to explain Warwick's military ineptness. It is true that he seems not to be heard of again, but his existence need not necessarily be in doubt. He was a survivor of Wakefield, that much seems true. He is said to have brought Warwick news of his brother's death there. However, he was captured and his life seemingly spared on the understanding that he would reveal Warwick's tactical plans to the Yorkists. If he had got word to the enemy that Warwick was preparing for a 'North South' engagement on Barnard's Heath, then the capture of the town takes on a special significance. It was a planned move in preparation for an advance against the Yorkist force from West to East.

EPILOGUE

With Henry now ensconced within the bosom of his family and the Lancastrian faction at least temporarily victorious, Warwick had an immediate problem. Although back at his power base in London, he was king-less and, without Royal prerogative, could not legally continue his Yorkist ambitions. Enter Edward Plantagenet. On Wednesday, March 4th, in the Great Hall of Westminster, the Royal robes were draped around him and he took the oath to become Edward IV of England.

Queen Margaret and her reunited King meanwhile, now on the outskirts of London, had failed in her negotiations with its leaders to enter, despite her assurance that she would see them well guarded. The prospect of several thousand booty hunting mercenaries loose within the city, however had brought increasing panic and, to quote from a contemporary account

"... They called for a brewer as their leader (perhaps John Lumbard, a Victualler) *and that day this place was in an uproar ..."*

Although her legal entitlement was perhaps well placed, Margaret decided not to follow her St. Albans' victory by forced entry and the uneasy calm which cloaked the capital was finally dispelled by her departure.

Yorkist retribution was to follow. On Palm Sunday, March 29th, by the banks of the

River Cock in Yorkshire, after the bloodiest battle ever fought on English soil, the Lancastrian army was decimated, its supporters largely killed or seeking sanctuary in Scotland, its cause at least temporarily in tatters.

AS THE ENEMY GETS CLOSER THE ARCHER COMES DOWN TO POINT-BLANK AIM

TOWTON, 1461

IF ANY MONTH within the turbulent history of England could be singled out as decisive, then that month was March of 1461 and, intimately associated with it, the man who bore its name: The Earl of March who, on the 4th day was proclaimed Edward IV, King of England.

The decision to oust Henry VI from office as sadly wanting in Affairs of State, had been taken at St. John's Field in London, where it is recorded that his perceived shortcomings were spelled out in front of a

> "... *great power of men* ... *whereupon it was demanded of the said people whether the said Henry was worthy to reign any longer, or no. whereunto the people cried hugely, and said 'Nay, nay.' Asked then whether they would have the Earl of March as King* ... *they cried out with one voice 'Yea, yea'.*"

That being so, on March 3rd, the people's decision — or, at least part of it — was ratified by council at Bayard's Castle in London and England welcomed Edward IV, son of the deceased Duke of York, as their new but yet, uncrowned King.

Understandably this re-arrangement of the Royal prerogative was quite unacceptable to the Lancastrian faction and it was pointedly observed that, although Edward undoubtedly held the sceptre of office, he had yet to receive the unction and the crown. This, according to an interested foreign observer, he would postpone until he had *"annihilated"* the other King and, inter alia, exacted vengeance for the untimely slaughter of his father at Wakefield.

Be that as it may, Edward was anxious to meet and deal decisively with Henry and his Lancastrian advisers; still smarting from the unexpected out-turn at St. Albans, he set about raising a suitable army for the purpose.

The undisciplined rabble that constituted a sizeable chunk of the Lancastrian force was now withdrawing northward, having — despite the forceful influence of Queen Margaret — been prevented from entering London. It was seen off the premises at a respectable distance by Lord Fauconberg, with a substantial body of archers, followed a day later by Edward himself and the rest of the army. Simultaneously, the Duke of Norfolk had been despatched post-haste to muster his formidable East Anglian contingent, a force that was later to prove so decisive.

Passing through the still smoking wreckage of burnt out villages and homesteads — wrecked by the Lancastrian moss-troopers en route for northern parts and reinforcement — the Yorkists first encountered their foe at Ferrybridge, a crossing point of the River Aire.

There are conflicting reports of what happened here. In one, the bridge was broken but unguarded; in another a strong Lancastrian force held it and crossing was achieved only after a bitter fight, with many slain on both sides. In yet another and, perhaps, a more reliable version, although the broken bridge was repaired and unguarded, the Yorkists — having crossed and camped — were attacked by Lord Clifford and a strong contingent of Lancastrian mounted spearmen (whilst asleep) and swept back across it with many casualties.

Whatever the position, when Edward with the main force arrived later that day (to be met by chaos), he sized up the situation and, dismissing Ferrybridge as an option (since this would now be strengthened to take the baggage train and cannon), chose to cross the river at Castleford, by so doing cutting off the jubilant Lancastrians and their leader, Lord John Clifford (whose father had died at St. Albans), en route to their encampment.

Thus they met at Dintingford Valley, somewhere between the village of Saxton and the Tadcaster/Ferrybridge road. A short, sharp fight took place, perhaps between Edward's mounted bowmen and the 'Flower of Craven': Northumbrian borderers — merciless men of vicious habit. During this contest, for some reason Lord Clifford removed his gorget and, receiving an arrow (legend says without a head) in his neck, expired on the spot.

With Ferrybridge avenged and honours now even, the Yorkists advanced until within sight of the enemy encamped on a plateau to the south of Towton and the north of Saxton (a relevant aside: had matters concluded differently, we would be writing of the Battle of Saxton, since the generally accepted site is broadly between the two villages).

Each side now substantially in position (although the Duke of Norfolk had yet to arrive) both armies lay down to sleep. The night was bitter and cover was negligible. A strong wind with eddies of snow blowing at first towards Edward's men, changed direction overnight and, when dawn broke on this winter world, a full snow storm had begun. This was to prove a vital factor in subsequent events.

The battle opened with the Yorkist army, still lacking the promised East Anglian contingent although, initially at least, the weather proved something of a compensation and matters, at first, went Edward's way. His archers, commanded by the vastly experienced Lord Fauconberg, opened with an arrow storm which, helped by the strong wind, landed well into the Lancastrian line, causing some casualties. The Yorkist archers then retired some distance and awaited the Lancastrian response. As expected this was prompt, although affected by the wind, for with visibility severely restricted the returning volleys fell short.

Edward Hall, a contemporary described the scene:

> *". . . The northern men, feeling the shoot, but by reason of the snow not perfectly viewing the distance between them and their enemies, like hardy men shot their sheaf arrows as fast as they might, but all their shot was lost and their labour in vain for they came not near the southern men by 40 tailors yards . . ."*

(Modern longbow archers shooting 'two-way' at Clout will be familiar enough with the result of loosing against the wind.)

With knowledge of their antagonists' position, the Yorkist archers now advanced, collected the furthest arrows and, adding them to their own sheaves, shot back until they saw, advancing through the snow towards them, the line of Lancastrian infantry and men-at-arms.

The struggle now began in earnest. Pressing forward strongly, the Lancastrians gained ground on the Yorkists' left flank, helped by the exertions of an unseen ambushing party positioned there. Although Warwick and the right flank held firm against the advance of Northumberland, slowly but surely Edward's troops on the left began to be forced back and, for a while, the outcome looked dangerously close to defeat for Warwick and his newly proclaimed King.

However, when all hope seemed to be failing, over the noise of battle Edward heard the sound of drums and saw, marching through the gloom of the late winter afternoon, the welcome banners and war pennants of Norfolk and his elite retinue of some 5,000 hard-bitten Easterners. Marshalling his road-weary but otherwise fresh troops without delay, Norfolk bore down upon the Lancastrian left flank, which began to give way under the impact.

Slowly the Yorkist left regained ground against the opposing right wing whilst, faced with fresh troops, well-led and determined, the Lancastrian left wing broke up and the battle line turned through 90 degrees. Controlled retreat gradually became rout and rout became flight, as the Lancastrian army slowly disintegrated and fled the scene. Many died whilst trying to cross the Cock beck, once a safeguard for their right flank but now an obstacle to their passage. Others were drowned in the river close to Tadcaster, where they themselves had broken down the bridge.

The fighting strengths of each army have been assessed by A.W. Boardman, whose recent research has been considerable. His view is that Henry VI and his commanders would have marshalled some 25,000 men, whilst initially and, before the Duke of Norfolk arrived with 5,000, Edward and Warwick would have mustered some 20,000, of whom it is said Welsh foot-soldiers under Sir William Herbert, reinforced by levies from Kent, formed the bulk.

In passing: Welsh legend named Edward's Standard bearer as one David Mathew from Llandaff; it was in fact Ralph Vestynden who subsequently received an annuity of £10 and upon whom this responsibility lay.

It is difficult, even impossible, to determine casualties after a battle such as this. Quarter was neither sought nor given and, as ever, killing, even of prisoners,[1] continued long after the outcome had been decided. George Neville, brother of the Duke of Warwick, wrote in a letter his belief that a total of 28,000 men had perished on both sides, proportionately more Lancastrians than Yorkists. Although many of these would have died during the Yorkist pursuit, this figure may be thought excessive by those who estimate a total participation of 50,000.

As happens in the aftermath of warfare, rumour and counter-rumour now abounded.

Where were Henry VI and Henry Beaufort, Duke of Somerset? Captured, it was said by one; whilst from another came the report that Henry had been cornered

---

[1] In this regard the reader is directed to BLOOD RED ROSES. ISBN 1-81247-025-2, a pragmatic account by eminent osteopathologists of skeletal remains recovered from a mass grave outside Towton.

"*. . . in a place in Yorkshire called Corcumbre; or a name something like it . . .*"
The report, made to Sir John Paston continued: "*. . . The place is besieged, and various squires of the Earl of Northumberland have gathered to attack the besiegers so that, in the meantime Henry VI could be smuggled out through a litte postern gate on the other side, and four thousand men of the North were killed in this attack . . .*"

Although with many vicissitudes the struggle simmered on for a further quarter century and Towton remained the bloodiest battle of the campaign, it was not the most decisive. To Ambion Hill, hard by Market Bosworth, would fall that distinction for, in 1485, on August 22nd, Henry of Richmond, with the aid of archery, wrested the crown of England from King Richard III in battle.

Peace — uneasy for a further decade — came slowly to this troubled country. The new dynasty attracted entrepreneurs anxious to advance their political ends by unseating Tudor Henry. Manipulated by their mentors, Lambert Simnel, Perkin Warbeck and Ralph Wulford each strutted their brief hour on the stage of history.

The imposter Simnel, pretending to be Edward, Earl of Warwick — who was in fact then imprisoned in the Tower — was proclaimed King Edward V in Dublin on May 24th, 1487, with the wholehearted encouragement of Margaret of Burgundy, sister to Edward IV, whose pathological hatred of Henry and his clan, ensured support for almost anyone in hose and cod-piece willing to take up arms against him.

Simnel had been discovered, to use a present-day term, by one Richard Simons, his teacher at Oxford and, had been persuaded of his noble birth. Supported by the Earl of Lincoln (whom the late King Richard had nominated heir) the Yorkist Lord Lovell and a parcel of German mercenaries provided by 'aunt' Margaret, Lambert I (alias King Edward V) landed his small force at the port of Furness in Lancashire.

Advancing through Yorkshire and picking up some reinforcements along the way, he crossed the River Trent below Fiskerton, and pitched his encampment some three-quarters of a mile south of the village of East Stoke, near Newark; there to await the arrival of the Royal army.

Although with fewer troops than expected, Lincoln and Simnel are believed to have mustered some 9,000 men, in comparison to Henry VII's smaller number of around 6,000. However, apart from the 1,500 Germans and, perhaps, an Irish contingent, Simnel's army was poorly armed and ill-trained. Despite a disparity in arms, numbers told: Henry's vaward was badly punished, losing very many men and rout was only avoided by the arrival of the main force.

After this initial success, battle was now joined in earnest. The rebels were first contained, then pushed back and finally, after a three-hour-long battle during which the German mercenaries put up a strong defence, they were forced to flee. Simnel and Richard Simon were captured; Lincoln, Martin Schwartz (the German commander) and the Irish captain Thomas Geraldine, were all killed.

Lord Lovell allegedly swam the River Trent, never to be seen again. Those who have visited Lovell Hall, in Oxfordshire, will know of the legend that his emaciated body was discovered in a secret room many years afterwards.

Henry behaved with what might be thought a curious magnaminity towards Simnel, eventually promoting him to Keeper of the King's Hawks, whilst, ostensibly as a priest, Richard Simon was allowed to go free.

Although the Battle of Stoke was essentially the final engagement in the wars of Royal succession, imposters were still an irritant. The Great CHRONICLE OF LONDON records:

> "... In this passing of time in the borders of Norfolk and Suffolk was a new mawmet apeared which named himself to be the Earl of Warwick, the which by sly and covert means essayed to win him some adherents. But all in vain. He was brought before th'Earl of Oxford, to whom he confessed that he was born in London, and that he was son to a cordwainer. ..."

Ralph Wulford, for that was his name, was hanged on Shrove Tuesday, 1499. One might think that Henry was now totally secure but, he had yet one more pawn with which to deal.

In 1491, a young Fleming, Perkin Warbeck, had arrived on the National scene claiming to be Richard, the younger of Edward's two murdered sons. Supported by factions opposed to Henry VII, he had remained a thorn in the Royal side for over five years, turning up in Kent, Scotland and finally Cornwall, where at Taunton in September 1497, he finally surrendered.

Warbeck was quite a different individual to Simnel, he was well aware of what he was about and Henry showed no magnaminity here. He was locked up in the Tower for the time being and, although he subsequently escaped, he was recaptured and beheaded in November, 1499.

The bloody wars of Royal succession, begun in the streets of St. Albans, had finally ended. The Tudor dynasty had begun and England was at last, albeit uneasily, at peace.

THE WARS ARE OVER
— TIME TO UN-STRING THE BOW

Sources referenced:
BATTLES IN BRITAIN. Wm. Seymour, 1975
THE WARS OF THE ROSES. J.R. Lander, 1990
THE MILITARY CAMPAIGNS OF THE WARS OF THE ROSES. P.A.Haigh; 1995
THE BATTLE OF TOWTON. A.W. Boardman, 1994
THE MEDIEVAL SOLDIER IN THE WARS OF THE ROSES. A.W. Boardman
WALES AND THE WARS OF THE ROSES. H.T. Evans: 1998
THE CHRONICLE OF LONDON.

Part 12

Resurgam in Pace

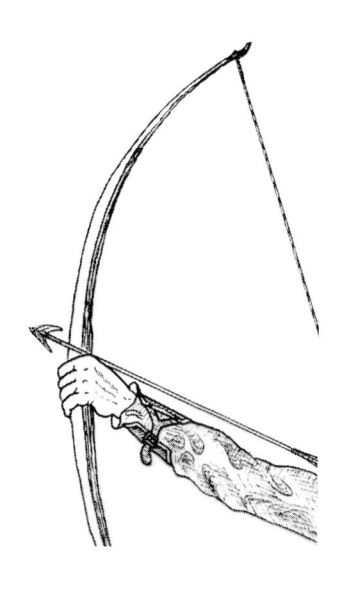

A Rest!
The fighting has finished. The Archer rests

PART 12

RESURGAM IN PACE

'RISE AGAIN IN PEACE!' A flamboyant title to this book's final Chapter perhaps, but one which is as relevant as yesterday and as current as today. For the long-bow is not only still with us, but thrives in the hands of those whose forefathers used it to such effect in those 'bowman-battles' of long ago.

There is no point during the long story of the bow at which one might say — with accuracy — "Here the war-bow finished — and here began archery as a pastime." Continental military influences ended the bow's use as a viable weapon in warfare; the Elizabethan edict of 1595 requiring re-training of archers was a belated recognition of the fact. But long before it ceased to be made for purposes of war, there were still many for whom exercise with the long-bow in the freedom of the countryside was the perfect antidote to city vapours.

Old soldiers, they say, seldom die, they just fade away. This is as true of the war-bow as it was of those who used it. Following William Neade's successful 1625 petition to Charles I on behalf of the 'Double Armed Man by the New Invention,' it was subsequently coupled with the pike as prescribed armament. Neade had the weapon demonstrated to Charles I at St. James Field (Park) by a member of the Artillery Garden of London (the Honourable Artillery Company) and, receiving the royal pleasure:

> "... solicited that worthy Societie in the ARTILLERY GARDEN in LONDON who hath practised it ever since. But because many of that worthy Society have not heretofore exercised shooting, it doth not take that perfection yet, which I hope time and practice will bring it unto, for it is the exercise of shooting that must make men perfect therein..."

Although modern experiment has proved the viability of the arrangement, the combination would have been unwieldy and its manipulation in battle conditions would have taxed even a trained archer. Despite some evidence for its subsequent use (there is reference to a 'Company of Bows with Pikes' in service at Hertford during the Civil War) and, for at least tacit Royal approval, it did not last.

That this coupling of bow and pike was in being as late as 1628 however, is apparent from a booklet 'A New Invention of Shooting Fire-shafts' published then for John Bartlet, a "True Patriot for the Common good of his native country of England,"

THE 'DOUBLE-ARMED MAN' (by the New Invention)
A combination of bow and pike contrived by William Neade[1]

[1] Although William Neade (described as an 'ancient archer') claimed to have invented this seemingly unwieldy arrangement, it is possible that the germ of the idea came from elsewhere. A poem by Thomas Churchyard, written as the foreword to Richard Robinson's 'history' of the archery Society of 'Prince Arthur's Knights' has this enigmatic verse.

> 'A rare device I will set out, to strengthen man and bow
> And when the plain device there of the world shall see and know
> The bow shall come again in fame, and win his wonted grace
> Look out of hand for my discourse, till then come, Bow in place.'

Churchyard was a practising archer and, although there is no direct evidence that he and Neade ever met, their lives overlapped and it is entirely possible that Neade's coupling of bow and pike involved the 'rare device' mentioned by Churchyard in his poem.

Neade mentions the advantage to an archer of the assistance which the angled pike offers in strengthening his bow arm when 'inconveniences' weakened it; 'being a reste for the Bowe-arme' and this suggests that perhaps medieval archers used their stakes in a similar fashion.

The 'British Archer', as depicted by Richard Oswald Mason in 1798. Armed with pike, sword, bow and arrow he was proposed as the answer to prospectively invading French.

Although Mason was not an archer when he designed his bow and pike combination — unlike William Neade, whose earlier 'Double Armed Man' design may have influenced him — Mason had the ear and the expertise of noted bowyer Thomas Waring on which to call and at whose Warehouse the pike might be seen.

Following the publication of his book 'Pro Aris et Focis' (for Hearth and Home) Mason was invited to become a member of the Toxophilite Society where he quickly became an average shot, a measure perhaps of his claim that daily practice for a month would make a bowman out of an ordinary citizen. He shot with the Society until 1802.

Interestingly, in his battlefield Drill, Mason proposed that prior to an order to shoot, distance from the enemy in score of yards should first be established by the most expert archers, or 'Flugelmen' (literally flight-men) placed on the right of the Battalion. 'Determined by Judgment of the Eye, and by the Assistance derived from Training.' One wonders idly whether some similar arrangement obtained in Medieval times?

Another of Mason's intended commands — that for nocking the shaft, ' Make ready poin,' is intriguing and again one puzzles whether this was of his own invention.

which both extolled the combination[1] and, proposed in addition that the bow should be used for the purpose of discharging fire-arrows. Instructions for the preparation of these was linked to a suggestion that for

"... *a brave and manlike sport* ..."

they be shot at tethered bulls during times of festival, instead of baiting them with dogs (an amusement of the time.)

The longbow was, moreover, carried as a weapon by City of London auxiliaries during the early years of the Civil War; whilst the Court of Aldermen revived and encouraged its use after the restoration of the Monarchy. Following an ostentatiously presented Competition in 1663, in front of the then Lord Mayor, shooting the 'standard arrow' and the 'flight arrow' for distance once more took place on Finsbury Fields.

The pike and bow combination was suggested again a century later, in 1798, by Oswald Mason — a patriotic citizen with, it would seem, a penchant for reviving old ideas — as an addition to the half pike; and in the early years of the 19th Century it was carried with an associated bayonet when the Archer's Division of the Honourable Artillery Company mustered. Although by then an obsolete anachronism, both its charisma and England's history excused its presence. Truly a long time a-dying.

Although regulations requiring practice remained as Statute Law well into the 19th Century, before repeal there is little doubt that rural archery declined after the need for training required by Statute law ceased — perhaps because other available pastimes were less demanding of physical activity. The gentry maintained an interest however and large bodies of archers regularly marched and shot in London during the latter years of the 17th Century.

'The Bowman's Glory,' whilst largely an account of the 1583 Procession and Tournament in Hoxton Fields, contains in its Postscript a brief note of the muster in 1682 of

"... *at least a Thousand Archers in the Field* (Tuttlefields) ..." *At this event, amongst other activity, three showers of whistling arrows were shot; and the author (Sir William Wood) records that "... now Gentlemen begin to be pleased with the Divertisement, and pleased with this Manly Recreation. ..."*

There was now a perceived need for organised activity in addition to independent archery by individuals. It has been customary to date the revival of archery as a pastime from the latter years of the 18th Century and, to link it closely with the Prince Regent. Whilst his interest was invaluable and demonstrably important in the context of Societies then created, in truth we should look for earlier beginnings; for Thomas Roberts, in an unpublished Note to his 'The English Bowman' mentions that

"... *The Toxophilite Society are now in possession of the silver badge made for the Marshall of the 'Fraternity of Archers of Queen Catherine'* (wife to Charles II) *by the contributions of Sir Edward Hungerford and others. ..."*

---

[1] "... *and if to rest the left hand on the pike, inable men to draw a stronger bowe, the ingenious device of scruing (screwing) both together will be best. ..."*

It would seem from the brief Notices in 'The Bowman's Glory,' that annual gatherings of gentlemen archers took place at least from 1661; suggesting that the revival of archery — as a genteel pastime —occurred a century earlier than is generally credited.

By 1652, the Society of Finsbury Archers had formed and, was shooting regularly on Finsbury Fields, for silver arrows and other plate. (Sir) William Wood (his formal elevation to knighthood may be a matter for conjecture, but it seems likely that he was dubbed by Charles II for his prowess with the bow) was closely associated with them and, in 1687, presented them with a Constitution of Rules. For a discussion of these Rules and their curious similarity to those of the 1673 Society of Scorton Archers of Yorkshire, see 'Further Reading.'

As an aside, it is perhaps out of keeping with the times that an archery Society should have begun during a period of civil strife and this may argue, perhaps, for an earlier formation. Pure conjecture, but Sir William's revision of the Rules — if indeed that is what he did — may have celebrated the occasion of their founding, perhaps their centenary and, if this had indeed been 1587, then there were certainly Archery Marks in Finsbury Fields at that time and, dedicated archers shooting at them together.

A little booklet prepared and published in 1601 for the

". . . ease of the skilfull, and behoofe of the yong beginners in the famous exercise of Archerie . . ."

listed 173 individual Marks, each sponsored by a person, or an Organisation, favourable to the activity. Thus, Churches, Inns, Livery Companies and Aldermen vied with each other to have their interest confirmed. Distances between Marks were given in scores of yards, with odd yards added alongside. Names were curious, many outside our comprehension today: 'Egpie,' 'Sea-Griphon,' 'Martins Marigold' and 'Thief in the Hedge,' all were there, each distance carefully listed, with the warning that

". . . you must shoote long ayme, because this is set downe by measure of the line . . ."[2]

In 1676, the Society of Finsbury Archers gave themselves the additional title of 'Queen Catherine's Archers,' and purchased, by subscription, the Badge known as the Catherine of Braganza Shield. William Wood held custody of this shield as Marshal to the 'Queen's Majesty's Regiment of Archers.' The shield, now a treasured possession of the Royal Toxophilite Society, rests on permanent display in the Victoria and Albert Museum, whilst its Cabinet is in the possession of the Society.

The selection of 1676 for an association with English Royalty is doubly interesting, for a Scottish Company of Archers — later to become the Sovereign's Bodyguard for Scotland — was founded in that year. A Constitution of Laws presented to the Privy Council for its approval, had received its blessing and these now bound together previously looser gathering of companions in the bow.

Difficulties with archery on Finsbury Fields became more and more apparent as the

---

[2] The alternative to 'long line' or exact measurement was 'pacing.' A pace can fall short of a yard by several inches. Two hundred paces (10 score) would cover some 185 yards.

17th Century turned into the 18th. Commercial London was expanding rapidly and good building land was at a premium. Walls were erected under the noses of the Honourable Artillery Company, whose responsibility the remaining Shooting Marks still were. Now in cold stone and no longer of arrow-friendly wood capped with crude carvings, they were used by the Company for musket practice. A map of the area drawn in 1745 clearly shows that, of the original 170 Marks, just 12 remained in place and these were soon to go.

The fate of these is conjectural. One survives and sits uneasily on the stairway within Armoury House. Rumour has it that others were broken up and used as landfill at the further end of the Garden; perhaps some future archaeology will reveal this as truth.

Although regularly inspected, it is believed that the last occasion on which the Marks were used for practice by the H.A.C. was 1792; although as late as 1819 orders were given for their examination. The Society of Finsbury Archers had virtually ceased to exist by the 1780's however and, with the formation of the Toxophilite Society in 1781, the few left joined the new Body, bringing what silver plate they had with them. After some 300 years, both the formal and informal exercise of archery in Finsbury Fields was over.

After the enthusiasm of the late 17th Century, the 40 or so years before formation of the 'genteel' archery societies in the 1780's, were lean in archery terms. Seemingly little happened generally, beyond the activities of the gradually diminishing number of Finsbury Archers and those who still shot at one or two of the northern provincial Clubs. Matters were to change however with the ever-blossoming interest in the activity by the Prince Regent and his myriad hangers-on. By 1791 there were some two dozen Clubs and Societies actively meeting, both individually and together, in annual Competition on Blackheath.

Common to most was Butt, or Rood shooting, at 120, 90, 60 and 30 yards; although Roving was practised by some and Papingo formed part of the itinerary of certain Scottish Clubs. One of the more senior English Clubs, the 1785 'Woodmen of Arden' — happily still extant — revived Clout shooting at nine and 10 score yards, coupling this with the Roods. Emphasis was largely upon distance shooting, Thomas Roberts, who shot on their ground, regularly achieving results in excess of 11 score yards.

Whilst 11 score (220 yards) was equivalent to the old minimum practice distance of the 16th Century, it had been frequently exceeded by those who shot on Finsbury Fields, where distances between Marks were seldom less than 12 score (240 yards) and most were around 16 (320 yards.) The longest Flight shot recorded in early 'modern' times was 22 score (440 yards) in 1663, made by a Mr. Girlington in controlled conditions on Finsbury Field; a century later, Mr. Rawson, a cobbler from Manchester, made 18 score (360 yards) and, later still, at the turn of the 18th century, Mr. Troward of the Toxophilite Society achieved 17 score, (340 yards) on Moulsey Heath. For comparison, the British Long-Bow Society's Flight record stands at present at 17 score and two yards (342 yards.)

Essays on archery were given by eminent men. Daines Barrington, in 1783 (Archaeologia Vol VII) and Walter Michael Moseley, in 1792, each extolled the virtue of shooting in the bow. Henry Oldfield published his 'Anecdotes of Archery' in 1791, to be followed a year later by Eli Hargrove, a bookseller in York, who published his similarly titled book, a slim volume, something along the lines of Moseley's Essay. This was supplemented 50 years later, in 1845, by a more detailed extension written by his son, in which the Shooting Rules and Constitutions of 51 of the then existing Societies and Clubs were set down.

Most of the 18th Century Societies were all-male affairs, manned by roistering young bucks to whom carousing was virtually a full-time activity and, who saw archery as a manly exercise perfectly suited to their image. Whilst these male dominant Clubs had 'Ladies Days,' at which wives and daughters were welcomed to shoot, it became increasingly difficult to keep the distaff side away altogether from what was, potentially, a propitious marriage market place. Although some Societies clung grimly to their independence, before long barriers had been breached and women were admitted.

Of the few early dual-sex Societies, the perapatetic Royal British Bowmen was perhaps pre-eminent. This prestigious Club was formed in 1787 through the energies of Lady Cunliffe, whose enthusiasm was seemingly sparked by a visit from a Gentleman archer, the identity of whom, although not revealed, perhaps thinly disguises Sir Ashton Lever, co-founder of the Toxophilite Society.

Containing within its ranks almost everyone with pretensions to be anyone in 18th Century Society, it met for shooting and conviviality at the Great Houses of its members in Flintshire and, across the Border in Shropshire. Enjoying Royal Patronage from George IV, first as Prince Regent and later King, it suffered a period of recession during the Napoleonic Campaign — as did many other Societies — re-starting after that was ended and continuing until the late 1880's, when the untimely death of the current Patron's son, by drowning, brought it to a halt.

Other Societies admitting women were shorter-lived affairs. The Union Society of Harlow, formed in 1790, with the Hertfordshire and the Hatfield Archery Societies of much the same date, drew ladies of the nobility and gentry into its folds but did not outlive the lengthy Napoleonic interlude.

A feature of the earlier clubs and, of the Royal British Bowmen in particular, was their attitude to the practice of archery. It was perceived as a 'rural' activity and as such both garb and food were simple. Costume for the ladies was of 'stuff' — material unsuited to garments for the well-to-do — and, for the men, trowsers (sic) of buff or green cloth, quite distinct from the sateen breeches of the London fop. The first song, sung by Mr. Hayman at the inaugural Acton Park Bow-Meeting, on June 25th, included the lines:

"... *Ah Stuff! 'there's the rub' & I vow I won't bear it,*
whilst there's Cambric and Silk Ma'am I wonder who'd wear it. . . ."

That sung at Wynnstay, in 1820, by Mr. Lloyd exhorted the gentlemen to:

"... *Come try the coat and waistcoat on. The cloth it comes from Poyser*
'Twill last out many a satin one, then don't be nice or Coy Sir . . ."

And, wear it they did. Simple clothing was a characteristic of the Society in its early years and when it reformed in 1819 this was once again a prominent feature.

The songs and ballads presented a microcosm of contemporary life. Although steam power had been around for some time, it was still a source of interest and often amusement to Regency Society at large.

> *"But if you're still shy, I must tell you that I*
> *Have a plan for a Cast Iron Doll*
> *To work by the steam of our Bacon and Bean.*
> *And sing Fol de Rol, Fol de Rol.*
> *"With this Songster of Metal, our Disputes we can settle*
> *Sure he'll be a most excellent Boon,*
> *With a Handel behind, like an Organ of grind,*
> *And Parker* (another Society balladeer) *to alter the Tune."*

In keeping with the rural image, the Society's staple food was bacon and beans; a potentially explosive mixture in its own right one might think, given the heat and activity invariably generated by the subsequent Ball

Of the equipment, understandably both bows and arrows underwent some change, particularly at 'mixed' Clubs. The 'recreational' bow had always enjoyed the distinction of superior finish, with embellishment of handle binding and, before such items were bought in bulk from the Continent, sometimes elaborately carved stringing horns (upper nocks). When archery became more and more accepted as a suitable, even a necessary social pastime, so bows dropped in draw-weight to meet the lesser demands of distance placed upon them.

Women habitually shot no farther than at 60 yards and their weapons became correspondingly lighter. The practice of marking draw-weights on bow limbs was now well-established and a serious 19th Century archeress would look for two bows, one lighter than the other, for each distance. With longer target and butt distances, men's bows of the early 19th Century were heavier in comparison to those of a generation later. The draw-weight of a bow (in the writer's possession, by bowyer Waring the Elder), is marked 69 which appears not to have been an unusual weight.

Innovations included the production of 'Carriage,' or 'take-down,' bows, ideal for transport within the limited space available in a gentleman's conveyance. Although there is some evidence for the use of hinged limbs, they were perhaps usually of the plug and socket type. A significant advantage would have been the stiffer handle, allowing each limb to work independently. It was the custom in the early 1800's for bows to 'work in the hand' — an arrangement which was altered in the 1850's by bowyer James Buchanan, who built up his handle sections in order to stiffen them, this 'invention' giving rise to the term 'Buchanan Dips.'

As the century progressed, arrow manufacture also changed; fletching profiles altered and, manufacture from 'pinus sylvestris' (Russian redwood, or 'red deal') became the norm, replacing native woods. Shafts were usually 'footed,' sometimes with exotic wood (snakewood was favoured for its fine figuring) but mostly with greenheart. Many arrows were crested with the owner's personal colour bands, a practice which lasted well into the 20th Century, stopping only after the end of the Second War, and the destruction by fire of the cresting record books.[3]

Although vestigial binding remained for many years, particularly on Continental arrows, fletches were now fastened in position by glue alone and no longer glued and bound as before. Full-horn and half-horn nocks finally replaced the inset slivers of horn that earlier had protected slots cut directly into the shaft.

Arrows which during the 18th Century and earlier had been 'paired' for Butt and Clout shooting, were now made in greater numbers for Target archery. Where two arrows had been shot at one 'end,' now three were used. Weight, measured by silver coinage, became a universal method of arrow comparison; the archaic distinction, by marking of Rood length on shafts between the fletchings, was by then seldom seen.

Brazed piles, created to fit shafts rather than vice versa, were still to be found as the 20th Century dawned, major arrow-makers preferring that method to turned piles. Although there is some evidence for the Continental manufacture and use of turned brass piles as early as the mid-18th Century, these were not to be available or accepted for general use until the close of the 19th Century.

The style of shooting, constant for so many years, also changed as Horace Alfred Ford, 12 times National Champion, applied scientific thought to his draw and release. He reasoned that an arrow drawn to a position beneath the chin had advantages over one drawn to the cheek, as was then common practice. Firstly, a greater accuracy was possible if the arrow nock lay directly under the aiming eye; secondly, the deeper resultant angle between eye, arrow point and drawing hand in relation to the point of aim improved the trajectory and allowed the use of a lighter bow. Archers who applied his teaching advanced their shooting, scores improved and it was not long before drawing under the chin became normal.

Experiments with rudimentary 'sighting aids' dated from the early 19th Century, notably in 1802/3 by the Reverend John Dilke, who dangled a piece of knotted twine from his little finger as an aid when shooting Clout; later on, in 1870, by James Spedding, of the 'Royal Tox.,' who introduced a rudimentary sight on his bow-limb. Notwithstanding artificial help, 'point of aim' — the aligning of the arrow head with a mark on the field or, for that matter in the clouds — was the standard method of aiming until the early years of the 20th Century and was mandatory in International Competition until a year or two after the Second War.

Whilst 'point of aim' archery may seem archaic and is so in purely modern terms, it was itself an innovation as late as Tudor times. Roger Askham notes its use in his book 'Toxophilus,' published in 1545 and questions its advantage over the then method of instinctive shooting.

> "... *And men continue the longer in this fault* (looking at the shaft) *because it is so good to kepe a lengthe withall: and yet to shoote streighte, they have invented some wayes to espy a tree or a hill beyonde the marke, or els to have some notable thing*

---

[3] A present-day Society which has maintained distinctive 'cresting' since its inception in 1785, is the Warwickshire based 'Woodmen of Arden.'

betwixt the markes; and ones I saw a good archer which did cast off his gere, and laid his quiver with it, even in the mid waye betwixt the prickes. Some thought he did it for safeguard of his gere: I suppose he did it to shoote streight withall. . . ."

Prior to the standardising of target shooting during the early years of the 19th Century, a number of forms of archery were practised by English and Scottish Clubs, most of which have now been re-introduced as the long-bow once more receives its deserved recognition.

Six forms of shooting are mentioned by Thomas Roberts in his 1801 book 'The English Bowman': 'Roving,' 'Hoyles,' 'Flight,' 'Butt,' 'Target' and 'Clout.' Of these, all but 'Butt' (or 'Rood') shooting presently form part of the modern long-bow calendar. However, even a type of this, the 'Palmer Round,' has survived to form part of the Programme of the Royal Toxophilite Society, where it is shot by a few hardy souls.

Mentioned by Roberts as a 'Game of Amusement,' Popinjay shooting is occasionally seen, although in this Country now almost invariably at 'roosts' of 'hens and chicks' on a horizontal and not a vertical mast. Roberts draws attention to the Papingo (a wooden dove) shot by the Ancient Society of Kilwinning Archers, who still annually 'ding doon the doo'; whilst Wand shooting has become popular again as a fitting conclusion to a Target Round.

Roberts also includes 'Pluck Buffet,' a game which is mentioned in the 'Little Geste of Robyn Hode.' Although the reference is obscure, it is the writer's opinion that this form of archery was linked to instruction — possibly for hunting purposes — and derived from the practice of 'shooting under the line'[4] where an arrow was forfeited if it fouled an overhanging gantry, or branch. A buffet by the Instructor following the forfeit would be a natural consequence.

By the early years of the 19th Century target faces had standardised. The 'Prince's Colours' (Prince Regent, later George IV) as they came to be known, were largely as they are today, although without the concentric rings forming the present-day '10 zone' International target face. Gold, red, blue (to replace the earlier inner white), black, and white.

Originally heraldically 'correct': metal (gold), followed by colour (red), followed by metal (white, or silver), followed by colour (black) and, finalised by metal (white, or silver), this sequence was broken when colour (blue) appeared, to follow colour (red).

An abortive attempt to alter colours was made by Charles John Longman of the Royal Toxophilite Society in 1885. The 'Longman Target' — had it been adopted — would have been largely in one neutral colour only (originally grey, but later altered to light blue) with conventionally coloured but, much narrower concentric rings. The centre spot was black. His proposals were unpopular though and the Longman Target got no further than a dusty garden shed. However, arising directly from his initiative,

---

[4] The principles are outlined in 'L'art d'archerie,' see Henri Stein: 'Archers d' Autrefois, Archers d' Aujourd'hui.' Paris 1925, or, in translation, 'The Archer's Register' 1902/3.

to avoid glinting in strong sunshine, from 1886 the central colour (gold) on all targets was painted matt and not gloss, or made up with gold leaf as previously.

Sizes of target faces were early standardised at four feet diameter for men andfor women shooting at 60 yards. Smaller diameters were appropriate for shorter distances — as they are today when shooting International Rounds — and, for many years, targets three feet in diameter served for archery at 50 yards.

Whereas in the 18th Century archery had been the prerogative of young 'bucks,' who saw it as a manly exercise to complement wining, dining and generally carousing, the presence of women-folk added the additional frisson of sexual encounter. There is little doubt that many liaisons, not all of them socially appropriate, arose from flirtation at Archery Meetings and the Balls and Masques that invariably followed.

Archery became sanitised and 'proper' however as the 19th Century rolled on. Private Meetings took place against a back-drop of gentility and picnic on convenient grounds, or at the houses of those of the leisured classes who made up much of the bow-shooting fraternity. And prominent at these, predatory mamas were to be found carefully eyeing eligible bachelors, before deciding at whom to launch their many marriagable daughters.

The Church was thought eminently acceptable as an occupation for prospective mating. Accordingly, the proportion of young Curates to the rest of the archery fraternity was considerable, a most satisfactory state of affairs for those to whom virginity was an inconvenient and, hopefully, a temporary condition. Every club of note had at least one clerical gentleman, sometimes many, amongst its members. Shropshire and Herefordshire seem to have beeen particularly favoured. The 'Archers of the Wye' mustered seven in 1876 and the 'Archers of the Teme,' six.

It is difficult, impossible even, for the young of today to understand, much less recognise, the Victorian and Edwardian distinction between single men and women and married couples. Bachelors and spinsters accepted their condition largely with equanimity. Flirtation had clearly defined boundaries understood by each; unrestrained promiscuity was unthinkable and, opportunity for acceptable liaison was carefully controlled by Mama. Our street-wise moral relaxation had yet to happen. The age of innocence had still to run its course and, to emphasise the fact, Victorian and Edwardian prizes reflected a clear-cut and fully understood distinction between maiden and matron, when awards for excellence were on offer for 'unmarried ladies.'

The fortunes of the traditional long-bow declined during the middle of the 20th Century. Technology, developed during two World Wars, brought fresh materials and, of more importance to archery in the round, a questioning by eminent engineering physicists of the status quo. Bows of steel and aluminium were ousting the old weapon from shooting lines across the competitive world whilst, in turn, these were replaced by bows that drew their origins from the horsed-archery of the Eastern Steppes. Replaced by man-made plastics and glass fibre, wood was now unfashionable and bowmaking skills, learned over generations, became irrelevant to the modern scene.

By foresight and good fortune, however, a Society was formed to safeguard the old weapon and save it from extinction. To reward those few who kept faith with it 50 years ago, the old long-bow has now returned in all its frustrating glory to delight and thwart.

May those who are its stewards long be spared to see it so.

Principal references consulted, and further reading:
TOXOPHILUS, OR THE SCHOLE OF SHOTINGE. Roger Askham. 1545. Reprint Edward Arber: 1902.
AYME FOR THE FINSBURIE ARCHERS. 'E.B.' & 'J.J.' 1601. Facsimile Reprint University Microfilms Inc.
THE DOUBLE ARMED MAN BY THE NEW INVENTION. Wm. Neade 1625. Facsimile Reprint: George Shumway York. Penn. 1971. SBN 87387 022 0.
A NEW INVENTION OF SHOOTING FIRE-SHAFTS. John Bartlet. 1628. Reprint Walter J. Johnson Inc. 1974. STC 14127.
THE BOWMAN'S GLORY. Sir Wm.Wood. 1682. Facsimile Reprint. S. R. Publishers. 1969 SBN 85409 552 7.
ANECDOTES OF ARCHERY. Eli Hargrove. 1792. Facsimile Reprint: Tabard Press 1970: SBN 901951 22 6
AN ESSAY ON ARCHERY. W.M. Moseley. 1792.
PRO ARIS ET FOCIS. R.O. Mason. 1798. Facsimile Reprint: Tabard Press 1970. SBN 901951 20 X.
THE ENGLISH BOWMAN. Thomas Roberts. 1801.
ANECDOTES OF ARCHERY. A.E. Hargrove 1845. York.
THE ARCHERS REGISTERS. Various. 1864 - 1866. 1876 - 1914.
ARCHERY, IT'S THEORY AND PRACTICE. Horace A. Ford. 1859. Cheltenham.
HISTORY OF THE HONOURABLE ARTILLERY COMPANY. Vol's I & II. Raikes. 1878. Bentley & Son.
HISTORY OF THE ROYAL COMPANY OF ARCHERS. Balfour Paul. 1875. Blackwood & Sons.
SEVENTEENTH CENTURY ARCHERY. H.D.Soar. 1992. Journal of the Society of Archer Antiquaries.
REGENCY ARCHERY IN SONG AND BALLAD, A SOCIAL DIMENSION. H.D. Soar: 1998. Journal of the Society of Archer Antiquaries.
SONGS OF THE ROYAL BRITISH BOWMEN. C. Hassall. 1998 (Privately Published)
THE ARROW-MEN OF AVON - BATH ARCHERS 1857-1882. 2nd Edn. 2000. H.D. Soar (Privately Published)

Your Notes

Your Notes

Your Notes

Your Notes

Glossary of Certain Words and Terms

Aigul(l)et(te) n	-	A metal point or tag associated with the securing of protective clothing.
Artillerie coll. n	-	in this context the bow. Derived from 'tiller(ing)'; the process of preparing the bow to bend.
Birding bow n	-	A lighter weapon used with 'bird arrows,' i.e., those fletched spirally to restrict distance and, armed with a blunt head.
Bivouac v	-	To camp overnight, often with minimal cover.
Brazed pile n:	-	A form of recreational arrow head in which a metal 'stopping' (the head) is surrounded by a sheet of thin metal, the whole being brazed to form a cylinder.
Butt (shooting v)	-	An earlier form of archery in which a pair, or a combination of pairs of permanent turf mounds bore paper target faces.
Chevauchée abstr n	-	A deliberate punitive mounted foray into enemy territory characterised by devastation
Clout (shooting) v	-	A disciplined form of distance shooting now conducted at nine score yards (men) and either six score, or seven score (women).
Foraging v	-	A foray into enemy territory for food, provisions, and fodder.
Flight arrow n	-	An arrow designed to be shot for maximum distance.
Goddams n	-	A pejorative nickname given to English and Welsh archers by the French by reason of their frequent use of the words God Damn!
Highstacked (cambered) v	-	A bow is said to be high-stacked (alt: high cambered) when its side is seen to be greater in depth than its frontal surface.
Hobbling v	-	An arrow is said to be 'hobbling' when its flight wobbles uncertainly.
Hoyle (shooting) v	-	An early form of 'roving' archery conducted at shorter distances and involving natural, rather than imposed Marks. e.g., hillocks, thistle clumps, etc.
Maul n	-	A weapon associated with military activity, carried by archers for driving in stakes and as an auxiliary weapon. An iron, or lead head mounted on a lengthy haft.
Meinie (menie) coll.	-	A gathering, in the context of hunting and/or warfare.

Of Bowmen and Battles — Glossary of Certain Words and Terms

Morice Pike n	-	A pole, some 18ft. in length, fashioned of ash and tipped with metal.
Nestroque adj	-	The enigmatic word or phrase uttered by Sir Thomas Erpingham as a preliminary to the battle of Agincourt. Anglicised as '(me)nie stroke' (menie cf. stroke - a horn, or trumpet call) it may have been an instruction to the trumpeters to sound the advance. Alt: now strike,' 'knee stretch'.
Noble n	-	Coinage, minted originally by Edward III approximating to 6s. 8d. (old money)
Nydam n	-	An area originally in Sweden notable for the recovery there in the 19th C: of two Viking longships, containing inter alia, a number of archery artefacts.
Popinjay/Papingo (shooting) v	-	An archaic form of archery at which simulated birds are shot from a vertical, or in modern times, also a horizontal pole. Papingo. an original Scottish variation involving a carved Dove extended from a Church Tower in Kilwinning, Ayrshire.
Paunch (to) v	-	To slit open the stomach revealing the internal organs.
Pavise n	-	A protective shield used formerly by crossbowmen when re-loading their weapons. Also by Markers to the Woodmen of Arden when Clout Meetings are shot.
Pole-axe n	-	A weapon consisting of a heavy axe head mounted upon a long ash shaft.
Prickers n	-	Medieval army reconnoitring Scouts.
Prick (shooting) vb	-	An archaic form of archery. The 'prick' was a white mark, or target.
Quarterstaff n	-	A rural defensive weapon. See frequent references in early ballads. esp: Robin Hood.
Rampier n	-	A defensive embankment.
Rood n	-	An archaic lineal measurement of either $5\frac{1}{2}$, or $7\frac{1}{2}$ yards. Rood shooting, alt: butt shooting was a feature of 18th and early 19th C: archery, usually conducted at 30, 60, 90, and 120 yards, each distance divisible by $7\frac{1}{2}$. (nb. a cricket pitch is 22 yards in length, divisible by $5\frac{1}{2}$).
Schiltron n	-	A defensive formation of Scottish pikemen.
Shoot long ayme v	-	An advisory instruction related to the distance between roving archery Marks
Standard arrow n	-	In medieval warfare the common English livery arrow or battle-shaft. In modern terms a (replica) war-arrow shot for distance by members of the British Long- Bow Society using heavy draw-weight bows..
Standfast adj	-	Abbreviated to 'Fast.' Originally an instruction to an onlooker to remain still whilst shooting was in progress. In modern times an instruction to an archer to cease shooting if safety is compromised.

Index

AGACHE, GOBIN: 81, 82
AGAPIDA, PADRE FRAY ANTONIO: 117
ANCIENT SOCIETY OF KILWINNING ARCHERS: 224
ANGLO-SAXON CHRONICLE, THE: 15
ANJOU, MARGARET OF (wife of HENRY VI): 197, 202, 204, 205, 206, 208
ARAGON, KATHARINE OF (wife of HENRY VIII): 128, 139, 140
ARGYLL, ARCHIBALD CAMPBELL, 2ND EARL OF: 168, 171
ARGYLL, ARCHIBALD CAMPBELL, 8TH EARL OF: 141, 142
ARMS, ASSIZE OF 1252: 7
ARNOT, ROBERT (PROVOST OF PERTH): 143
ARTOIS, ROBERT OF: 71, 176
ARUNDEL, HUMPHREY: 116
ARUNDEL, WILLIAM FITZALAN, 9TH EARL OF: 202
ASKAM (ASCHAM), ROGER: 5, 223
ASSHETON, SIR RICHARD: 211, 212
ATHELING, EDGAR, THE: 12
AUDLEY, SIR JAMES: 186, 187

BAKER, GEOFFREY LE: 184
BALLIOL, EDWARD: 54, 56, 57, 59, 157
BALLIOL, JOHN (KING OF SCOTLAND): 42,
BARRINGTON, DAINES: 220
BARRETT, ALEXANDER (HIGH SHERIFF OF ABERDEEN): 171
BARTLET, JOHN: 215
BAYEUX TAPESTRY: 21, 22, 23
BEAUCHAMP, GUY: 47
BEAUFORT, EDMUND (DUKE OF SOMERSET): 197, 198, 199
BEAUFORT, SIR HENRY (DUKE OF SOMERSET): 210
BEAUFORT, SIR HENRY (DUKE OF DORSET): 198, 200
BEAUMONT, SIR HENRY: 152, 153, 155
BEDFORD, JOHN, DUKE OF: 95, 96, 101, 103
BENHALE, SIR ROBERT: 59
BERE, SIR KINARD DE LA: 37
BERKELEY, THOMAS LORD: 109
BERKELEY, WILLIAM FITZHARDING, LORD: 110, 111, 113
BLOIS, CHARLES, COMTE DU: 71, 73, 74, 176
BOARDMAN, A.W.: 210

BODY, WILLIAM: 115, 116
BOHUN, SIR HENRY: 152, 155
BOHUN, SIR HUMPHREY DE (EARL OF HEREFORD & ESSEX): 66, 152
BOHUN, SIR WILLIAM DE (EARL OF NORTHAMPTON): 71, 72, 73, 74, 81, 176, 179, 180
BOLINGBROKE, DUKE OF LANCASTER: 147, 162, 187
BONVILLE, WILLIAM, LORD: 206
BOTILLER, JOHN LE (EARL OF WILTSHIRE): 198, 201
BOURBON, DUKE OF: 191
BOUSSAC, MARSHAL DE (CONSTABLE OF FRANCE): 102
BOUCICCAUT, MARSHAL: 190
BOWYERE, IVO LE: 7
BRABANT, SIR CLIGNET DE: 193
BRADBURY, PROFESSOR JIM: 21
BRANDON, HENRY (DUKE OF SUFFOLK): 123
BRET, CAPTAIN: 124
BRITISH LONG-BOW SOCIETY, THE: 6, 220
BRUCE, DAVID (KING OF SCOTLAND): 54, 56, 147, 156, 157
BRUCE, EDWARD: 150
BRUCE, ROBERT (KING OF SCOTLAND): 49, 53, 54, 57, 147, 150, 152, 153, 155
BUCH, CAPTAL DE: 185
BUCHANAN, JAMES: 222
BUCKINGHAM, HUMPHREY STAFFORD, DUKE OF: 198, 200, 201
BURGAVENNY, LORD: 124
BURGUNDY, DUKE OF: 202
BURGUNDY, MARGARET OF: 211

CAITHNESS, EARL OF: 171
CAMBRENSIS, GERALDUS: 6
CAREW, GEORGE (VICE-ADMIRAL): 120
CAREW, MARY: 121
CASK, LORD OF: 55
CASSILIS, DOUGLAS KENNEDY, 1ST EARL OF: 168
CASTILE, PEDRO (THE CRUEL) KING OF: 128, 133, 136
CATHERINE, daughter of OWAIN GLYN DWR: 38
CATHERINE, PRINCESS OF FRANCE: 193
CHARLES, DAUPHIN OF FRANCE: 92, 98, 101, 105
CHARLES I: 215
CHARLES II: 219

CHARLES V, KING OF FRANCE: 133
CHARLES V, KING OF SPAIN: 119
CHARNY, GEOFFREY DE: 186
CHRONICLE OF LONDON, THE: 34, 35, 37, 60, 92, 95, 105, 129, 154, 164, 187, 201, 212
CHURCHYARD, THOMAS: 216
CLARENCE, THOMAS, DUKE OF: 89, 90
CLERMONT, MARSHAL: 185
CLIFFORD, LORD JOHN: 209
CLIIFFORD, LORD ROBERT: 152, 153, 155
COBHAM, SIR REGINALD: 81:
COMTE D'AUSSI: 166
CONSTABLE, SIR MARMADUKE: 168
CRAWFORD, JOHN LINDSAY, 6TH EARL OF: 168, 170
CRESSINGHAM, SIR HUGH: 44, 45, 46
CUNLIFFE, LADY: 221
CUNNINGHAM, CUTHBERT (EARL OF GLENCAIRN): 168
CYNAN (father of GRUFFYD): 27

DACRE, THOMAS (3RD BARON OF THE NORTH): 167, 170
DAFYDD (brother to LLEWELLYN THE LAST): 33
DAGWORTH, SIR THOMAS: 176
D'ALBRET, CHARLES (CONSTABLE OF FRANCE): 190
D'ALENCON, DUC: 103, 190
D'ANNEBAULT, ADMIRAL CLAUDE: 119, 120, 121
D'ARC, JOAN: 85, 98, 99, 100, 101, 102, 105
DARCY, SIR GEORGE: 168
D'AUDREHEM, MARSHAL: 133, 134, 136, 185
DE BOHUN, SIR HENRY: 152, 155
DE PIENNE: 139
DE POITIER, COMTE (DUKE OF NORMANDY): 182
DERBY, HENRY GROSMONT, EARL OF: 71, 75, 77, 78, 79
DESPENSER, HUGH: 47, 81
D'ESTRACELLES, JACQUES: 181
DEVEREUX, SIR WALTER: 37
DEVON, THOMAS COURTENAY, 7TH EARL OF: 198
D'HARCOURT, GEOFFREY (aka GODFREY): 80, 179, 180
DIARMUID, KING OF IRELAND: 28
DILKE, REVD. JOHN: 223
D'ISLE, COMTE LE: 75
DON TELLO: 134,
DORIAN, OTTONE: 179
DOUGLAS, ALEXANDER: 96
DOUGLAS, ARCHIBALD (EARL AND REGENT): 57, 58, 60
DOUGLAS, ARCHIBALD "TYNEMAN": 147
DOUGLAS, JAMES ("THE BLACK"), 2ND EARL OF: 152, 153, 155, 159, 160

DOUGLAS, SIR WILLIAM OF LIDDESDALE: 156
DRUMMOND, SIR JOHN: 142, 158
DUDLEY, JOHN, DUKE OF NORTHUMBERLAND: 123
DUDLEY, JOHN, EARL OF WARWICK: 117
DUDLEY, LORD: 198
DU GUESCLIN, BERTRAND: 133, 134, 136
DUNCAN, EARL OF FIFE: 54
DUNOIS, CAPTAIN: 100
DURHAM, LORD: 200

EDMUND, PRINCE ('CROUCHBACK') (son of HENRY III): 129
EDWARD, KING (THE CONFESSOR): 12,
EDWARD I: 7, 31, 34, 42, 43, 45, 47, 132, 147
EDWARD II: 47, 49, 50, 53, 150, 152, 153, 154, 155
EDWARD III: 53, 54, 56, 57, 58, 59, 65, 66, 67, 71, 79, 80, 81, 82, 92, 137, 156, 175, 176, 177, 179, 180, 181, 187
EDWARD IV (EDWARD PLANTAGENET, EARL OF MARCH): 197, 206, 208, 209, 210, 211
EDWARD V: 197
EDWARD VI: 115, 123
EDWARD, BLACK PRINCE, THE: 79, 81, 82, 128, 133, 134, 135, 136, 179, 180, 181, 182, 184, 186
EDWIN, EARL OF MERCIA: 12, 13, 15
ELEANOR, OF PROVENCE (HENRY III's sister): 129
ENRIQUE (half brother to PEDRO THE CRUEL): 133, 134, 135, 136
ERPINGHAM, SIR THOMAS: 193
ERROL, WILLIAM HAY, EARL OF: 168, 170
ETHELRED, KING (THE REDELESS): 12

FASTOLF, SIR JOHN: 102, 103
FALKIRK, LENNOX, EARL OF: 44, 45
FAUCONBERG, WILLIAM NEVILLE, LORD: 208, 209
FAY, GODEMARS DU: 81, 181
FEVRE, JEAN LE: 190
FITZHARDING, MAURICE: 110, 111
FITZWALTER, ROBERT: 7
FORD, HORACE ALFRED: 223
FORMAN, SIR JOHN: 171
FRANCIS I, KING OF FRANCE: 120
FRANKTON, STEPHEN DE: 33
FROISSART: 75, 77, 97, 181
FYCHAN, OWAIN AP GRUFFYD (OWAIN GLYN DWR): 31, 35, 37, 38, 159, 162, 164

GAUCOURT, LORD DE HARFLEUR: 87
GAVESTON, PIERS: 47
GEORGE IV: 220, 221, 224
GERALDINE, THOMAS: 211
GILBERT, EARL OF GLOUCESTER: 152, 153, 155

xlii

GIRLINGTON, MR: 220
GLASDALE, CAPTAIN SIR WILLIAM: 99, 100
GOCH, MEIRION: 28
GODWIN, EARL OF WESSEX: 12, 19
GODWINSON, GYRTH: 22
GODWINSON, KING HAROLD II: 12, 13, 15, 16, 17, 19, 20, 21, 22, 23
GODWINSON, LEOFWIN, 22
GODWINSON, TOSTIG, EARL OF NORTHUMBRIA: 12 13, 15, 16, 17
GRAHAM, JAMES (5TH EARL & 1ST MARQUIS OF MONTROSE): 115, 128, 141, 142, 143, 144
GRENVILLE, SIR RICHARD: 116
GREY, LADY JANE (QUEEN JANE): 123,
GRUFFYD AP CYNAN (PRINCE OF GWNEDD): 26, 27, 28, 29, 30
GRUFFYD, LLEWELYN AP (LLEWELYN MAWR): 31, 45, 47, 129 130
GRUFFYD, LLEWELYN AP (son of DAFYDD AP GRUFFYD): 33
GRUFFYD, LLEWELYN AP (LLEWELYN THE LAST):, 31, 45
GRUFFYD, OWAIN AP (son of DAFFYDD AP GRUFFYD): 33
GWENLLIAN (daughter of LLEWELLYN AP GRUFFYD), 33
GWCHARKI: 28, 29

HAINAULT, JOHN DE: 179, 181
HALL, SIR EDWARD: 209
HALLE, SIR FRANK: 75, 78
HARCLAY, SHERIFF ANDREW DE: 49, 50, 51
HARGROVE, ELI: 221
HARPER, SIR GEORGE: 124
HAYMAN, MR: 221
HENRY I: 7
HENRY III: 7, 129, 130, 131, 132
HENRY IV (DUKE OF LANCASTER, HENRY BOLINGBROKE): 147, 162, 187
HENRY V: 86, 87, 89, 90, 91, 92, 137, 162, 187, 189, 190, 191, 193, 194, 197
HENRY VI: 95, 197, 198, 202, 208, 210,
HENRY VII (DUKE OF RICHMOND): 28, 166, 197, 211, 212
HENRY VIII: 28, 119, 120, 123, 128, 137, 138, 139, 140, 166, 167
HERBERT, SIR WILLIAM: 210
HEREFORD AND ESSEX, HUMPHREY DE BOHUN, EARL OF: 50, 155
HEREWARD THE WAKE: 26
HERLEVE: 12, 28
HIRE, CAPTAIN LA: 102

HERON, LADY (wife of SIR WILLIAM HERON): 166
HERRIES, ANDREW (2ND BARON): 170
HOLLAND, JOHN (EARL OF HUNTINGDON): 86, 89
HOME, ALEXANDER, EARL OF: 168
HOOD, ROBIN: 3, 4, 67, 68, 69
HOWARD, EDMUND: 168, 170
HOWARD, THOMAS (ADMIRAL): 167, 168, 169, 170
HOWARD, LORD THOMAS: 125
HUGO, THE BRAVE (EARL OF SHREWSBURY): 28, 29
HUGO, THE STOUT (EARL OF CHESTER): 28, 29
HUNTLEY, ALEXANDER GORDON, EARL OF: 170
HYWISH, MATILDA DE (wife of SIR RICHARD): 7
HYWISH (HUISH), SIR RICHARD DE: 7

ISABELLA (mother to EDWARD III): 53, 54,
ISHI (Last of the Yana Indians): 11
ISLEY, SIR HENRY: 124

JAMES II (KING OF SCOTLAND): 201
JAMES IV (KING OF SCOTLAND): 166, 167, 170, 171
JERNINGHAM, SIR HENRY: 123
JOHN, KING OF BOHEMIA: 179
JOHN, KING OF ENGLAND: 31
JOHN II (KING OF FRANCE): 184, 186, 187
JOHN, LITTLE: 4

KET, ROBERT: 116, 117
KEITH, ROBERT (EARL MARISCHAL OF SCOTLAND): 153
KILPONT, LORD JOHN GRAHAM: 156, 157
KING ARTHUR: 35, 38
KYLTER, WILLIAM: 116
KYRIELL, SIR THOMAS: 206

LANCASTER, HENRY, DUKE OF: 182
LANCASTER, JOHN OF GAUNT, DUKE OF: 134, 135
LANCASTER, THOMAS, EARL OF: 47, 49, 50, 51
LENNOX, FALFIRK, EARL OF: 44, 45
LEVER, SIR ASHTON: 221
LINCOLN, BISHOP OF: 53
LINCOLN, EARL OF: 211
LISLE, VISCOUNT THOMAS TALBOT: 109, 110, 113, 114, 120
LLOYD, MR: 221
LONG, 'BLACK WILL': 111, 113, 114
LONGMAN, CHARLES JOHN: 224
LOTHIAN, WILLIAM KERR: 5TH EARL OF: 142
LOUIS XII (KING OF FRANCE): 137, 139
LOVELACE, CAPTAIN (SQUIRE OF KENT): 202, 205, 206
LOVELL, VISCOUNT FRANCIS: 211

MACCLESFIELD 100: 7
MACDONALD, ALASDAIR MACCOLLA: 141, 142, 143
MADERTY, DAVID DRUMMOND, MASTER OF: 142
MARCH, EDWARD PLANTAGENET, EARL OF (see EDWARD IV)
MARGARET (THOMAS TALBOT'S GRANDMOTHER): 110
MARY I, QUEEN ('BLOODY MARY'): 123, 124, 125
MASON, OSWALD: 216, 217
MATHEW, DAVID: 210
MAUNAY (MANNY), SIR WALTER: 64, 67, 77, 79, 175, 176
MAXIMILIAN I, HOLY ROMAN EMPEROR: 137, 139, 140, 166
MONTFORT, JOHN DE: 71
MONTFORT, HENRY DE (son of SIMON pére): 130, 132
MONTFORT, SIMON DE (pére): 128, 129, 130, 131, 132
MONTFORT, SIMON DE (son of SIMON pére): 130
MONTROSE, JAMES GRAHAM, 5TH EARL & 1ST MARQUIS): 115, 128, 141, 142, 143, 144
MONSTRELET, ENGUERRON: 190, 193
MORAY, THOMAS RANDOLPH, EARL OF: 152, 153, 155, 156
MORLEY, SIR ROBERT: 67
MORTIMER, EDMUND: 37, 38, 164
MORTIMER, ROGER: 53, 54, 57, 131
MOSELEY, WALTER MICHAEL: 220
MUCH (miller' son - outlaw): 4
MURRAY, ANDREW: 44, 45

NEADE, WILLIAM: 215, 216, 217
NEVILLE, GEORGE (ARCHBISHOP OF YORK): 210
NEVILLE, JOHN (LORD MONTAGUE): 206, 206
NEVILLE, RALPH (EARL OF RABY): 156
NORFOLK, JOHN HOWARD, DUKE OF: 209
NORFOLK, THOMAS HOWARD, DUKE OF: 123
NORTHAMPTON, WILLIAM PARR, MARQUIS OF: 117
NORTHUMBERLAND, SIR HENRY PERCY, 2ND EARL OF: 156, 157, 158, 159, 161, 164, 165
NORTHUMBIRA, MORCA, EARL OF: 12, 13, 15
NORWAY, HARALD SIGURDSON (HARDRADA), KING OF: 12, 5, 16, 17
NORWAY, MAGNUS (BAREFOOT), KING OF: 29, 30
NYDAM: 6

OLDFIELD, HENRY: 221
ORDER OF THE GARTER: 181
ORLEANS, DUKE OF: 191
ORRE, EYSTEIN: 17
OXFORD, THOMAS DE VERE, EARL OF: 71, 179

PEACOCK, THOMAS LOVE: 26
PELHAM, NICHOLAS (later SIR): 119, 120, 121
PELHAM, SIR WILLIAM: 121
PEMBROKE, EARL OF: 125
PEMBROKE, LAWRENCE HASTINGS, EARL OF: 75, 77, 78
PENDRAGON, UTHER: 35
PHILIP, PRINCE OF SPAIN: 123, 126
PHILLIP VI, KING OF FRANCE: 68, 71, 80, 82, 156, 175, 177, 179, 180, 181
PIERRE, LANCELOT: 190
PLANTAGENET, RICHARD (DUKE OF YORK): 197, 198, 199, 200, 201, 202
POLE, SIR ALEXANDER DE LA: 100
POLE, SIR JOHN DE LA: 100
POTHON, CAPTAIN: 102

RAWSON, JAMES: 220
RICHARD II: 35, 162, 187
RICHARD III (Previously DUKE OF GLOUCESTER): 197, 211
RICHEMONT, COUNT OF: 191
ROBERT, DUKE OF NORMANDY ('THE DEVIL'): 12
ROBERT (HIGH STEWARD OF SCOTLAND): 156. 157
ROBERTS, THOMAS:: 220, 224
ROBINSON, RICHARD: 216
ROGER OF CLIFFORD: 50
ROKESBY, RALPH: 124
ROYAL BRITISH BOWMEN: 221
ROYAL TOXOPHILITE SOCIETY: 224
RUSSELL, LORD JOHN: 116
RUTHIN, LORD GREY OF: 35, 37

SALISBURY, RICHARD, EARL OF: 89, 90, 96, 97, 198, 199, 200
SANCELLES, THIERRY: 181
SAVAGE, CHRISTOPHER: 168
SAVEUSES, SIR GUILLAUME DE: 193
SCALES, LORD: 100, 118
SCATHLOCK (SCARLET), WILL: 4
SCHWARTZ: MARTIN: 211
SCOTT, SIR WALTER: 197
SETON, ALEXANDER: 153
SHREWSBURY, ABBOT OF: 162
SICILY, ROBERT, KING OF: 175
SIMNEL, LAMBERT (ALIAS EDWARD V): 211, 212
SIMONS, RICHARD: 211, 212
SMITH, SIR JOHN: 117
SOMERSET, EDWARD SEYMOUR, EARL OF: 115, 116, 117
SOUTHWELL, SIR RICHARD: 125
SPEDDING, JAMES: 223

SPENCER (DESPENSER), SIR HUGH: 81
SPRINGHOUSE, SIR EDMUND: 90
STAFFORD, RALPH, EARL OF: 55
STAFFORD, SIR RICHARD: 182
STANLEY, SIR EDWARD: 167, 168, 171
STATUTES OF WINCHESTER, 1285: 7
STEWART, JAMES (GUARDIAN OF SCOTLAND): 44, 45
SUFFOLK, POLE DE LA, EARL OF: 100, 101, 202

TALBOT, LORD JOHN: 99, 100, 102, 103
TALBOT, THOMAS, EARL OF LANCASTER: 47, 49, 50, 51
TANNER, JOHN: 34
TEWDYER, RHYS AP: 28
THOMAS, STEPHEN: 86
TIPTOFT (TIBOTOFT), ROBERT DE: 31
TRAHEARN: 27, 28
TROWARD, MR: 220
TUDOR, MARGARET: 166
TWENGE, SIR MARMADUKE: 45

UMFRAVILLE, SIR GILBERT: 92
UMFRAVILLE, SIR INGRAM DE: 153

UMFRAVILLE, SIR THOMAS DE: 158

VESTYNDEN, RALPH: 210

WALLACE, WILLIAM: 42, 43, 44, 45, 46, 47, 147, 148, 149
WARBECK, PERKIN: 211, 212
WARWICK, RICHARD NEVILLE, EARL OF: 198, 199, 200, 202, 204, 205, 210
WARING, THOMAS (THE ELDER): 217, 222
WARRINGTON, SIR ROBERT: 200
WAURIN, JEAN: 190, 191, 195
WEMYSS, DAVID (LORD ELCHO): 142, 143
WHITNEY, SIR ROBERT: 37
WILLIAM I ('THE CONQUEROR'), DUKE OF NORMANDY: 6, 12, 13, 17, 19, 20, 21, 22, 23
WILLIAM II ('RUFUS'): 29
WOOD, SIR WILLIAM: 219
WORCESTER, THOMAS PERCY, EARL OF: 162, 163
WULFORD, RALPH: 211, 212
WYATT, SIR THOMAS: 123, 124, 125, 126

YORK, ARCHBISHOP OF: 54, 156
YORK, SHERIFF OF: 51

YOUR NOTES

REIGNING MONARCHS OF ENGLAND AND SCOTLAND DURING THE PERIOD COVERED BY THIS BOOK

EDWARD THE CONFESSOR.	1042 to 1066	
HAROLD II	1066 to 1066	
WILLIAM I 'The Conqueror'	1066 to 1087	
WILLIAM II 'Rufus'	1087 to 1100	
HENRY I	1100 to 1135	
HENRY II	1154 to 1189	
RICHARD I 'Coeur de Leon'	1189 to 1199	
JOHN	1199 to 1216	
HENRY III	1216 to 1272	
EDWARD I 'Longshanks'	1272 to 1307	
EDWARD II	1307 to 1327	deposed
EDWARD III	1327 to 1377	
RICHARD II	1377 to 1399	deposed
HENRY IV	1399 to 1413	
HENRY V	1413 to 1422	
HENRY VI	1422 to 1461	
EDWARD IV	1461 to 1483	
EDWARD V	1483 to 1483	
RICHARD III	1483 to 1485	
HENRY VII	1485 to 1509	
HENRY VIII	1509 to 1547	
EDWARD VI	1547 to 1553	
JANE (Lady Jane Gray)	1553 to 1553	
MARY I 'Bloody Mary'	1553 to 1558	
ELIZABETH I	1558 to 1603	

KINGS OF SCOTLAND

JOHN BALLIOL	1292 to 1296
ROBERT I 'The Bruce'	1306 to 1329
DAVID II	1329 to 1371
ROBERT II 'Stewart'	1371 to 1390
ROBERT III	1390 to 1406
JAMES I	1406 to 1437
JAMES II	1437 to 1460
JAMES III	1460 to 1488
JAMES IV	1488 to 1513
JAMES V	1513 to 1542
MARY	1542 to 1567
JAMES VI	1567 to 1625

NATIVE PRINCES OF WALES

LLYWELYN AP IORWERTH (Llewelyn Mawr - The Great)	d. 1240
LLYWELYN AP GRUFFYD (Llewelyn Olaf - The Last)	d. 1282
OWAIN AP GRUFFYD FECHYN (Glyn Dwr)	1350 to 1416

Your Notes